MIGRATION, CULTURE CONFLICT, CRIME AND TERRORISM

Advances in Criminology
Series Editor: David Nelken

Titles in the Series

Deleuze and Environmental Damage: Violence of the Text
Mark Halsey

Re-Thinking the Political Economy of Punishment: Perspectives on Post-Fordism and Penal Politics
Alessandro De Giorgi

Globalization and Regulatory Character: Regulatory Reform after the Kader Toy Factory Fire
Fiona Haines

Family Violence and Police Response: Learning From Research, Policy and Practice in European Countries
Edited by Wilma Smeenk and Marijke Malsch

Crime and Culture: An Historical Perspective
Edited by Amy Gilman Srebnick and René Lévy

Power, Discourse and Resistance: A Genealogy of the Strangeways Prison Riot
Eamonn Carrabine

Hard Lessons: Reflections on Governance and Crime Control in Late Modernity
Edited by Richard Hil and Gordon Tait

Informal Criminal Justice
Edited by Dermot Feenan

Becoming Delinquent: British and European Youth, 1650–1950
Edited by Pamela Cox and Heather Shore

Migration, Culture Conflict and Crime
Edited by Joshua D. Freilich, Graeme Newman, S. Giora Shoham and Moshe Addad

Critique and Radical Discourses on Crime
George Pavlich

Migration, Culture Conflict, Crime and Terrorism

Edited by

JOSHUA D. FREILICH
John Jay College of Criminal Justice, New York, USA

and

ROB T. GUERETTE
Florida International University, USA

Routledge
Taylor & Francis Group
LONDON AND NEW YORK

First published 2006 by Ashgate Publishing

2 Park Square, Milton Park, Abingdon, Oxon OX14 4RN
711 Third Avenue, New York, NY 10017, USA

Routledge is an imprint of the Taylor & Francis Group, an informa business

First issued in paperback 2017

British Library Cataloguing in Publication Data
Migration, culture conflict, crime and terrorism. -
(Advances in criminology)
1.Emigration and immigration - Social aspects 2.Immigrants
- Cultural assimilation 3.Immigrants - Crimes against
4.Immigrants - Crimes against - Prevention 5.Terrorism
6.Marginality, Social
I.Freilich, Joshua D. II.Guerette, Rob T.
364'.086912

Library of Congress Cataloging-in-Publication Data
Migration, culture conflict, crime and terrorism / edited by Joshua D. Freilich and Rob T. Guerette.
p. cm.
Includes index.
ISBN 0-7546-2650-4
1. Crime--Social aspects. 2. Terrorism--Social aspects. 3. Emigration and immigration--Social aspects. 4. Immigrants--Social conditions. 5. Alien criminals. 6. Culture conflict. 7. Crime--Religious aspects. I. Freilich, Joshua D. II. Guerette, Rob T.

HV6181.M54 2006
304.8--dc22

2006005842

ISBN 978-0-7546-2650-3 (hbk)
ISBN 978-1-138-27788-5 (pbk)

Contents

List of Figures

List of Tables

About the Authors

Aronowitz, Alexis A.: PhD, Consultant, United Nations Office on Drugs and Crime

Brettfeld, Katrin: University of Hamburg, Department of Criminology

Britz, Linsey: Department of Justice Studies, Kent State University, OH, USA

Eckert, Roland: Professor of Sociology, University of Trier, Germany

Erez, Edna: LLB; PhD, Professor and Chairperson, Department of Justice Studies, Kent State University, USA

Freilich, Joshua D.: JD; PhD, Associate Professor, Sociology Department, John Jay College of Criminal Justice, New York City, NY, USA

Guerette, Rob T.: PhD, Assistant Professor, School of Criminal Justice, Florida International University, Miami, FL, USA

Kleimann, Matthias: Criminological Research Institute in Lower Saxony, Germany

Kühne, Hans-Heiner: PhD, Professor, European and International Criminal Law, University of Trier, Germany

Miyazawa, Koichi: Professor Emeritus for Criminal Law, Criminology and Philosophy of Law, Keio University, Japan

Natarajan, Mangai: PhD, Professor, Sociology Department, John Jay College of Criminal Justice, New York City, NY, USA

Newman, Graeme R.: Distinguished Teaching Professor, School of Criminal Justice, University at Albany, NY, USA

Opesso, Matthew R.: Institute for Graduate Clinical Psychology, Widener University, DE, USA

Osten, Philipp: Assistant Professor for Criminal Law, International Criminal Law and German Law, Keio University, Japan

Pfeiffer, Christian: Director, Criminological Research Institute in Lower Saxony, Germany

Reich, Kerstin: University of Tübingen, Germany

Shoham, Shlomo Giora: Professor, Faculty of Law, Tel Aviv University, Israel

Sokullu-Akinci, Fusun: Faculty of Law, Department of Criminal Law. Istanbul University, Turkey

Tarhanli, Turgut: Professor of Public International Law, Director, Istanbul Bilgi University Human Rights Law Research Center, Turkey

Wetzels, Peter: Department of Criminology, University of Hamburg, Germany

Windzio, Michael: Criminological Research Institute in Lower Saxony, Germany

Acknowledgments

The editors thank Istanbul Bilgi University for hosting the conference that made it possible for the authors of these chapters to come together to share and discuss matters pertaining to migration, culture conflict, crime and terrorism.

Introduction

Joshua D. Freilich
John Jay College of Criminal Justice

Rob T. Guerette
Florida International University

This anthology comprises selected chapters from the third international conference on migration, culture conflict, crime and terrorism held in Istanbul, Turkey in October 2003.[1] Since the initial conference held in 1999 these topics have only increased in importance. In addition to other events, the terrorist attacks in the United States on 9/11, and March 11, 2004 in Spain, underscore the need to better understand and respond to problems stemming from culture conflicts. The present volume builds upon the first two conferences and through scientific scrutiny makes sense of recent developments.

While the book originating from the first conference (Freilich, Newman, Shoham and Addad 2002) garnered favorable assessments (Antonopoulos 2005; Vazsonyi 2003), the reviewers pointed out areas for future research focus. Antonopoulos called for an examination of the media's role in the migration-culture conflict-crime nexus and greater consideration of the historical context from which these issues arise (2006: 226). Taking this into account, the present volume includes chapters which examine the influence of media on crime perceptions and other issues within the context of historical developments. Although the focus of selected chapters ranges widely, covering topics such as religion, culture, the media, terrorism, transnational and organized crime, offending, and victimization, all in some fashion intersect with migration and illegal conduct. Taken together, the chapters represent an encompassing overview, in both breadth and depth, on these matters.

Depending on the context, views on immigration and its consequences vary considerably. Some contend that criminal participation by migrants is the result of environmental factors found in the host country that are beyond the control of migrants themselves. Since new immigrants often reside in poverty and experience

---

1 The conference was sponsored by Istanbul Bilgi University. This meeting followed the first two international conferences on migration, culture conflict, and crime that were held in Israel in 1999 (Freilich, Newman, Shoham and Addad 2002) and Germany in 2001 (Freilich and Newman 2002).

racial disadvantages in the host country, it is claimed that these conditions, operating through strain or cultural/learning adaptations, lead to higher offending rates among immigrant groups. In other words, the poor social conditions and the marginalization of immigrant groups in the host society contribute to and facilitate the migrant-crime relationship (Newman, Freilich and Howard 2002).

Conversely, many native-born citizens blame immigrants for all that is wrong in their communities. Despite research to the contrary (Lee 2003; Martinez 2002; Tonry 1997), migrants are accused of committing more crime than the host population, and taking unfair advantage of government benefits (Buchanan 2002). Many argue that the migrant/crime association results from a selection process, since criminals are more likely than others to migrate (Newman, Freilich and Howard 2002). Research has also found that more heterogeneous societies have higher crime rates (Howard, Newman and Freilich 2002a, 2002b). As a result of these fears, many countries have seen an increase in the popularity of groups that advocate for legal migration to be curtailed or eliminated. It is claimed that foreigners do not wish to assimilate and seek instead to supplant the indigenous traditions with their own culture (Huntington 2004; Raspail 1985). It is also contended that specific migrants, akin to the Trojan horse, serve the interests of outside powers and seek to attack the host nation from within. Right-wing political parties and movements in many nations argue that Arabic and Islamic immigrants pose such a threat and should be monitored closely, and ultimately deported to their countries of origin, to prevent future 9/11s.

Although many nations have long adopted policies that allow foreigners to be repatriated under certain circumstances (the United States, for instance, deports non-citizen felons, after they have completed their prison sentences, and has stripped citizenship from naturalized citizens found to be disloyal), these statutes usually apply after specific *actions* (i.e., crimes) have been committed. Contemporary calls, like those issued by the National Front in France to banish Arabic migrant communities (DeClair 1999), in contrast, are a form of national profiling that are based upon *who* the non-citizens are. Relatedly, in some countries angry citizens accuse their government of ignoring the immigration issue and are taking matters into their own hands. In the state of Arizona in the United States, for example, some citizens have formed private paramilitary organizations that patrol the Mexican border to enforce immigration laws (and detain illegal migrants) as well as prevent drug smuggling (Marizco 2004). Critics warn that it is only a matter of time before these groups degenerate into vigilante groups and commit hate crimes (Hendricks 2004).

In other instances, however, migration is viewed favorably and is associated with positive consequences in the host country. Today in Russia and similar to the past practices of many European nations, the shortage of laborers has led to liberalized immigration policies and a warmer reception for migrants who fill the need for workers. Though not currently the case, during the mid-1900s the United States adopted a program that allowed migrant workers into the country to accommodate laborer shortages during and after the Second World War. Referred to as the Bracero program, over a 22-year period more than five million workers were imported to work at farms and ranches in 24 states (Welch 2002). Thus, views of immigration, its implications, and how it is responded to, are dictated by the larger economic, political and social context.

To some extent, how nations respond to migration processes also affects the negative and positive consequences of immigration. The Director General of the International Organization for Migration (IOM) writes that, "if properly managed, migration can be beneficial for all states and societies. If left unmanaged, it can lead to the exploitation of individual migrants, particularly through human trafficking and migrant smuggling, and be a source of social tension, insecurity and bad relations between nations" (McKinley, 2004: 3).

There is clear evidence of an increasing trend among national governments to strengthen their management of the immigration process (McKinley 2004). In 2000 the United Nations adopted protocols against transnational organized crime, which included human smuggling and trafficking, which marked the first such measure by the UN in this area. Further, there have been efforts by the European Union to pressure transit countries that fail to restrict the flow of migrants or do not crack down on human traffickers (Simons 2002). Citing the ever increasing diversity and complexity of the migration landscape the IOM recently released a model for nations to use in managing immigration (see Figure I.1). Comprising four primary parts – Migration and Development, Facilitating Migration, Regulating Migration, and Forced Migration – the model was offered as a guide for a "comprehensive" as opposed to an ad hoc approach to migration management. Importantly, the IOM model tackles the need for countries to address the various aspects of migration simultaneously. If policies aimed at any of these parts are to be successful, however, greater understanding of the nature of migration in various contexts is needed. The chapters in this anthology address many of the areas identified by the IOM model. In addition, since this conference was organized in the post 9/11 world, many of them explore issues surrounding terrorism from a variety of perspectives. The chapters have been grouped into four topical categories – Religion, Culture and Terrorism; Migration and Offending Issues; Organized Crime, Trafficking and Refugees; and Responding to the Victimization of Migrants.

Migration, Religion, Culture and Terrorism

The post 9/11 period has highlighted and associated together in the public mind the issues of migration, religion, and terrorism. There is little doubt that many nations seek to control immigration in the name of safeguarding their country against terror. Part I of this book examines the interactions between and among these issues. To a large extent, terrorism is an outgrowth of migration and religion. Routinely, terrorism (and other forms of violence) are attributed to extreme religious ideologies, such as fundamentalist and or apocalyptic views of Islam, Judaism, Christianity, or racist fringe off-shoots such as Christian Identity, Hinduism and other faiths (Jurgensmeyer 2000; Stern 2003).

Hans-Heiner Kühne, in Chapter 1, identifies the dissonance between the status of terrorists as criminals and most governments' policy of treating terrorism as a war. He asserts that terrorists lack authority to pronounce war and therefore deserve the status of criminals. Yet, many governments embrace policies that call for a "war" on terror that allows them to deal with terrorists through war-time and military procedures and thereby deny these individuals the rights afforded under criminal processes. Kühne calls a warning to be wary of this trend. He argues that the current war on terrorism has led to a repressive shift in national penal law systems even when there is no discernible domestic terrorist threat and that it has blurred the difference between domestic crime issues and external, military, and security considerations.

Roland Eckert argues, in Chapter 2, that terrorism emerges as a result of humiliation or when one's collective idenitity is threatened. He explains that migration sometimes, by disrupting one's sense of self, leads individuals to embrace fundamentalist and traditionalist belief systems that provide stability to their lives. Unlike Huntington's thesis, however, Eckert maintains that it is not always the case that orthodox/traditional religious beliefs cause conflict, but that sometimes this causal order is reversed. In other words, conflict may cause participants to discard their more peaceful identities in favor of apocalyptic and traditionalist religious teachings/identities that encourage violence. Indeed, a number of scholars have recently made this claim in regard to the Chechen campaign against the Russians, which originated as a secular dispute. The solution, then, is to promote mediation and conflict resolution strategies.

Meanwhile, in Chapter 3, noted criminologist Shlomo Giora Shoham provides a sweepng historical and cultural analysis of the clash between fundamentalist Islam and the West that, besides responding to Antonopoulos's call for more attention to the historical context, applies his personality theory to shed further light on these significant matters. Shoham's masterful journey ends on a hopeful note. He argues that a dialogue based upon mutual respect which results in a reconciliation between these two cultures is indeed possible, once militant Islam realizes that its use of terrorism will not bring it any closer to its goals (see also Dershowitz 2002).

Finally, Freilich, Opesso and Newman, in Chapter 4, change our focus from the causes of the migrant/terrorist association, to an analysis of how governments responded it. Their study outlines the legislative and policy changes pertaining to non-citizens that Australia, Canada and the United States enacted in response to the 9/11 attacks. Freilich et al's investigation indicates that although the three countries balanced the same factors (e.g., individual liberty and public safety, economic interests and national security), they differed in the premium they placed on them. They conclude that the United State, and to some extent Australia, placed national security interests above economic and personal liberty concerns, while Canada privileged economic interests. It appears that each country's political context, and personal history with migrants and terrorism influenced their legislative and policy responses.

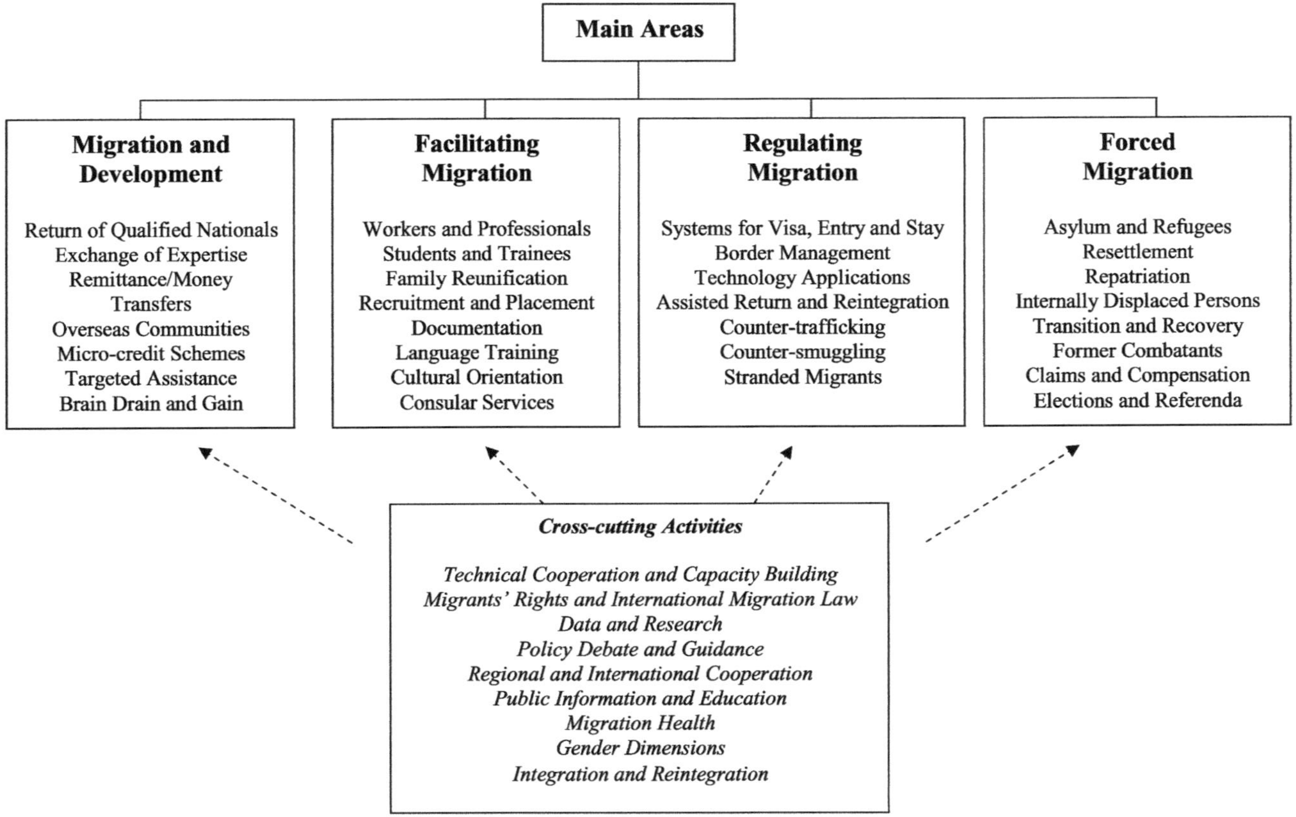

Figure I.1 IOM Model for the Management of Migration
Source: Adapted from McKinley (2004).

Migration and Offending Issues

Criminologists and others have long engaged the issue of whether or not migrants commit more crime than the native-born population. Unlike other studies that examine this issue in terms of ethnic, or national origin distinctions, Katrin Brettfeld and Peter Wetzels, in Chapter 5, examine the association between religious background, migrant status, and crime in Germany. Their findings are important because they too illustrate the importance of the context in which perceptions are shaped. The common European sterotype that more religious Muslims commit more crime was not empirically supported. In most cases, there were no significant behavioral differences between Christian and Muslim youths. More religious Islamic youths were more likely, however, to have positive attitudes toward violence, while more religious Christians were less approving. This difference, as well as the finding that there were higher levels of family violence among Muslim youths, may be due to the more traditional gender roles in the Muslim community. It is clear that future research is needed on this issue.

In an overview of juvenile crime among immigrants found in Chapter 6, Kerstin Reich identifies the relationship between the context in which immigration occurs and how immigrants are perceived in Germany. When there was a need for workers, immigrants were welcomed and ushered into the country. When financial resources were low and unemployment rates were high, however, the immigrants were perceived as a social problem. Reich empirically confirms that immigrant juvenile crime is increasing in Germany. Through qualitative data, Reich also explores the issue of "imported" versus "home grown" criminality (see also Newman, Freilich and Howard 2002), and finds that participation in crime tends to increase with time spent in the host country and that immigrant juveniles tend to identify strongly with their original nationality. He concludes that better integrating young migrants into the host country's mainstream society would be an effective crime prevention strategy.

Moving to a smaller cross-section of the immigrant population, Koichi Miyazawa and Philipp Osten provide an overview of foreign nationals held in the Japanese penal system in Chapter 7. They discuss the obstacles prison administrators face in facilitating the integration of immigrants with distinct language and cultural orientations. This is interesting because it identifies an overlooked dimension of immigrant integration. While most attention has been placed on increasing immigrant assimilation into conventional society, Miyazawa and Osten's examination implies a need to learn more about the impediments of integration for those migrants brought into criminal justice institutions.

Finally, Pfeiffer, Windzio and Kleimann in Chapter 8 examine how the media influenced the public perception of crime inside Germany which partially addresses Antonopoulos's call for greater consideration of the role of the media. Their study indicates that many people's perception of the crime problem did not match reality. For example, most people estimated the number of burglaries to be much higher than the actual number. The authors demonstrate that these incorrect perceptions, which include the notion that foreigners are to blame for an increasing crime rate, are partially the result of sensational media reporting. Pfeiffer et al found that these incorrect perceptions led to greater public support for harsher punishments, and the to the imposition of more severe penalties in general, and it appears against non-citizens in particular, as well.

Organized Crime, Trafficking and Refugees

A number of countries have responded to the current anti-migrant environment and have recently lowered the number of migrants they legally admit. Similarly, many nations have also reconsidered their policies that govern refugees, asylum seekers, and others claiming to have fled political persecution. Issues related to asylum seekers, and organized crime and transnational trafficking have therefore assumed a prominent place on the migrant research agenda. Alexis A. Aronowitz in Chapter 9 provides an overview of the UN Research Project, "Coalitions Against Trafficking in Human Beings in the Philippines". Aronowitz defines key terms, discusses the broader problem of illegal migration in general and the survey instrument used in the study in particular. Her subsequent thorough review of each step in the trafficking process is important, since trafficking is a worldwide problem. Aronowitz concludes that there must be a collaborative effort on the part of governments, victim organizations, and non-governmental organizations to combat this issue. Fusun Sokullu-Akinci builds on Aronowitz's study and, in Chapter 10, comments on the the involvement of organized crime in trafficking in Turkey. She not only discusses the causes of organized crime, but more importantly, sets forth a detailed listing of policy initiatives to combat it.

Lastly, Turgut Tarhanli discusses the legal dimension of refugees and asylum seekers in Turkey in Chapter 11. Tarhanli's piece examines and compares Turkey's legal provisions that govern asylum and refugees requests with international law. He finds a synthesis between the two and argues that to accord with Turkish national and international human rights doctrine, refugees and asylum seekers should not be hastily expelled, deported or returned to countries from which they have escaped. Tarhanli argues that sufficient time must be allotted for the investigation of the claims, and that the refugees and asylum seekers must also be granted access to judicial procedure to validate their claims.

Responding to the Victimization of Migrants

Another dimension of managing migration deals with responding to and assisting immigrants victimized both during the migration process and after their arrival in the host country. It is incumbent upon government to respond to victimization among both authorized and unauthorized immigrants. In Chapter 12, Rob T. Guerette characterizes the issue of death among migrants in the United States as they attempt unauthorized entry from Mexico. Noting the increasing trend of migrant deaths around the world, Guerette identifies the possible role of situational crime prevention as a means to reduce and prevent deaths within the migration process. The utility of this approach, he argues, is that it operates within the current context of greater border policing and provides an immediate response without relying on reversal of restrictive immigration policies. This idea is intriguing because it not only identifies the need to manage this emerging facet of migration but also because it calls for the application of a method largely used to prevent conventional crimes to this transnational issue.

Shifting to victimization within the host country, both Natarajan and Erez and Britz identify the need to improve the ability of institutions to assist immigrant women who are victims of domestic violence. Erez and Britz study the experiences of social services providers, legal advocates and lawyers in dealing with battered immigrant women in Chapter 13. Through a national survey conducted in the United States, they found that battered immigrant women often have difficulty accessing social services and the criminal justice system for assistance. They argue that effective advocacy and intervention for battered immigrant women should include the development of collaborative working relationships among legal practitioners, social workers, domestic violence advocates, cultural consultants, and non-traditional community leaders and organizations. Finally, Natarajan in Chapter 14 presents a case study of a problem-solving approach to assist battered women in India. The model entails the use of an all female police unit specially trained to respond to the unique needs of abused women. A primary focus of the program is to provide better access to police services for victims of abuse. While the model was used with a native population, Natarajan points out that the utility of such an approach with battered immigrant women is equally relevant, especially given the reluctance of immigrant women to seek help. Together, both studies shed light on yet another dimension of managing immigrant populations and further underscore the unique requirements that immigrant populations place on preexisting institutions in host countries.

Conclusion

In comparison to other foci of scientific inquiry, the quantity of research examining migration, culture conflict, crime and terrorism has yet to come of age. While those working in this frontier have made significant progress, much more work is clearly needed. The chapters in this anthology further our understanding of a variety of issues surrounding migration. At the same time, they also illuminate the complexities of managing migration and make apparent the challenges all nations currently face. As globalization continues governments will find it increasingly necessary to manage the process and impact of immigration. To be successful, governments will need to be both cognizant and informed of its many dimensions. It is hoped that future research builds upon this volume, and continues to investigate these very important matters.

References

Antonopoulos, G.A. (2005), "Book Review of Freilich, J.D., G. Newman, S.G. Shoham and M. Addad (eds), *Migration, Culture Conflict, and Crime*, Burlington: Ashgate, 2002", *British Journal of Criminology* 45: 225–47.

Buchanan, P.J. (2002), *The Death of the West: How Dying Populations and Immigrant Invasions Imperil our Country and Civilization*, New York: St. Martin's Press.

DeClair, E.G. (1999), *Politics on the Fringe: The People, Policies, and Organization of the French National Front*, Durham: Duke University Press.

Dershowitz, A. (2002), *Why Terrorism Works: Understanding the Threat, Responding to the Challenge*, New Haven: Yale University Press.

Freilich, J.D. and G. Newman (2002) (guest eds), Special issue on Migration and Crime, *International Journal of Comparative and Applied Criminal Justice* 26(2): 137–325.

Freilich, J.D., G. Newman, S.G. Shoham and M. Addad (2002) (eds), *Migration, Culture Conflict, and Crime*, Burlington: Ashgate.

Hendricks, Tyche (2004), "Militias Round up Illegal Immigrants in Desert", *San Francisco Chronicle*, at http://www.sfgate.com/cgi-bin/artcile.cgi?file=/c/2004/0531 (accessed May 31, 2005).

Howard, Gregory J., Graeme Newman and Joshua D. Freilich (2002a), "Population Diversity and Homicide: A Cross National Amplification of Blau's Theory of Diversity', in Freilich, J.D., G. Newman, S.G. Shoham and M. Addad (eds), *Migration, Culture Conflict, and Crime*, Burlington: Ashgate.

Howard, Gregory J., Graeme Newman and Joshua D. Freilich (2002b), "Further Evidence on the Relationship between Population Diversity and Crime", *International Journal of Comparative and Applied Criminal Justice* 26(2): 203–29.

Huntington, Samuel P. (2004), *Who Are We: The Challenges to America's National Identity*, New York: Simon & Schuster.

Juergensmeyer, M. (2000), *Terror in the Mind of God: The Global Rise of Religious Violence*, Berkeley: University of California Press.

Lee, Matthew (2003), *Crime on the Border: Immigration and Homicide in Urban Communities*, New York: LFB Scholarly Publishing.

Marizco, Michael (2004), "Echoes of Wild West in One Man's Border War", *Arizona Daily Star*, at http://www.dailystar.com/daolystar/dailystar/14622.php (accessed March 21, 2004).

Martinez, Ramiro (2002), *Latino Homicide: Immigration, Violence, and Community*, New York: Routledge.

McKinley, Brunson (2004), "Managing Migration: The 'Four-Box Chart'", *Migration, International Organization for Migration*, December: 3–4, at www.iom.int (accessed February 28, 2005).

Newman, G., J.D. Freilich and G.J. Howard (2002), "Importing and Exporting Criminality: Incarceration of the Foreign Born", *International Journal of Comparative and Applied Criminal Justice* 26(2): 143–63.

Raspail, J. (1985), *The Camp of the Saints*, Petoskey: Social Contract Press.

Simons, Marlise (2002), "Britain and Spain Seek Backing for European Policy on Migrants", *New York Times*, May 23, Foreign Desk, Section A, p. 7, col. 1.

Stern, Jessica (2003), *Terror in the Name of God: Why Religious Militants Kill*, New York: HarperCollins.

Tonry, Michael (1997) (ed), "Ethnicity, Crime, and Immigration: Comparative and Cross-National Perspectives", *Crime and Justice: A Review of Research*, vol. 21.

Vazsonyi, A. (2003), "Book Review of Freilich, J.D., G. Newman, S.G. Shoham and M. Addad (eds), *Migration, Culture Conflict, and Crime*, Burlington: Ashgate, 2002", *International Criminal Justice Review* 13: 202–4.

Welch, Wayne (2002) *Detained: Immigration Laws and the Expanding I.N.S. Jail Complex*, Philadelphia: Temple University Press.

Winterdyk, John and Liqun Cao (2004) (eds), *Lessons from International/ Comparative Criminology/Criminal Justice*, Toronto: de Sitter Publications.

PART I
Migration, Religion, Culture and Terrorism

Chapter 1

Terrorism Rediscovered: The Issue of Politically Inspired Criminality

Hans-Heiner Kühne
Universities of Trier and Westminster

Introduction

Crime for political reasons – be they sincere or an abusive pretext for illegal behavior – is a phenomenon nearly as old as crime itself. Criminal acts in this context have been directed against representatives of the political system and anybody else whose victimization could prove detrimental to the system. History tells us that the more established states become, the more they define actions which threaten the prevailing system as criminal. Tribal quarrels which began as a struggle for predominance changed to internal warfare and from there into high treason. For instance, in the end of the 19th century early Russian revolutionaries used bombs in a context we would call terrorism today. Subsequently, we can document numerous conflicts especially in Europe, Africa and Asia in which criminal acts have been committed as a means of terror in an effort to invoke political change. Quite a number of these activities were successful and as the former terrorists or revolutionaries rose to power, their former criminal behavior retroactively changed into honorable liberation combat. The redefining of these individuals from criminal terrorist to liberator opened the way for them to become more or less respected politicians.

The Political Motivation of Criminal Acts

This leads directly to the question of defining terrorism and distinguishing it from combat for freedom as well as from simple criminality. Perhaps most apparent is that terrorists and freedom fighters could be considered criminals when they violate criminal laws. However, they might differ from simple criminals in terms of their motivation. Whereas criminals are perpetrating crimes for their own good, terrorists and revolutionaries insist that they are fighting for ideas, which ultimately will bring prosperity and happiness to everyone. The quality of their alleged philanthropic ends, in their eyes, justifies the evil means they apply.

This may have been the reason for specific provisions, which have in the history of penal law opted for respectful sanctions for these "men of good will". For instance, in Germany until 1969 instead of prison the penalty for politically inspired criminality was *Einschließung*, a kind of arrest without the stigma of a normal prison (custodia honesta). The predecessor of this regulation was a practice of the 18th and 19th century under which "political criminals" could be sentenced to *Festungshaft*, which entailed confinement in a reasonably comfortable fortress. The goal was to prevent political activities of individuals who were looked upon as endangering the interests of the ruling class, mostly the feudal lords of the epoch. It has to be admitted, however, that these comfortable forms of confinement were mostly but not exclusively reserved for political crimes which mainly consisted of the publication of "wrong ideas" and political agitation.

Potential Doctrinal Excuses for Acts of Political Criminality

Putting aside these peculiarities, at the level of substantive law in cases of manslaughter and other serious criminality, there might be some exemptions by excuse or justification when acts are committed for political and altruistic reasons. But there is no penal law in the world which grants justification or excuse for killing people other than for reasons of *self-defense* or *war*. Self-defense in most terrorist or revolutionary assaults does not apply. The very meaning of terrorism is to victimize people who are not aware of the assault and hence are without protection, let alone aggressive, which could allow terrorists to claim self-defense.

Much more complicated is to decide whether these acts – however deplorable they might be – are legally justified as combat activities of war. There has hardly been any revolutionary or terrorist group in history that did not insist on declaring themselves to be at war with the system they were fighting against. Yet, consistently the states involved have denied such undertakings for obvious legal and political reasons. Groups emerging from inside the country cannot be conceded a legal status of their own, enabling them to declare war against their own state. Such a situation could only be assessed differently in cases of full blown civil wars. For many reasons states try to avoid, however, an avowal of civil war since it would revalorize the inner enemy as well as display a definite loss of the state's control and autonomy. To give just two examples, this is why the United Kingdom has never acknowledged the IRA as a party to civil war just as Germany did not do so with the Red Army Faction (RAF).

Yet, it remains to be decided what forms of terrorism and under what circumstances they might be regarded as legitimate acts of freedom fighting. Both options lack a definition of their prerequisites. In the case of civil war, it is mostly a political question which is decided upon by political discretion. If there is declaration of civil war, either by the state concerned or some other recognized authority, what formerly might have been considered terrorism now retroactively changes into legal acts of war. However, it is uncertain under what circumstances such a transition occurs. This situation makes it extremely difficult to talk about terrorism and morally condemn it. Moreover, it might be the reason for the lack of any universal definition of terrorism.

A New Paradigm: War on Terrorism

Recently we have begun to speak about the "war on terrorism". This is not just a *façon de parler*, a mode of expression but, indeed, a new terminology with a very distinct and substantial aim. While refraining from historically and politically tracing back that terminology, it is meant to tear down the barriers between fighting crime and waging war.

Waging War and Fighting Crime

First, let us examine the differences between waging war and fighting crime. In the process of fighting crime, states may only impose sanctions on persons on the basis of a formal judicial trial of which the basic guarantees are laid down in a number of international covenants like the European Commission on Human Rights (ECHR) or the UN Covenant on Civil and Political Rights (CCPR) or the UN Declaration on Human Rights. Thus, any state needs a judicial justification to impose a penalty on a person.

In war, however, as soon as it is declared, the state is permitted to kill the enemy without further justification. Additionally, in war-time there is a worldwide consent that states, in the name of domestic security during war-time, may sanction their own people without or with restricted participation of the ordinary judicial system. Hence, during war it becomes easier to bring sanctions against individuals. Needless to say war gives permission to use the death penalty even in those countries which have abolished it in their judicial system. In other words, there are hardly any restrictions for the state to pursue its enemies if it is waging war.

Returning to the newly invoked term "war on terrorism", it only can mean that terrorists are set free from judicial guarantees, considered outlaws and may be prosecuted and killed by anyone authorized to do so by the state. Hereby a new international legal dimension is being opened up. That is, *the concept of a unilateral war*. The enemy is no longer a party to a conflict but an evil being, holding no rights or enjoying any respect, whereas the state denominating and defining terrorism and terrorist organizations holds the privilege of a party to a war with little obligation to judicial process and free to employ nearly any means of repression and extermination.

This is not the place to elaborate concisely on the viability of such a one-sided concept under international law, although it does seem to be lacking any internationally accepted basis. At the same time the criminological and pragmatic arguments weighing the worldwide dangers of terrorism against the achievements of human rights' protection and judicial guarantees cannot be exhaustedly discussed here. But it cannot be denied that since times of pre-enlightenment there has never been such a one-sided aspiration of power from the side of the state, nor has the state ever been so free in fighting evil-doers.

The new ideology that only preemptive strikes will prevent the risk of terrorist attacks also unleashes the state's power from any legal bond; not even a suspicion of a criminal act or a verifiable danger to a person or to society is needed to justify intervention. It will be hard to draw a line between these activities and those of a totalitarian, fascist state. It might even become controversial whether such a fight against terrorism is not terrorism itself.

At the end of the day it is all about the question of which of the two parties has relied on the right and true values. But, history and philosophy have shown us that the plurality of value systems, be they of religious or rational character, do not allow for such a simple differentiation. Additionally there have hardly been any terrorists in history who have not referred to generally or widely accepted values.

Thus, the "war on terrorism" leads to an unsolvable controversy about the right and true values of those involved. It also precludes those states from using the most important argument for their actions. That is, that the suspension of legal process invoked while fighting terrorism displays and proves their moral and just position.

Political and Legal Consequences of the Concept of War Against Terrorism

Societies that are under direct threat of terrorism, like the United States and Israel, refer to the war on terrorism while they ignore most of the guarantees civilized societies have agreed upon in responding to crime. Other states, which are under no imminent threat and have no cause to act accordingly, are also undertaking similar actions of suspending judicial process under the guise of the "war against terrorism". This is particularly evident among common attitudes of European penal law cultures. Germany, for instance, provides a useful example.

Shortly after September 11 the German minister of the interior came up with two packages of drafts for the "Fight against Terrorism and Improvement of International Security". The core of those proposals consisted of new or enlarged coercive measures making the police and the prosecutorial authorities considerably stronger than they had been even under the amendments of the mid-1990s established to fight organized crime. These two packages passed through parliament without any controversial discussion or opposition. There was not even the slightest attempt to explain why and how 9/11 could have deteriorated the German situation of domestic security. Neither has there been any explanation of how the new laws could help fight this non-described new terrorist threat.

The worldwide shock of 9/11 helped the passing of these laws without discussion. Just the headlines promising intensified efforts to fight terrorism were ample justification. The Zeitgeist was flying high above any possible clouds of doubt or controversy. In fact, these two packages were anything but custom-made provisions to improve prevention and prosecution of terrorism. They simply were – with some rare exceptions – the remnants of earlier drafts on organized crime, which did not pass the parliamentarian discussions as they were deemed to be unduly repressive and disputed as to their efficiency. The Zeitgeist brought them up again and determined politicians gave them a new meaning without changing their substance.

Three years after passing the anti-terrorism packages we are able to retrospectively examine them. We are even able to admit that Germany has neither experienced any additional threat of terrorism after 9/11 nor that there has been any crucial gap of legal instruments to respond to such threats. Yet, these laws have remained in effect. It is likely that any new spectacular terrorist attack anywhere in the world, directed against the new alliance of the "good guys" states, will open the gates for further repressive legislation which will neither reduce terrorism nor improve its prosecution.

So the worldwide rediscovery of terrorism is being used as an instrument to vindicate intensified repression in former liberal states. Beginning in the late 1980s, the catchword putting penal law on the move around the world was "organized crime", since September 11, 2001, it is terrorism. But the new catchword is much more dangerous as it destroys the limits between fighting crime and fighting wars. Under the pretext of terrorism, domestic security becomes an issue of external security thus alleviating or even ignoring legal and judicial restraints.

To summarize this discussion the following points are provided:

1. Although a number of former terrorists have become respected politicians there is no penal law which justifies or exempts such behavior. Terrorists cannot, on their own authority, refer to their situation as one of war thus justifying their atrocities as acts of combat. Hence, terrorists are criminals and have to be treated accordingly.
2. The term "war on terrorism" has introduced a new paradigm which claims an array of war like activities from the side of the state, while denying terrorists the rights and guarantees they enjoy as criminals. This concept of a one-sided war until now has lacked legal verification, at a national and international level, and presents the danger that states fighting terrorists can hardly be discriminated from the terrorists they are fighting against.
3. Terrorism has become the new catchword around the world used to justify the repressive shift of national penal law systems even when there is no discernible domestic terrorist threat. Further, this shift serves to blur the borders between domestic issues of fighting crime and external security issues of waging war.

After all this, two questions remain:

1. What can be done to help those nations which are plagued by terrorism?
2. How do we accommodate terrorists who become statesmen and what does this mean for the definition of and the fight against terrorism?

Repression Versus Prevention: The Limits of Penal Law

Turning to the first question, it should be remembered that police law and penal law are not a cure but only function as a supportive instrument to reduce and control criminal acts. Hence, there is no chance in relying solely on intensified repression. Further, we know that people who have nothing left to lose will try everything and the threat of punishment will do little to deter them. Because of this, any law or authority will be impotent if people are without hope. This characterizes the limits of any legal order and its repressive and preventive means, and leads us directly to the reasons for terrorism.

It is, after all, the reasons for terrorism that have to concern us. Shlomo Giora Shoham elaborates on the reasons of terrorism (see below, Chapter 3). If we follow his ideas and take entropy as a term measuring disorder and deficits in a society, we will realize societal shortcomings relevant for the formation of terrorism which include:

1. education;
2. economy;
3. respect of individual rights;
4. political autonomy and public participation in political processes.

Education in this context plays a crucial role. First, it is the source for competence, which opens doors to economic success and a decent political system. But education serves at the same time as a most powerful weapon against terrorist ideologies. All of these ideologies are in a certain way fundamentalist, that is, they are reducing the understanding of the world to an intellectual minimum thus explaining life in an extremely simplistic way. That life appears as an easy black and white picture where good and a bad can be discerned without difficulty. Needless to say, the simplifiers are always on the side of the "good guys".

These extremely banal world visions, be they of socialist, fascist or religious hues, will hardly be accepted by people whose education has widened their philosophical perspectives. Serious social injustice as well as a lack of participation in the political process is also a strong incentive. However, even for the educated to turn to such black and white views (as they make it easier to decide to rise against such a system) denies its legitimacy. Here matters of human rights and political participation interact negatively with the issue of education. Fighting the roots of terrorism therefore is a highly political issue of giving a solid educational, economic, and political structure to a society where terrorism exists.

The Moral Question

The last but by far not least question is about the impact of the volatile change of identity from terrorist to statesman on our understanding of terrorism. There is ample historical evidence, some more recently, which indicates that no matter how heinous the act of terror committed by an individual it will not prevent the possibility of a promotion to statesmanship. Unfortunately, there are no guidelines, value systems or other factors that predict such a promotion. It appears to remain completely random or at least at the political discretion of some powerful states to decide that the cause of the terrorist is valid. Upon such recognition, so to say, the criminal past is wiped out. Even considering the hazardous character of such a process it is not hard to understand that it still may give sufficient incentives for people in deprived situations to turn to terrorism as a political means. Historically, it has repeatedly been demonstrated that these causal processes work appallingly well, in fact.

Conclusion

The only way to prevent such a motivation to terrorism would be an international ban on specifically described acts of terrorism which would be prosecuted by an international court even in cases where the perpetrator has reached a high political position as head of state or minister.

The definition of such crimes, however, would be no easy task since it would have to be based on a definition of the limits of self-defense against legal injustice and against unjust or even illegitimate states. The problems of legitimacy versus legality and of natural law versus statutory law are some of the most complicated and oldest questions in legal science. How far to the right must a state reach to defend itself against tyranny? This is a question which has plagued mankind since the beginning of the existence of states. It has been documented widely in literature beginning with the classic Greek dramas, continuing with the revolutionary literature of the late 18th century up to modern writers who use the recent experience of totalitarian societies to display the dilemma of morality within the application of intolerable legal action and justice. Given the difficulty of this issue, we cannot expect an international draft proposing a solution to this problem within a short period of time.

This is further complicated as politicians will be extremely reluctant to sign a covenant which might force them into accepting the legitimacy of movements which for political reasons they would prefer to define as terrorist organizations. The simple call for more crime fighting and war waging against terrorism, so far, is designed to hide all of these problems.

Chapter 2

Culture or Conflict? Migration, Culture Conflict and Terrorism

Roland Eckert
Trier University

In response to the threat of totalitarian regimes in the 20th century, perfection of the state's ability to wield power and control opinion was viewed as the greatest threat to peace and freedom. During the last 15 years, however, this outlook has changed dramatically. Decaying state structures and ongoing civil wars in many parts of the world demonstrate, as during the time of Thomas Hobbes, that the state's monopoly on the use of force is a necessary (though not sufficient) precondition for peace and freedom. September 11, 2001, made clear once and for all that the use of political force by nonstate agents extends through global networks into the industrialized nations of the West. The main form taken by this force is terrorism, whose specific mechanisms and motivations therefore demand analysis. While this examination may contribute to a short-term remedy it could perhaps facilitate long-term prevention strategies.

Terrorism is part of a strategy of "asymmetrical warfare" that avoids open battle with the powers of the state but seeks to provoke a harsh response in an attempt to trigger waves of solidarity and support within those population groups of which the protagonists claim to be the avant-garde (Waldmann 1998). Since the late 1960s terrorism has become more internationalized and dependent upon financing from private businesses and other fundraising techniques (Hoffman 2002). Nonetheless, the strategy of many terrorists did not change. Their immediate goal is not "victory" but rather the spread of fear and terror, which in some cases may indeed cause the enemy to retreat. The success of terrorism depends upon a number of factors, such as:

1. whether the terrorists can win sympathy or even solidarity among specific segments of the population, i.e., whether they command or can attract collective solidarity;
2. what level of costs the other side is prepared to accept; and finally
3. the recruiting of terrorists is linked with transformations of subjective identity that depend on a plethora of preconditions.

Both the creation of collective solidarity as a background and precondition for terrorism and the transformation of the identity of actors do not usually precede conflicts, but instead form an integral part of the events concerned. Although the creation of collectives and the transformation of identities are closely linked, they also may diverge. Terrorism in Germany during the 1970s, for example, was successful in transforming the identity of the protagonists but failed to harness collective solidarity because people expressed sympathy not with the revolution but with the state under attack (Eckert 1978).

How does the creation of collective solidarity and the transformation of identities work? Human beings usually have a wide range of identities, and are therefore constantly adapting their behavior to their current situation as a family member, employee, neighbor, member of a club, and member of a religion, ethnic, racial or national community. Any such group membership implies limits that exclude other possible affiliations: if I am this mother's son, then I am not someone else's; when acting as a doctor, I am not a patient; if I belong to this political party, then I do not belong to another at the same time. Affiliations in direct everyday interaction are rendered relatively clear and trivially plausible by their complementary roles. Membership in imagined communities such as a religion, collective world view, ethnicity, class, or nation, however, depends upon many more factors since it is required to stabilize symbolic borders that are not necessarily manifest or plausible in everyday life.

This is why religious communities have always fought against mixed marriages. Two processes in particular can be used to cement imagined communities. First, symbolic borders can be ideologically reinforced by essentializing the corresponding group affiliation (e.g., "true" Germanness, the "pure doctrine", "hindutva") (Wetzstein, Reis and Eckert 1999). Second, such borders become much more pronounced as a result of conflicts, especially life-threatening disputes with other communities. In such conflicts individuals are reminded in existential and all-encompassing terms of their protection by and solidarity with a collective, even if previously they would only rarely, under certain conditions, have identified with it. It is therefore not simply collective identities with divergent traditions that generate conflicts, but it is conflicts (whatever their object) that generate or are used to radicalize collective identity (Eckert 2003). German nationalism emerged during the Franco-Prussian wars, Kurdish nationalism increased in response to the central state's definition of the Kurds as "mountain Turks". As Marx argued, class consciousness is not linearly related to class structures as such, but constitutes itself in concrete conflicts (between workers and capitalists).

How does this happen? Conflict reinforces one dominant collective identity among many others by means of fear and hope. The more we (as Albanians, for example) are forced to seek protection or the more we attempt (as Serbs) to safeguard the land of the Holy Monasteries, the more we commit ourselves to an ethnic category and are categorized as such by others. Psychologists of perception speak of a heightening of contrast that occurs during stressful conditions. The greater the fear, the more important it is to know which side someone is on. Neighborhoods and circles of friends are swiftly cleansed of potential enemies. Realms of good and evil are defined. Contrary to what Carl Schmitt (1933) believed, the distinction between friend and foe is not the "essence of politics", but is rather a consequence and an instrument of conflict aggravation. Although initially there may be room to compromise over some issues (such as access for an ethnic or religious group to civil service or recognition of a minority language), what is ultimately at stake is the "essence" of the collective identity, which engenders its own concrete signals and conflict scenarios on this basis. This results, for example, in Ayodhya being posited as the birthplace of a Hindu god as a way of entering into symbolic and real conflict with Muslims. The more energy and time that are invested in such an idea, the higher the cost in human life, the "holier" the idea becomes, and the more difficult de-escalation becomes. This is how groups are formed that possess collective solidarity, a capacity for suffering and a readiness for violence, while acting in a "cosmic struggle" (Juergensmeyer 2000: 242).

Not all members of a potential collective participate at the same time or in the same way in this process of essentialization of the communal identity. A range of different interests emerge, such as those of the war profiteers, whose social standing and material situation is enhanced by the state of conflict. Their interests will often clash with those of former notables whose business depends critically on peace. They also may differ from the collective's sympathizers living elsewhere, who contribute significantly to the financing of such movements although their everyday life is not affected, as shown by the funding of the IRA by Americans of Irish origin.

Since participation patterns cannot be reduced to economic interests, it raises the question of the transformation of identity among the actors. Sacrificing one's life to a cause is rarely rational, though it may be so if there is no other option, which may often be true in the case of child soldiers and juvenile attackers. Sacrificing one's life becomes entirely rational if one identifies totally with the religious, revolutionary, ethnic, or national collective in question (Berghoff 1997). This could occur in two ways. First, training can lead to this total identification, especially in juveniles (Elwert 2003), but I consider a more important influence to be humiliation and experiences of victimization and violence by the other side. According to Juergensmeyer (2000: 187), "religion and violence are seen as antidotes to humiliation", and "In many of the cases … not only have religion's characteristics led spiritual persons into violent situations, but also the other way around: violent situations have reached out for religious justification" (Juergensmeyer 2000: 161). Both violence suffered and violence exercised change a person's world view. They do so by posing inevitable questions without supplying clear answers. The same experience can generate both thoughts of self-assertion via revenge as well as thoughts of nonviolence, and the former will be the more probable outcome so long as there is no external judicial body to which either side can appeal and which is willing to help.

What are the links between migration and violent conflict? Sometimes the connection is obvious, especially when native people in a country with high immigration feel threatened. In Germany, the arrival of five million immigrants between 1988 and 1992 led both to rising fears of an overwhelming foreign presence and to increasing numbers of xenophobic attacks to be stimulated (Eckert 2002). State-sponsored transfer of population groups from Java to South-Kalimantan sparked the ensuing ethnic conflict. Israel's settlement policy in the occupied territories is likely to have similar, aggravating, effects on that conflict.

Things become more complicated when we examine how migrants themselves contribute to ethnic and inter-communal conflict. There are certainly many Irish in the United States, Hindus in Britain, Kurds in Germany, and Muslims around the world that support their ethnic or religious movements, even violent ones. But these same people have learned to operate with different identities, and have adapted to various situations and accordingly focused their ethnic or religious identity on the corresponding holidays and festivals.

But precisely this "sectioning off" of ascriptive identity is ambivalent. The inherent process of abstraction from conventional everyday culture could lead to both relativization and radicalization of communal identity. According to one estimate, only a small number of North African immigrants in France are practicing Muslims. At the same time, this group includes a considerable number of Islamists. Their fundamentalist development is due precisely to their removal from local and family traditions and their independent interpretation of the Koran. Similar causes have been documented for the emergence of the fundamentalist Caliphate movement in Germany (Schiffauer 2000). Migration creates a life situation that poses many questions without prescribing specific answers. One possibility is a radicalization of group affiliation. In terms of cultural theory, this can be interpreted as a phenomenon of the selectability of meaning. This applies not only to achieved social positions, but also to ascribed attributes such as gender, religion, and ethnicity which become subject to individual choice – at least in terms of meaning for the individual. Via the media, television, and the Internet, a global market in identity models is established. The attribution of existential meaning, even to ascribed identities, is an act of choice in this field. Gandhi's dhoti, the ultra-orthodox attire of New York Jews, the Mao-look of the May 1968 generation, the dreadlocks of Rastas and the prophet's robe of Islamic chiefs are all symbols and forms of self-stigmatization in the sense of a chosen tradition. This also means that fundamentalism is not a traditionalist response to modernization, but a modern answer to the dwindling status of tradition.

In this light, it is not just the continuing existence of archaic group affiliations that jeopardizes the triumph of Kant's vision of a cosmopolitan society – it is thoroughly modern processes of selectable identity susceptible to *radicalization in* and *via conflicts* that generate a threat to world peace. Huntington's concept of a "clash of civilizations" is incorrect. Increasing contact between cultures leads to a range of reactions – the return to specific traditions to "blood and belief, faith and family" (Huntington 1996: 126) is only one possible option and not necessarily the dominant one. In addition, in most cases fundamentalism is not violent (Marty and Appleby 1991: 814). Conflicts do not simply result from a return to traditional values. They may have quite different causes, including the struggle for land, water or a share in the state's exploitation machinery, as well as conflicts over public morals and cultural hegemony.

But conflicts, however they arise and whatever they are about, turn violent, if there are no institutions within which they can be carried out by other means. Such unregulated conflicts (Dubiel 1992; Hirschman 1994) intensify the process of establishing unambiguous identities, the construction of friend and foe, of good and evil. Contrary to what Huntington claims, initially it is not the shift to traditional identities that produces conflicts, but conflicts which produce, among other things, a reduction in the diversity of identities to those that appear to safeguard personal integrity and dignity – and these *can* (but may not) be fundamentalist ones. Due to colonialist and post-colonialist conflicts in the Middle East we observe a "consumption" of various ideologies: Nationalist, socialist and now religious ones. Terrorism is therefore not the expression of a specific culture (be it Basque, Irish, Tamil, Chechen, Hutu, or Saudi), it is primarily a means of extreme political struggle. Further, it is also both a consequence and a cause of differences between communities radicalized by unregulated conflicts. Juergensmeyer concludes "that war is the context for sacrifice rather than the other way round" (2000: 169). For these reasons, entering into the spiral of revenge is hardly a promising approach, and certainly not sufficient. No doubt, not all conflicts can be regulated, especially if they are protracted. Yet in the long term the fight against terrorists will only succeed if it is possible to halt the radicalization of the communities whose avant-garde the terrorists claim to represent. In this dispute, conflict resolution (Eckert and Willems 1992), mediation and under certain circumstances the type of power mediation employed in the former Yugoslavia are the only sustainable solutions.

References

Berghoff, Peter (1997), *Der Tod des politischen Kollektivs. Politische Religion und das Sterben und Töten für Volk, Nation und Rasse*, Berlin: Akad.-Verlag.

Dubiel, Helmut (1992), "Konsens oder Konflikt – die normative Integration des demokratischen Staates", in: Kohler-Koch, Beate (ed.), *Staat und Demokratie in Europa: 18. Wissenschaftlicher Kongreß der deutschen Vereinigung für Politische Wissenschaft*, Opladen: Westdeustcher Verlag.

Eckert, Julia (2003), *The Charisma of Direct Action: Power, Politics and Shiv Sena*, Delhi: Oxford: Oxford University Press.

Eckert, Roland (1978), "Terrorismus als Karriere", in: Geißler, Heiner (eds), *Der Weg in die Gewalt*, Munich and Vienna: Olzog.

Eckert, Roland (2002), "Hostility and Violence Against Immigrants in Germany", in Freilich, Joshua D., Graeme Newman, S. Shoham, S. Giora and Moshe Addad (eds), *Migration, Culture Conflict and Crime*, Aldershot: Dartmouth Ashgate.

Eckert, Roland and Helmut Willems (1992), *Konfliktintervention – Perspektivenübernahme in gesellschaftlichen Auseinandersetzungen*, Opladen: Leske + Budrich.

Elwert, Georg (2003), "Charismatische Mobilisierung und Gewaltmärkte. Die Attentäter des 11. September", in Sack, Detlef and Gerd Steffens (eds), *Gewalt statt Anerkennung? Aspekte des 11.9.2001 und seiner Folgen*, Frankfurt am Main, Berlin, Brussel, New York, Oxford, Vienna: Peter Lang.

Hirschman, Albert O. (1994), "Wieviel Gemeinsinn braucht die liberale Gesellschaft", *Leviathan: Zeitchrift für Sozialwissenschaft*, 2(22): 293–304.

Hoffman, Bruce (2002), *Terrorismus – der unerklärte Krieg. Neue Gefahren politischer Gewalt*, Frankfurt: Fischer Taschenbuch Verlag.

Huntington, Samuel P. (1996), *The Clash of Civilizations. Remaking of World Orders*, New York: Touchstone.

Juergensmeyer, Mark (2000), *Terror in the Mind of God. The Global Rise of Religious Violence*, Berkeley, Los Angeles and London: University of California Press.

Marty, Martin E. and R. Scott Appleby (1991), "Conclusion: An Interim Report an a Hypothetical Family", in: Marty, Martin E. and R. Scott Appleby (eds), *Fundamentalisms Observed*, Chicago and London: University of Chicago Press.

Schiffauer, Werner (2000), *Die Gottesmänner. Türkische Islamisten in Deutschland. Eine Studie zur Herstellung religiöser Evidenz*, Frankfurt am Main: Suhrkamp.

Schmitt, Carl (1933), *Der Begriff des Politischen*, Hamburg: Hanseatischer Verlag.

Waldmann, Peter (1998), *Terrorismus. Provokation der Macht*, Munich: Gerling-Akad.-Verlag.

Wetzstein, Thomas A., Christa Reis and Roland Eckert (1999), "Die Herstellung von Eindeutigkeit – Ethnozentrische Gruppenkulturen unter Jugendlichen", in Dünkel, Frieder and Bernd Geng (eds), *Rechtsextremismus und Fremdenfeindlichkeit*, Mönchengladbach: Godesberg Forum Verlag.

Chapter 3

The 21st-Century Kulturkampf: Fundamentalist Islam Against Occidental Culture

Shlomo Giora Shoham
Tel Aviv University, Israel

I thank God that my sons Oudai and Qoussai and my grandson Moustafa have sacrificed themselves for this country.

Saddam Hussein – A recorded message to the Iraqi people.

Introduction

Prior to September 11, 2001, the scourge of fundamentalist Islam was mostly felt by Israelis; victims of the Taliban in Afghanistan, suppressed students in Iran, and by slaughtered villagers in Algeria. After September 11, the political hierarchies in the United States and Britain, among other nations, realized that a war was going on – fought with different weapons, but overwhelmingly frightening and quite effective – between fundamentalist Islam and Western culture. How did this start? Why has it been overlooked and what may be expected to happen? To begin, however, we must clarify some preliminary questions. What were the sociocultural processes that preceded these outbursts of war that most observers prefer to denote as terrorism? What is the conceptual infrastructure with which this war may be analyzed? Finally, can this war be dealt with by conventional methods or do novel tactics and strategies have to be devised? Since we hold the present war to be a sequel to a harsh cultural conflict that raged throughout the ages between the Islamic more Tantalic social characters and the occidental largely Sisyphean social characters we have to deliberate on the concepts of Tantalic and Sisyphean social characters. These are related to our personality theory that we have developed in extenso elsewhere (Shoham 1979).

This theory identifies two opposing personality types: the "participant" and the "separant". "Participation" means the identification of the ego with people, objects or symbols outside the self, and the desire to lose one's separate identity in fusion with these externals. "Separation", of course, implies the opposite. These two character types define the extremes of a continuum of personality types.

Our personality theory also posits three main developmental phases. The first is the process of birth. The second, the crystallization of an individual ego by the molding of the "ego boundary". The third phase, a corollary of socialization, is the achievement of an "ego identity". The strain to overcome the separating and dividing pressures never leaves the human individual. The striving to partake in an all-encompassing whole is ever present and takes many forms. If one avenue towards its realization is blocked, it seeks out another. Total participation or fusion is, by definition, unattainable. In addition to the objective impossibility of participation, the separant trait acts as a countering force, both on the instinctive and interactive levels. At any given moment of our lives, there will be a disjuncture between our desire for participation and our subjectively defined distance from our participatory aims. We call this gap the "Tantalus Ratio", that is, the relationship between the longed-for participatory goal and the distance from it, as perceived by the ego (Shoham 1984: ch. 10).

Another basic premise of the theory concerns the fixating of separant and participant personality types. This is related to the stage of development, a later orality, when a separate self crystallizes out of the earlier undifferentiated whole. There is an ontological baseline by which the self is defined by the non-self – the outside object. The coagulation of the self marks the starting point for the most basic developmental dichotomy.

Two separate developmental phases can be distinguished: the first, from birth and early orality until the point at which the ego boundary is formed around the emerging individual separatum; and the second, from later orality onwards. In the first phase, any fixation that might occur, and thereby imprint some character traits on the developing personality, is not registered by a separate self capable of discerning between the objects, which are the sources of the fixation-causing trauma, and itself as recipient. The entity which experiences the trauma is a non-differentiated whole. However, if the traumatizing fixation occurs at the later oral phase, the self may well be in a position to attribute the cause of pain and deprivation to its proper source: the objects. We therefore propose a personality typology that is anchored on this developmental dichotomy of pre- and post-differentiation of the self (Shoham 1984: ch. 10).

The process of molding the separate individual determines the nature and severity of the fixation, which in turn determines the placement of a given individual on the personality type continuum. However, the types themselves are fixed at different stages in the developmental chronology; the participant at pre-differentiated early orality and the separant after the formation of the separant self. The participant factor operates, with a different degree of potency, on both these personality types, but the quest for congruity manifests itself differently with each polar personality type. The participant aims to achieve congruity by effacing and annihilating himself, by melting back into the object and regaining the togetherness and non-differentiation of early orality. The separant type aims to achieve congruity by overpowering, or "swallowing", the object.

Social Character

When our core personality continuum is applied to the characteristics of groups or cultures, it relates to a social character. The family and other socializing agencies transmit the norms and values of the group, which the individual then internalizes. It is important to note at the outset, however, that a social character as the composite portrait of a culture is never pure. It portrays only essentials, not peripheral traits. One culture may absorb the social character of its conquerors. This social character may thence be classified along a continuum similar to our personality core continuum. The separant pole can be denoted as Sisyphean, after the Greek stone-manipulating Titan; we denote the participant pole as Tantalic, after the stationary, inner-directed and abstract demi-god. Thus the social character constitutes the cultural dimension of the personality continuum.

Patterns of Culture and Social Character

The classification of cultures along a continuum and their relationship to a given personality structure necessitate two basic assumptions. First, that those cultures possess generalized traits that may be measured and ranked on a predetermined typology or scale. Second, that these traits could be related to the character of the individual. By adopting both these assumptions, we find ourselves in good or bad company, depending on taste or value judgment. Spengler and Toynbee have adhered to both these assumptions in their works on the growth and decline of cultures (Spengler 1954; Toynbee 1987). Indeed, Spengler compares the ages of cultures to the ages of man: "Every culture," he says, "passes through the age phases of the individual man. Each has its childhood, youth, manhood and old age"(Spengler 1954: 107). Oswald Spengler and Arnold Toynbee thus introduced the dynamic temporal dimension to the study of culture.

The current anthropological conception of culture as the "superorganic" (see Kroeber 1952: 22–30) pattern of symbols, generated by the interaction of groups and individuals and transmitted by learning, lends itself to abstract classifications. The crucial question is: are the patterns Platonic ideals projected by the mind of the anthropologist onto the rarified ether of abstraction, or are they generalized descriptions of processes actually taking place in societies? If culture "is what binds men together" (Ruth Benedict, cited in Kluckhorn 1962: 62) and it does so by "symbolating" human interaction (Reis Leslie White, cited in Kluckhorn 1962: 26), that is, by relating forms and appearances to qualities and attributes, then it already involves, by definition, the abstraction and ordering of "Gestalts" (Kroeber 1963: 101). In other words, the processes of cultures are themselves manifested in arranged patterns. This may also be gleaned from some of the key concepts in the definition of culture. A symbol is a value – or meaning-laden sign (White 1949: 25); and meanings and value judgments are readily expressed in generalized patterns. The "superorganic" is manipulated by tools, and the means chosen to achieve cultural goals are regulated by norms. Yet rules and norms themselves are constructs that are choice objects for paradigms and classifications. Prima facie, therefore, we may accept the feasibility, contrary to the vehement objections of some ethnographers, of ordering cultures into generalized configurations and patterns, or to use Spengler's flowery language, of painting the portrait of a culture (Spengler 1954: 101). Indeed, Ruth Benedict and her cultural-relativist colleagues have demonstrated how patterns may be identified by the direct observation of cultures. Furthermore, Claude Levi-Strauss and his structuralist school have shown that cultural processes in "savage" societies are coincidental to the classificatory passage from things to symbols, notably the totemic generalizations from the concrete to the abstract (Levi-Strauss 1966). The structuralists thus identify in societies not only patterns, but whole systems of functions underlying overt cultural processes. For Benedict, cultural patterns stem from "unconscious canons of choice that develop within the culture ... so that it selects some segment of the arc of possible human behavior and, so far as it achieves integration, its institutions tend to further the expression of its selected segment and to inhibit opposite expressions" (Benedict 1934: 54, 220).

These habits, symbols, values, cultural goals and the means to achieve them, crystallize into "total culture patterns" (Kroeber 1963: 125–30) by which cultures may be identified. The ordering of cultural patterns into schemes, paradigms, continua, and matrices may vary according to the purpose or theoretical orientation of the observer. There can be no universal criterion for measuring the validity of the classification of culture patterns. The value of a classification should be determined by the specific aims and needs of a given theoretical concern. This is aptly stated by Claude Levi-Strauss as follows:

> The real question is not whether the touch of a woodpecker's beak does in fact cure toothache. It is rather whether there is a point of view from which a woodpecker's beak and a man's tooth can be seen as "going together" (the use of this congruity for therapeutic purposes being only one of its possible uses) and whether some initial order can be introduced into the universe by means of these groupings. (1966: 9)

We may thus observe in the literature, a vast array of cultures that serve an ad hoc aim of the researcher. On the micro level, we may find F.L.K. Hsu's classification of cultures by their dominant dyads. Japan, according to his criteria, is a father/son-dominated society, whereas American culture is dominated by the husband/wife-dyad (Hsu 1969: 86). On the macro level, Riesman and his associates identified the traditional, inner-directed societies within a scheme related to transitional growth and economic development (Riesman, Glazer and Denney 1953). The typology that is closest in its general objectives to our own, is of course the one presented by Benedict, following Spengler's cultural relativism. The cultural-relativist method of identifying dominant social characters within a culture, which may be arranged between two poles of a continuum, suits our methodological purposes. By this method, we may characterize a culture according to its position on the continuum. This position is never static because it shifts with time and social change.

Next, we address the nature and viability of a social character. According to Fromm, a social character does not consist of those peculiarities that differentiate people, but of "that part of their character structure that is common to most members of the group" (1942: 277) The social character is, therefore, a common attribute of individuals, ingrained in them by socializing agents, which display the characteristics of a culture. Riesman, who uses mutatis mutandis, Fromm's definition of social character, relies for the sources and genesis of this social character on Erikson, who claims that "Systems of child training ... represent unconscious attempts at creating out of human raw material that configuration of attitudes which is the optimum under the tribes' particular natural conditions and economic-historic necessities" (Riesman, Glazer and Denney 1953: 19). Erikson's mesh of social Darwinism with Marxist material dialectics is too concrete and harsh in our view as an explanation for the volatile concept of social character. We prefer to see the social character as a "collective representation" in the sense used by Levy-Bruhl (1966: 3–5), of acts, symbols, and transitions from the concrete to the abstract displayed by groups in their interaction with the individuals which comprise them, or with other groups. This involves the transmission of the social character from the group to its young, and from generation to generation by a process of learning and socialization, and not by heredity, as postulated by Jung (1944: 616). The social character is the psychological type of a character as displayed by a collectivity, and not by the individuals comprising it. Yet, when this social character is implanted in the individual by the group, it provides the necessary link between the phylogenetic and otogenic bases of the personality structure.

Activitist and Quietist Cultures

Every classification fulfills the specific aims of a given theoretical structure. Our purpose is to determine the inter-relationship of the Sisyphean–Tantalic personality type continuum with the separant-participant continuum of cultures. Consequently, we have to define our cultural continuum and describe the polarities of our social characters, and this, to be sure, is no mean task. The "portrait of a culture", depicts only the predominant cultural traits and patterns, but every culture is perforce pluralistic and displays, to varying degrees, aspects of the opposite polar type, as well. This is the main reason why a continuum is the most suitable means of describing the polarity and range of social characters.

The polarization into Sisyphean-separant and Tantalic-participant social characters has influenced the *Weltanschauung* of observers from time immemorial. The first characteristic which distinguishes a separant culture is an orientation toward action. The second contrast is between unity and plurality. The participant culture decrees that one has to rid one's thoughts of the illusory perceptions of the senses in order to reach the monistic wholeness behind the deceptions of plurality. Consequently, the Parmenidean sphere, representing all-present wholeness is also the three-dimensional mandala that is the prevailing symbol of the Far Eastern participant cultures. The separant conception of reality follows Pythagoras, and of course Heracleitus, who saw the universe as ordered into measured pluralities that

Separant	*Participant*
Object-manipulation	Self-manipulation
Reason	Intuition
Flux	Constancy
Plurality	Unity
Action	Resignation

Figure 3.1 Polar Patterns of Social Character

follow the universal formula of sequence and dynamic harmonies within inter-related boundaries. The third polarity contrasts the ideal of constancy in the participant cultures with the idea of relationship in the separant culture. If plurality is illusion and the veil of Maya and the sole reality is unity, then all relationships are also illusory because unity cannot interact with itself. Moreover, for participant cultures, relationship is not only deceptive, but also the source of evil, sorrow, and pain. For separant cultures, on the other hand, relations with space and time and with other human beings are the frame of reference of human life, and have to be coped with by integration, adjustment, and solidarity. The fourth contrast relates to the emphasis of separant cultures on reason, on those formulae and models that explain man and his universe. The participant cultures tend to distrust and reject logic, relying more on intuition and revelation. The fifth polarity which we have found useful is that between the separant tool orientation, for instance, a culture geared toward the manipulation of objects and the participant symbol-oriented culture, in which ideas and belief systems are centered on inwardly contemplating individuals immersed in "doing their own thing."

Our five polar characteristics of social characters are summarized in Figure 3.1. These patterns are by no means exhaustive, but rather illustrative. They point out the highlights of a given social character, but do not constitute a precise definition.

Our use of a continuum to describe social characters means that no culture may be tagged by one definitive label. Consequently, in every participant social character there are separant patterns, and vice versa. In Judaism, for instance, Yom-Hakipurim, the Day of Atonement, is a participant ritual in which the individual strives to partake of divinity through self-humiliation and effacement. Yom Hapurim, the feast celebrating the deliverance of the Jews from Haman, Ahasuerus's evil Wazir, is written in Hebrew like the Day of Atonement less one syllable: ki. This led the Lurianic Kabbalists to link the two holidays: the Day of Atonement being Yom ki Purim. The lots cast by children and adults on the festival of Purim were compared with the lots of life and death cast by God on Yom Hakipurim, the Day of Atonement. And yet, Purim is a separant ritual of frenzy in which individuals strive to reach each other through the ecstatic togetherness of wine, song, and dance (see *Encyclopaedia Judaica* 1971, vol. 13: 1390). The pure separant or participant culture does not exist in reality, but the signs that indicate the presence of one or the other type of social character may be arranged on several continua, representing various cultural areas.

At the separant extreme, we may place the north-western European societies imbued with the Protestant ethic which burst forth in the full-blown flames of the "American Dream". On the participant pole we find cultures dominated by the Hinayana Buddhist doctrines of quietist self-annihilation.

It might well be that the separant-activist trends of north-western European cultures have their origins in the ethos of the Germanic tribes who conquered their way across Europe, carrying Thor's hammer as a symbol of power. They even dispensed with the fear of the after-life by having Odin, the god of battle, send his armor-clad maidens, the Valkyries, to carry the slain warriors to eternal bliss in Valhalla. There is no doubt, however, that the concern with achievement, the manipulation by force of less powerful societies, and the scientific conquest of nature which marked the rise of north-western European societies in the last centuries, were boosted by the Protestant ethic. A separant trend runs through Luther's sanctification of work as a sacred calling, Calvin's stress on achievement as proof of predestined worth, Hegel's doctrine of action as the necessary bridge between subject and object, and Marx's decree to harness all means of production in order to mold man's (dialectical) future. The separant culture is Sisyphean because its aim of incorporating and controlling spatio-temporality within itself is unattainable. Hyperactivity often channels itself into routine and aimless ritualism, social engineering is more likely to lead to the social death of totalitarianism or the robotic zombies of Orwell's *Nineteen-Eighty-Four*, and the scientific manipulation of matter seems to achieve the suffocation of air, the death of water and the perfection of artifacts for mass murder. Yet, the separant striving to reach Utopia through the dialectics of action is never-ending, like the pushing of the Sisyphean rock.

We may, at this stage, anticipate critical reactions to our focus on religion as an anchor for the identification of cultures along our continuum. However, this focus is warranted both by theoretical considerations and empirical findings. First, religious affiliation has been found to correlate with many attitudes and modes of behavior, as well as with the structure and contents of social institutions (see McClelland 1961). Religion is a significant identification tag, although many other social institutions, norms and cultural goals are also relevant for our classification. Most, if not all, of our pairs of polar patterns are reflected in the religious doctrine of a given culture. Most of human history, to risk a sweeping generalization, has been related, influenced and often totally dominated by religion. The "unchartered region of human experience", to use Gilbert Murray's fortunate phrase (1955: 4–5), is the domain of religion. Although the areas of our "positive knowledge" are greatly expanding, most of the swift human journey from an involuntary beginning to an unknown end is governed by confusion and chaos. Consequently, religion has reigned supreme in human societies throughout history. Even Marxism has been denoted a "secular religion", and Bertrand Russell (1947: 383) has made the following ingenious analogies:

Yahweh = Dialectical Materialism
The Messiah = Marx
The Elect = The Proletariat

The Church = The Communist Party
The Second Coming = The Revolution
Hell = Punishment of the Capitalists
The Millennium = The Communist Commonwealth.

Yet, if we try to place Communist China, still adhering to the Marxist secular religion, on our space continuum, we may decide that its position is not on the far separant pole because it still retains some vestiges of the Taoist and Buddhist participant social characteristics.

On the participant extreme of our continuum, we have placed Hinayana Buddhism, of the Southern Theravada school. The Hinayana is the "small vehicle", as condescendingly labeled by the Mahayana Buddhists who called themselves the "great vehicle". The Hinayana rejects temporal existence as a burden because all action and interaction is irritation, friction, and suffering (dukkha) (SEE Humphreys 1952: 81). Second, the Samsara, the cycle of growth, fruition and decay that is the essence of the individual's separate condition, produces disharmony and desire, the harbingers of evil. Third, plurality is an illusion generated by the perception of the separate self. Nirvana, therefore, is achieved by the annihilation of the individual self and "awakening", into the blissful reality of unity (Humphreys 1952: 88–9). We may identify in the Hinayana doctrine at least four out of our five main patterns of the participant social character: quietist inaction, rejection of temporality, self-effacement and the belief in the omnipresence of unity behind the veil of plurality. Although Hindu yoga is near to the participant pole, it is somewhat removed from the extreme position of the Hinayana.

The social characters like the personality types may be arranged along a continuum with the extreme Sisyphean and Tantalic social characters at its two poles. The social characters which embraced during the last millennium and a half the Muslim creed's ethics and way of life tend more or less towards the Tantalic pole of our social character continuum, whereas the occidental cultures tend to move towards its Sisyphean pole.

The relationship between the self and its human and objective environment is, therefore, conceived within the context of a Buberian dialogue. If an I–thou encounter occurs, there is a sense of revelation and meaning. If a dialogue is not effected, the self feels that its environment is menacing, opaque, and absurd. A dialogue may be affected, according to Buber, only if the self opens up voluntarily to the other. When the choice has been made, and the self enters into a dialogic relationship with another human being, or into an authentic relationship with words, music, or a painting, the alternatives – to use a quantum mechanical simile – collapse, and the relevant mental energy is infused exclusively into the dialogical relationship. Technically, we have availed ourselves of Niels Bohr's conceptualization of the complementarity between divergent dualities to describe the possibilities of linkage between man, on the one hand, and energy-matter, on the other. Bohr says:

> Evidence obtained under different experimental conditions cannot be comprehended within a single picture, but must be regarded as complementary in the sense that only the totality of the phenomena exhaust the possible information about the objects...Indeed this circumstance presents us with a situation concerning the analysis and synthesis of experience which is entirely new in physics and forces us to replace the ideal of causality by a more general viewpoint usually termed "complementarity". The apparently incompatible sorts of information about the behavior of the object under examination, which we get by different experimental arrangements, can clearly not be brought into connection with each other in the usual way, but may, as equally essential for an exhaustive account of all experience, be regarded as "complementary" to each other. (1937: 291)

Bohr intended his complementarity principle to apply not only to pairs of quantitative parameters (the measurement of both at the same time barred by the uncertainty principle), but also to the bonding of contradictory parameters in biology, psychology, philosophy, and especially ethics. Hence, for instance, the complementarity between value judgments and collapse of alternatives would induce us to see evil after we have made an indeterministic choice to opt for evil. Per contra, if we elect to see good, we shall see good. If we concentrate on one alternative, the other collapses; if we set out to observe good, we tend to ignore evil, and vice versa. The complementarity principle in the field of cultural norms may be envisaged in the following manner: Every organism needs a system-in-balance to function and survive. This holds true for artifacts as well as human aggregates.

The link between consciousness and the objective world was masterfully metaphorized in the following Hasidic tale, as told by S.Y. Agnon to Gershom Scholem:

> When the Ba'al Shem had a difficult task before him, he would go to a certain place in the woods, light a fire, and meditate in prayer – and what he set out to perform was done. When a generation later the Maggid of Meseritz was faced with the same task he would go to the same place in the woods and say: We can no longer light the fire, but we can still speak the prayers – and what he wanted done became reality. A generation later Rabbi Moshe Leib of Sassov had to perform this task. And he too went to the woods and said: We can no longer light the fire, nor do we know the secret meditations belonging to the prayer, but we do know the place in the woods to which it all belongs – and that must be sufficient; and sufficient it was. But when another generation had passed and Rabbi Israel of Rishin was called on to perform the task, he sat down in his golden chair in his castle and said: We cannot light the fire, we cannot speak the prayers, we do not know the place, but we can tell the story of how it was done. And, the story-teller adds, the story which he told had the same effect as the other three. (Scholem 1941: 350)

This Hasidic tale was interpreted by Scholem as portraying the decay of the Hasidic movement and the transformation of its values (Scholem 1941: 350). Our interpretation is different: We hold that the Ba'al Shem Tov (the Besht) – the charismatic founder of the Hasidic movement – taught that the optimal performance of man's tasks in this world is a praxis: a combination of action and meditative prayer or spiritual concentration.

The link between subject and object has been one of the most relevant psycho-philosophical problems from time immemorial. Solomon Maimon, the disciple of Kant, posited the matter in metaphoric terms: "To find a passage from the external world to the mental world is more important than to find a way to East India, no matter what statesmen may say" (*Encyclopaedia Judaica* 1971, vol. 11: 743). Still, our concern is more pragmatic: We wish to understand how the mental revelation of an Archemedian "Eureka" is structured into an objective creation. We hypothesize that this creative linkage is affected by a mythogenic structure, the meaning of which has, of course, to be presently explained.

We hold that myths structure meanings for human behavior and serve as motivation and prime movers for both individual and group behavior. As myths are projected models of human behavior at all levels, they may be records of past experience as well as a structuring for future longings and goals. Myths are also expressions of both overt behavior and of covert dynamics; of the here and now as well as of transcendence. The dimensions of myths may also vary greatly, ranging from micro-myths, like names of persons and places representing meaningful experiences or quests, to meta-myths representing the polar type of human behavior on both the individual and group levels such as the myths of Sisyphus and Tantalus. They vary with time and place. Every society and culture has its own indigenous mythology. Myths move in time from sacred myths recorded before history to modern myths, like master detectives Sherlock Holmes and Hercule Poirot, or the master spy, John Le Carré's Smiley, or even Superman, who realizes the dreams of omnipotence among the downtrodden, henpecked inhabitants of Metropolis.

Myths can relate to individuals. The offering of Isaac and Iphigenia, signifying the sacrificial enmeshing of the young within the normative system of society, are two examples. Then there are group myths like the adventures of the Olympian gods and the tribal exploits of the German Æsir. The Nazi movement may indeed be studied as a collective myth when the collective worms, to use Goebbels's macabre simile, become effectively a fire-spitting dragon (Shoham 1995: 25).

We follow in the giant footsteps of Claude Levi-Strauss, who claimed that myths are a connecting structure between divergent polarities like the raw and the cooked (1964: 9). However, we attribute to mythology, as a structure, wider and deeper functions. Piaget has described the function of a structure, thus:

> A system of transformations is characterized by the laws of this system (in contradistinction to the attributes of its individual components). The system is preserved and enriched by the actions of these transformations, but they do not lead to outright components, which are outside the (structured system). In short, a structure is characterized by holism, transformation, and self-regulation. (1971: 5)

It is important to note that once the structure has been formed, we get used to it by processes of feedback. The earlier and longer one has had a structure, the more it is cherished through the dynamics of cognitive dissonance and is normalized and mythologized. Established structures lend security, familiarity, and confidence. Hence, normative upheavals and ideational revolutions are painful and relatively rare.

Since we try to understand the Kulturkampf of fundamentalist Islam against Western culture within the context of culture conflict it would be useful to examine this culture conflict frame of reference. Thorsten Sellin says:

> Culture conflicts are sometimes regarded as by-products of a cultural growth process – the growth of civilization – sometimes as the result of the migration of conduct norms from one culture complex or area to another. However produced, they are sometimes studied as mental conflicts and sometimes as the clash of cultural codes. (1938: 34)

The theoretical premises of culture conflict may be expanded both on the relatively well-cultivated social level and the meagerly explored personal one. It would be rather fruitful to guide our analysis by the following trichotomy:

1. Culture conflict as mental conflict. These normative conflict situations would take place, presumably, within the arena of the personality of the potential criminal or deviant prior to his first criminal act or his initial "recruiting" to a deviant subculture. These internal conflicts and their subsequent first overt manifestations are crucial in the differentiation process of defining a person to himself and to his relevant others as delinquent and deviant. This is the rather abrupt transfer from the "right" side of the legal and social barricade to the "wrong" one.
2. The gradual deeper integration of an individual within the criminal or deviant group and his corresponding rejection of the "legitimate" or "square" normative systems involves rather elaborate conflict processes: the narrowing of socioeconomic opportunities, the rupture or jeopardizing of marriage and other domestic affiliations, the stigmatizing rejection and counter-rejection of friends, community, voluntary associations, and most of the former membership and reference groups. The last step in this process is full-fledged membership in the criminal or deviant group. The resolution of the internal conflicts with the "right" side of the barricade at this advanced stage of deviance is by severing most relevant normative ties with it.
3. The third level of analysis is the perennial favorite of culture conflict theorists: the fluctuations of crime rates in a given community for a given time, the genesis and volume of special types of crime and deviance, urbanization, industrialization, internal and external migration, disintegration and secularization of traditional and tribal structures, and the *ex-definitione* link among most of the other forms of social change and the conflict of conduct norms.

A Frame of Reference

A frame of reference is a common boundary of phenomena that have an empirical common denominator. The common denominator may not necessarily characterize the whole phenomenon under consideration; it would be sufficient that a part of its factual manifestation would fit into the common boundary of the frame of reference. By exclusion we may note the culture conflict premise is not a theoretical system in the engulfing Parsonian sense, nor is it of similar scope to the conflict theory of society, which society (according to the expounders of Simmel's thought) is held together in dynamic equilibrium by diverging normative discord. Moreover, we hold that culture conflict is also not a "middle range theory" by which Merton denoted the relatively limited theories applied to rather narrow and well-defined areas of study. Culture conflict is both wider and deeper and at the same time less systematic than a middle range theory. The latter operates on one level of analysis whereas culture conflict may include in its premises phenomena that occur on different planes of a space which need not have clear-cut delineations.

Levantinism

Before we launch our own analysis of the clash between fundamentalist Islam and Western civilization we would like to examine previous attempts at explanation. The extreme manifestation of the Levantine is behavior based on the external forms and attributes of a culture, while at the same time being ignorant of or disregarding its contents and intrinsic values. It is manifest among members of oriental and Eastern cultures exposed to European culture. The Middle Eastern Levantine adopts occidental languages, dress and mannerisms. He takes care to furnish his house based on the latest ads. He is not acquainted with, nor has he had the opportunity, to become interested in European literature, art or history, and he has not internalized the values of European culture.

In many instances, Levantinism results from a failure to imitate or rebel. Individuals or groups in a society regard the adoption and absorption of a more advanced and progressive culture as a panacea for all miseries and social ills. Eventually the task proves too formidable or the internal cultural mixture is thought to be impossible, and the innovation or rebellious zeal to integrate with the so-called "enlightened" culture deteriorates into a superficial and shallow imitation of its external manifestations. On the group level, this can take the form of an Atatürk or a Zaglul Pasha burning with the fervor of making Turkey and Egypt modern occidental nations, but ends in the pitiful image of Levantine bourgeoisie in Alexandria and Constantinople whose original oriental values and culture are still latent below the surface. The group's reaction toward this behaviour is far from derogatory, because usually those who display the external trademarks of an advanced and modern culture belong to the social elite and are idolized by the ignorant multitudes.

The aetiology of Levantinism can generally be traced to a failure of innovation. The Afro-Asian intellectual, the South American revolutionary and the idealistic communist bring from abroad – or from books – new ideas, techniques and schemes for raising the standard of living, eliminating malaria, trachoma and syphilis, introducing more efficient and less corrupt bureaucracies, and installing a postal service or a telephone system that really works. Reality, however, is rarely cooperative: there are no roads for the heavy trucks to convey equipment; there is no money or trained workers to construct the roads; very few people understand technical matters; the population is so entrenched in its traditional routine that few avail themselves of new services – or are even interested in them. The Western idea of hard work and the concepts of accuracy or even of time itself are foreign, undesirable or meaningless – what is the big hurry? So the great dream deteriorates into rusty, unused, broken equipment, the clerks continue their perennial slumber undisturbed, while the timetables and efficiency charts are slowly covered with dust from the scorched desert plains or with entangled vines from the humid jungle. The innovator is discouraged, deflated and disgusted, and succumbs to his private hibernation retreat surrounded by the external remnants of his dream, a few gadgets, a few beverages, a few clothes and half-baked knowledge sent over to him from the faraway "progressive" culture. This is the main current of individual Levantinism.

With time, emulators of occidental cultures realized that they were in love with a mirage. There can be no admixture between their indigenous cultures and Western culture, especially when the latter exploits the former through political or economic colonialism. Freedom fighting and wars of independence marked most of the second half of the 20th century. Furthermore, the conflictual encounter with Occidental culture and the relatively shallow absorption of their patterns of cultures and norms was linked to a disintegration of the familial and traditional normative structures of Muslim societies. Middle Eastern and North African Muslim societies witnessed the disintegration of familial ties and the exposure of their young to drugs, alcohol, pornography, gambling and prostitution, all of which they attributed to the encounter with the West. Hence, fundamentalist Islam howled a rallying cry back to the purist Islamic norms of family asceticism, thrift and sexual mores. The enemy, the wiedergeist, the devil – was the Occident, the harbinger of all those ills. Hence, jihad should be waged to the bitter end against Western nations, culture, religion, technology, art and literature.

Huntington says that Westernization and modernization are two parameters that are only tangentially correlated. Westernization would enhance modernization of indigenous cultures. But then, when economic and technological progress reaches a fair level of political, military and economic might and independence, a sense of dignity and self-esteem sets in stimulating pride in one's roots and traditions and rejection of occidental values and of Western culture as a whole (Piaget 1971: 86). On the personal level the clash between Western values and norms and indigenous traditional ones that are liable to give way and disintegrate, temporarily leads to a value vacuum, and to alienation and anomie that may lead to the embrace of fundamentalist Islam. This could create a renewed sense of belonging – "rootedness" and "ego-identity", in the Eriksonian sense (Piaget 1971: 87). Our stance, however, differs from the culture conflict frame of reference as applied to the clashes between Western and Islamic cultures and their resolutions as described by Huntington. He bases himself on research by Ronald Dore (Shoham 2000), whereby the first generation elite of a newly independent colony are educated in the former colonial power's universities, and thus bring back with them an admiration and adherence to

Western norms and culture. However, second generation youth, studying at home in their indigenous languages, are influenced by their own culture and religion and hence are more likely to adhere to fundamentalist Islam. We, however, claim that the second generation is still uncertain and confused from parental influence on the one hand, and local culture, on the other. Hence, the second generation is culturally passive, and rarely does it actively reject Western culture. Usually, this role is assumed by the third generation, who are sure of their origin, firmly anchored in their indigenous culture and fiercely proud of their heritage, which they consider far superior to any occidental normative system. They are the natural candidates to fight Western culture and embrace fundamentalist Islam (Shoham, Shoham and Abd-El-Razel 1966).

The rejection of Western mores and values by Muslim fundamentalists despite their willingness to accept Western technology in industry, science, medicine as well as in the military, is mainly due to the fact that the largely Sisyphean diachronic arriviste tool-oriented West does not really agree with the Tantalic, synchronic, passive and meditative East. Unlike regimented, stratified and specialized Christianity, Islam is unified holistically and embraces the whole human life, both individual and group. The Muslim's customs, mores, morals and laws are regulated in the realm of the family, tribe, nation, subject and object, physics and metaphysics, faith and logic. Huntington claims that Islam is well on its way to dominate holistically the Muslim's life, the way Marxism ruled the body, soul and society of its adherents in a totalitarian manner (1996: 137). The Muslim Brotherhood aims and – in many Islamic societies succeeds – in dominating the educational systems, from kindergarten to university, and thus infiltrates in a relatively short period the social and political infrastructures of a large number of Muslim nations.

Muslims, points out Huntington, are more likely to resort to violence to deal with internal and external conflicts. The *New York Times* counted 59 ethnic conflicts in 1993, half of which involved Muslims. In 1993–94, Muslims were involved in 26 out of 50 ethno-political conflicts. Ruth Seaward found that of the 12 wars waged in 1992 with at least 1,000 deaths, 9 were between Muslims and non-Muslims. The most frightening statistic is that the mean military strength of Muslim countries, as measured by material and manpower on a predetermined scale, is 11.8 compared to 7.1 for non-Muslim nations, and military expenditure in Muslim countries accounts for an average of 17.7 percent of the national budget compared to 12.3 percent in other countries (Huntington 1996: 347–8). Indeed, Din Muhammad Beseif, The Law of Muhammad, as decreed by Islam – is by way of the sword.

Another parameter, which is very rarely related to human behavior, is the entropy gradient of the second law of thermodynamics. This law was formulated for physics and mechanics by the Frenchman Sadi Carnot in 1827 and by the German Rudolf Clausius in 1868, respectively. The law states that in a closed system, entropy (the dissipation of energy) must ultimately reach a maximum. Entropy then ordains that in closed systems the physical or chemical processes will degrade (Schneider and Kay 1994). The second law of thermodynamics also states that work is dissipated into heat but that heat cannot be completely converted into work. This is the principle of irreversibility in nature (Schneider and Kay 1994: 27). This law of entropy increases with nature, becoming more disordered and thus determining the diachronic "arrow of time". However, the work that is most relevant to our present context was carried out by Ilya Prigogine and his associates.

Prigogine's ideas are applied in our context by use of the two dynamics of fluctuations and bifurcations, which he describes. According to Prigogine, fluctuations are disorders within the subsystems of systems. When these fluctuations become very violent through resonance or feedback they can shatter the organization of the system. This process, which happens in a system that is far from equilibrium, is the "bifurcation" junction. At this crossroad, it is up to the organism, in our case the human being, to choose indeterministically to react in a manner that is evolutionarily adaptive and thus reach an "order through fluctuations", or choose not to intervene or react in a non-adaptive manner with catastrophic results for the system (Prigogine and Stengers 1967: 73).

If we apply these dynamics to human society we may claim that the transformations and exchange of energies between social characters obey the rules of thermodynamics and entropy: Muslim societies in the Middle East and North Africa have perennially been Tantalic participant social-characters of low entropy, while occidental cultures have mostly been close to the Sisyphean pole of social characters with high entropy. When the West invaded Muslim societies by sheer force of colonialism, economic domination, or technological, scientific or managerial superiority, an influx of violent fluctuations occurred leading to a bifurcation junction with nefarious, evolutionary non-adaptive and structurally destructive results for the Muslim societies. First, traditional Muslim values of asceticism, frugality, self-sufficiency, lack of worldly ambition, cohesion of family, tribal mores, sexual virtuousness and belief in God – were assaulted and harassed by the carnivorous, covetous, ambitious occidental invaders. Second, industry, oil, conspicuous consumption, fast food, hedonism and present orientation, brought an avalanche of high entropy, waste, pollution and the tyranny of diachronic time in low entropy societies that lacked the means and structures to deal with these ecological catastrophes. Kemal-Pasha Atatürk, Reza Shah Pahlevi, Zaglul Pasha and many others who tried to emulate the West destroyed the low entropy infrastructure of their societies but could not possibly build, erect and transform their cultures into high entropy Western type social characters, thus their societies slumped into what Halper calls incoherence. The Levantine's shallow absorption of Western culture, on top of the ruins of traditional norms and values, makes for an incoherence of *Weltauschauungen* crippled "ego-boundary" and resultant low self-esteem, powerlessness, meaninglessness, alienation, anomia and accidia (Halpern 1977). All this may be the consequent pathological states for societies of low entropy and for the individuals who comprise them and who have been invaded, harassed and subjugated by social characters of high entropy. We must make a conceptual clarification, however, in order to understand the alienating havoc wrought by Sisyphean high entropy cultures when clashing with Tantalic low entropy cultures.

The Return of Accidia

We propose a conceptual revival of "accidia" ("acedy" or "accidie") to denote an individual's breakdown of involvement with social norms and values, just as "anomie" ("anomy" or "anomia") has been resurrected from 16th-century usage to denote normative disintegration in society. The need for a distinct and specific concept of accidia stems primarily from the fact that anomie was conceived by all its exponents, from Emile Durkheim to Merton and beyond, as an attribute of groups, not individuals. For Durkheim, anomie was a collective hangover from a social (mainly economic) shock. The effect of this on individuals is almost taken for granted: the normative enclosure has burst open. This conception of anomie is focused, therefore, on a societal state and the individual's confrontation with it is secondary; the individual himself is left in the shade and his subjective state of mind is entirely disregarded.

The dynamism of our conception of accidia rests in its being the final link in a triadic chain. The three elements of the chain are as follows. First there occurs an initial normative gap between previously internalized norms and newly transmitted ones. Second, there is a congruity-motivated involvement by the subject to bridge this gap. And finally, if this involvement effort fails, there is a value breakdown, a disengagement – or, to use current slang – the subject mentally "cops-out". Our dynamic conception of accidia is anchored on the congruity principle, which is a basic ego defence mechanism that motivates human beings to resolve their normative conflicts and thus re-establish their otherwise threatened cognitive balance and consonance.

Pious saints like the Talmudic Reish-Lakish and the Catholic Augustine were notorious lechers in their youth; the switch from a "life of sin" to a life of religious fanaticism and apostasy is quite common. The accidiac, however, would tend to agree with Sartre that "it seems that Man is incapable of producing more than an impotent God" (Kaufman 1958: 259). Similarly, when the examining magistrate brandishes a crucifix at Meursault, his natural reaction – is in fact barely to react at all. The Existentialist outsiders are anaesthetized to all value-systems and commitments, particularly religious ones (including committed atheism). Similarly, accidiacs, to use Camus's Judge-penitent's simile in *The Fall*, would like some of Dante's angels to be neutral in the fight between God and Satan (Camus 1956: 87).

Among the types of alienation presented by Seeman, the nearest to our present exposition is "self-estrangement". The latter is quite in line with our conceptualization insofar as it relates to Erich Fromm's description of a mode of experience in which the person experiences himself as an alien and has become estranged from himself (Seeman 1959: 534). This is similar to the element of self-objectification, which we have identified as one of the components of accidia. However, Seeman considerably relies on an "other-directedness" element in his conceptualization of self-estrangement. The former, as expounded by Ortega y Gasset and David Riesman, is a very common personality trait among individuals comprising "the mass society" and "the lonely crowd". Other-directedness makes for "joyful obedience" and a

Dale Carnegie-type contentedness. But for the accidiac, other-directedness is non-existent. Albert Camus's Meursault regards the judge who is trying him for murder, the courtroom and its audience as having hardly anything to do with him. At most his trial appears to him as a game (Camus 1958: 103). He assumes the spectator and not the participant role, and at times is interested in the proceedings because it is his first time at a criminal trial. Sometimes he even feels de trop – at his own trial (Camus 1958: 105). The Judge-penitent in *The Fall* is also "playing at doing things, and not doing, being and not being there" (Camus 1956: 87). The accidiac regards his environment as an arena where games are staged incessantly, but where he is a watcher and not a player. To him, man is a game player dabbling in semi-serious games, but the accidiac himself is not one of the players. Accidia is a hangover of the Tantalic low entropy social character that was dissipating in his leveling encounter with a high entropy Sisyphean social character.

The aetiology of so called Third World societies is linked very significantly to the invasion of high entropy, sociopolitical and economic patterns of cultures into low entropy societies which cannot contain the resultant destructive fluctuations. These assault and destroy the traditional normative infrastructure with nothing but brute force, violence, corruption, managerial abuse and stifling mindless bureaucracy to take its place. The mineral and other natural resources in which the Third World is rich, work to its detriment in a positive feedback cycle. The low entropy Third World countries do not have the technology to mine and process their natural resources, hence the high entropy Western nations are doing so. They erect petrochemical plants, mining industries; wood processing projects which enhance an accelerated urbanization, which takes the form of huge shanty towns. These processes destroy the traditional villages and create a vast population of poor, homeless, undernourished and diseased people (Rifkin 1980: 188–93). Since most of the food and consumer goods and gadgets are imported, they are handled either by Western agents and distribution companies aided by the local corrupt hereditary or by the military-backed oligarchy. This is the frightening saga of the aftermath of the violent encounter between the high entropy West and the low entropy Third World. Moreover, since low entropy countries are unable to develop their own industries, invading high entropy aggressive salesmen induce the already impoverished shanty town dwellers to buy more consumer goods that they cannot afford, hence they are sucked into the vicious circle of never-ending debt to "the company store".

Since oil revenues in the Middle East and North Africa go to a small minority of power crazed and money debauched potentates, most Muslim countries seem to have the pomp and ostentatious lavishness reminiscent of *The Thousand and One Nights* – for the exclusive consumption of corrupt and degenerated despots, with few resources allocated to social welfare, socialization, medicine and education for human rights and their awareness. Of course, this results in even greater poverty, more subjugation, less democracy, and less freedom for women. The only refuge left for the downtrodden masses seems to be the sole solaces that cannot disappoint and let down: Allah and the Koran. Since the shallow absorption of Western culture inherent in Levantine dynamics made for a distorted perception of Western social characters, particularly as reflected by colonial bureaucracies or greedy executives of Western conglomerates, an us/them dichotomy has been created in the self/other perception of the Muslim populace. Consequently, those who fall back onto purist Islam create a vision of themselves as worthy martyrs, mostly crushed, subdued and enslaved by the Western *wiedergeist*, usurper, Satan. Hence, all means are appropriate to combat this demonic trespasser. No moral scruples, legal restraints or pity should curb the fight against the hellish adversary. Since the United States and its ally, the *Wise Men of Zion* (this tsarist forgery is a runaway bestseller in the Muslim Middle East and North Africa), have never shown any compassion to their Muslim victims, the war against them should be to the bitter end. This is the ideology, war plan and strategy of Al Qaeda, Hizbullah, Hamas and their ilk. Because the war against the West is a jihad, no human can declare an armistice; only Allah can decide on the conduct of the war against the accused foes through his emissaries: Osama bin Laden, Sheikh Hassan Nassralla and Sheikh Ahmed Yassin. This also conforms with the work of entropy theorists, such as Prigonine and Hermann Haken (Portugali 2000), who point out that when an extreme choice is followed in a bifurcation all other alternative possibilities undergo a cognitive collapse as if they never existed.

Conclusion

Finally, we are left the question of whether it is possible to avoid, halt or curb this catastrophic collision between Islamic cultures and Western civilization. To approach this question seriously, we must divide it into two: First, do we have a model or experience of changing a low entropy culture into high entropy? Second, could such a model or experience be applied to the clash between Islam and occidental culture? We have an answer to our first query in the form of two examples, one a micro illustration of the absorption of Jewish immigrants in the hills of Jerusalem; the second, the ongoing experience of East Asia vis-à-vis modernization, social management and economic development.

The official ideology and strategy of the Jewish Agency in the 1950s was to force new immigrants, who at the time were mostly from low entropy cultures, to discard quickly the traditions, norms and values of their countries of origin and absorb the normative system of Israel, which at that time was largely a high entropy community. Consequently, at the new immigrant settlement of Beit Shemesh, located near Jerusalem, Jewish Agency bureaucrats took great pains to create a "true melting pot", mixing all manner of ethnic groups so they would abandon the culture and norms of their countries of origin and become integrated Israelis as quickly as possible. Thus, a Yemenite family was settled near a Moroccan one, and both were placed opposite the asbestos shed of an extended Iranian family. This strategy resulted in strife, tension and social conflict, as well as twice the rate of delinquency in Beit Shemesh as compared to Jerusalem. Per contra, when the bureaucrats might have been away, sick or inattentive, a whole tribe of Kurdistani Jews replete with their leaders, rabbis, gabbais (community functionaries), cantors, soothsayers and witchdoctors settled on a hill near Jerusalem and named their new abode "Ness-Harim", Miracle on the Mountain. At first, when the nurse came to offer medication to the sick, she was scolded and chased away. Gradually the tribe members learned that antibiotics were as effective as the incantations of the witchdoctor. Thence, every box of medicine had to have the benediction of the witchdoctor before actual use by tribe members. When people finally realized that the medicine was effective even without the blessing of the witchdoctor they were immediately assigned to irrigate the old orchard, which didn't need irrigation to begin with. Today, with the coming of age of the third generation, delinquency is no longer part of the landscape at Ness-Harim, the tribal village. It is flourishing economically. Many second and third generation members are doctors, lawyers, senior army officers, and the rest are successful farmers who grow fruit, grapes and olives, and raise chicken, cattle and goats using the latest science and technology.

On the Sabbath and on holidays, the entire tribe comes to the synagogue and kisses the hand of the barely literate tribal octogenarian headman. Here the low entropy tribe has absorbed the high entropy patterns of the absorbing culture, yet the normative and traditional structures, having remained intact, did not allow the fluctuations caused by the absorption of innovations to disrupt the tribe. Hence, the fluctuations resulted in bifurcations, which adaptively enhanced the evolutionary synthesis and cultural growth of the whole tribe and its individual members. On the other hand, the traditional normative infrastructure of the Beit Shemesh families was disrupted because of the absorption of high entropy patterns of culture-generated fluctuations, which played havoc with the new immigrant families and their members.

On the macro level we have Japan, China and the so-called Four Tigers – Hong Kong, Taiwan, South Korea and Singapore – initially all low entropy cultures that absorbed high entropy modernization and technology. Because they succeeded in keeping intact their traditional normative structures the fluctuations of modernization did not disrupt their infrastructures but instead bifurcated into evolutionary adaptation and synthesized into economic boom and cultural growth. Kishore Mahbubani informs us that it took Britain 58 years and the United States 47 years to double GDP. Japan required 33 years; Indonesia, 17; South Korea, 11; and China, 10 (cited in Huntington 1996: 77). This brings to mind Napoleon's warning that we should let China sleep because the world will be sorry if she awakes. Western conglomerates must have difficulty sleeping when they consider that China and the Four Tigers already have enjoyed annual economic growth of approximately 8 percent. This remarkable feat was possible because modernization, industrialization and scientification were kept in check and balance by traditional Confucian values of asceticism, thriftiness, hard work, family cohesion, and individual responsibility for the welfare of the community Huntington 1996: 133). Hence, high entropy patterns of culture generated fluctuations in the low entropy absorbing structures, but the Confucian values served as shock absorbers, and the fluctuations led to a bifurcation of growth and adaptive viability.

In sum, on both the micro level on the macro level, it is possible to achieve a viable and adaptive synthesis between low entropy and high entropy. Fundamentalist Muslims must realize with Camus that revolutions failed: the French Revolution ended with the Terror; the German Revolution, with Auschwitz; and the Russian Revolution, with the Gulag (Camus 1962). Also, the West realizes that the days of colonialism and economic exploitation of low entropy countries are just about over. Eventually, President Bush, the Israeli security forces, and anti-terrorism units around the world will demonstrate to militant fundamentalist Muslims that terrorism will not achieve its disruptive goals. The only way is viable synthesis between low entropy cultures backed by traditional normative infrastructures absorbing (in a controlled manner) the fluctuation-generating high entropy pattern of cultures resulting in adoptive evolution and growth. In the 10th and 11th centuries, Jews and Muslims lived in Spain in a mutually fructifying symbiosis; later Christians joined in a convevencia (a living together) with Alfonso X (El Sabio), which kindled the renaissance in Europe, the expansive discoveries of new worlds, and the Age of Enlightenment. Fundamentalist Muslims, and for that matter their Western adversaries, must realize the profound wisdom of Rabbi Akiva, the second-century sage, who said: "The forces of the world are determined, but Man is endowed with the Freedom of choice" (Berko n.d.). Hence, the stochastic bifurcation is given but a clear choice should be made between suicide, destruction and bereavement, and viability by dialogue and growth through the complementarity of opposites.

References

Benedict, Ruth (1934), *Patterns of Culture*, New York: Mentor Books.

Berko, Anat (n.d.), "The Moral Infrastructure of Chief Perpetrators of Suicide Terrorism", unpublished PhD thesis.

Bohr, Niels (1937), "Causality and Complementarity", *Philosophy of Science*, 4: 291.

Camus, A. (1954), *The Stranger*, New York: Vintage Books.

Camus, A. (1956), *The Fall*, New York: Vintage Books.

Camus, A. (1962), *The Rebel*, Harmondsworth: Penguin.

Dore, Ronald (2000), "Unity and Diversity in Contemporary World Culture" in Shoham, S.G., *God is the Shadow of Man*, New York: Peter Lang.

Encyclopaedia Judaica (1971), Jerusalem: Keter.

Fromm, Erich (1942), *Escape from Freedom*, New York: Farrar & Rinehart.

Halpern, Manfred (1977), "Four Contrasting Repertories of Human Relations in Islam", in Brown, L. Carl and Norman Itzkowitz (eds), *Psychological Dimension of Near Eastern Studies*, Princeton: Darwin Press.

Hsu, Francis L.K. (1969), *The Study of Literate Civilizations*, New York: Holt, Rinehart & Winston.

Humphreys, Christmas (1952), *Buddhism*, Harmondsworth: Penguin.

Huntington, Samuel P. (1996), *The Clash of Civilizations: Remaking of World Orders*, New York: Touchstone.

Jung, C.G. (1944), *Psychological Types*, London: Kegan Paul.

Kaufmann, W.A. (1958), *Critique of Religion and Philosophy*, New York: Harper & Brothers.

Kluckhohn, Clyde (1962), *Culture and Behavior*, New York: Free Press.

Kroeber, A.L. (1952), *The Nature of Culture*, Chicago: University of Chicago Press.

Kroeber, A.L. (1963), *Anthropology: Culture Patterns and Processes*, New York: Harcourt, Brace and World.

Levi-Strauss, Claude (1964), *Le Cru et le Cuit*, (Mythologiques, vol. I), Paris: Plon.

Levi-Strauss, Claude (1966), *The Savage Mind*, Chicago: University of Chicago Press.

Levy-Bruhl, L. (1966), *How Natives Think*, New York: Washington Square Press.

McClelland, D.C. (1961), *The Achieving Society*, Princeton: Van Nostrand.

Murray, Gilbert (1955), *Five Stages of Greek Religion*, New York: Doubleday.

Piaget, Jean (1971), *Structuralism* (trans. Chaninah Maschler), London: Routledge and Kegan Paul.

Portugali, Yuval (2000), *Self-Organization and the City*, Heidelberg: Springer Verlag.

Prigogine, L. and L. Stengers (1967), *Myth, Religion and Mother-right*, Princeton: Princeton University Press.

Riesman, D., N. Glazer, and R. Denney, (1953), *The Lonely Crowd*, New York: Doubleday/Anchor Books.

Rifkin, Jeremy (1980), *Entropy*, London: Routledge and Kegan Paul.

Russell, Bertrand (1947), *History of Western Philosophy*, London: Allen & Unwin.

Schneider, E.D. and J.J. Kay (1994), "Life as a Manifestation of the Second Law of Thermodynamics", *Math Computer Modeling*, 19(6–8): 25–48.

Scholem, Gershom Gerhard (1941), *Major Trends in Jewish Mysticism*, Jerusalem: Schocken Publishing House.

Seeman, H. (1959), "On the Meaning of Alienation", *American Sociology Review*, 24: 534.

Sellin, T. (1938), *Culture Conflict and Crime*, New York: Social Science Research Council.

Shoham, S.G. (1979), *The Myth of Tantalus*, St Lucia: University of Queensland Press.

Shoham, S.G. (1984), *Rebellion, Creativity, and Revelation*, Middlesex: Science Reviews Ltd.

Shoham, Shlomo Giora (1995), *Valhalla, Calvary and Aucshwitz*, Cincinnati: Bowman & Cody Academic Publishing.

Shoham, Shlomo G., Nahum Shoham and Adnan Abd-El-Razek (1966), "Causality and Complemantarity", *British Journal of Criminology*, October, pp. 391–409.

Spengler, Oswald (1954), *The Decline of the West*, London: Allen & Unwin, vol. 1.

Toynbee, A. (1987), *A Study of History*, Oxford: Oxford University Press.
White, L.A. (1949), *The Science of Culture*, New York: Farrar, Strauss & Cudahy.

Chapter 4

Immigration, Security and Civil Liberties Post 9/11: A Comparison of American, Australian and Canadian Legislative and Policy Changes[1]

Joshua D. Freilich
John Jay College of Criminal Justice

Matthew R. Opesso
Widener University

Graeme R. Newman
University at Albany

Introduction

This chapter examines the post 9/11 legislative and policy changes pertaining to non-citizens in Australia, Canada, and the United States. The terrorist attacks on September 11, 2001 in New York City and Washington DC claimed 3,000 lives from all over the world, caused financial damage (some estimates calculated the direct costs as exceeding 50 billion dollars), psychological trauma, and negatively affected the global economy. Unlike other acts of terrorism, many people around the world perceived these assaults as more than an attack against a single country. Most countries condemned the 9/11 attacks, and the leading French newspaper *Le Monde*, even published a front-page headline that proclaimed, "We are all Americans".

Since the perpetrators of the 9/11 attacks were non-citizens, many countries focused their attention on foreigners (Meissner 2002). In this study, we examine how the United States, Canada and Australia responded to these attacks. The United States was chosen because the attacks were perpetrated on American soil, and Australia and Canada were selected because they are English speaking "immigrant nations". The three countries are geographically dispersed in two continents and prior to 9/11

1 This work was supported, in part, by a grant from the City University of New York PSC-CUNY Research Award Program.

had different immigration histories, statutes, and policies. Canada's policies favored "productive" immigrants who benefited their economy, while the other nations were more receptive to family reunification and/or refugee requests. The four major types of post 9/11 legislative and policy changes pursued by the three nations against their non-citizens were:

1. operations abroad;
2. detainment and treatment of alleged foreign terrorists;
3. border security, visa application, refugees and asylum seekers;
4. internal measures.

After discussing the responses of each nation and comparing them, we conclude by offering suggestions for future research.

Post 9/11 United States Legislative and Policy Responses to Non-Citizens[2]

American Operations Abroad

The United States engaged in military operations against the foreign individuals, groups, and nations it claimed supported international terrorism in general and the 9/11 attacks in particular. America attacked Afghanistan after it refused to turn over Osama Bin Laden, the Al Qaeda leader that organized the September 11 attacks. The American bombing campaign combined with increased military aid to the insurgent Northern Alliance led to the defeat of the ruling Taliban and its replacement by a pro-American government. A few thousand American and allied troops remain in Afghanistan engaging in sporadic fighting while searching for the surviving Al Qaeda and Taliban leadership.

The Central Intelligence Agency conducted a "targeted operation" in Yemen in 2002, where a pilot-less drone fired a missile that destroyed a car and killed its six occupants, said to be Al Qaeda operatives. The next year, the United States attacked Iraq, toppled Saddam Hussein's ruling Ba'ath party, and eventually apprehended Hussein himself. President Bush ordered this engagement because he believed Saddam Hussein had supported Al Qaeda and other international terrorists, and pursued weapons of mass destruction. Over 150,000 American and allied soldiers remain in Iraq battling Hussein loyalists, Al Qaeda-inspired insurgents, and others.

Supporters of President Bush argue that these proactive operations enhanced American security and incapacitated or removed governments, groups, and individuals who threatened the United States. Critics claim, however, that President Bush's unilateral actions isolated the United States from most of the world community, and America is therefore as vulnerable as it was pre-9/11.

---

2 This analysis focuses on the federal government response and does not examine policies enacted by the individual 50 states.

American Detainment and Treatment of Alleged Foreign Terrorists

The United States detained hundreds of foreign-born suspected Al Qaeda operatives during these overseas operations and sometimes treated them harshly. The *Washington Post* and *New York Times* reported that American forces occasionally beat suspected terrorists immediately after their capture. During the interrogation process some detainees were subjected to stressful circumstances such as blindfolding, noise, lack of sleep, forced standing, harsh lighting, extreme climate changes, and temporary withholding of food, water and medical care. A few detainees were threatened that they would be turned over to their countries of origin for torture if they refused to cooperate. The United States was, in fact, accused of handing over some detainees to Middle Eastern nations known to employ torture against suspected terrorists, to obtain sought-after information (Bonner, Van Natta Jr. and Waldman 2003; Priest and Gelman 2002; see also Heymann 2002). According to the *Washington Post*, one United States official stated that "the understanding is we don't kick the [expletive] out of them. We send them to other countries so they can kick the [expletive] out of them." Another official conceded that he rendered detainees "with his eyes wide open" they would be tortured (Priest and Gelman 2002). Other American officials denied the allegations and explained that Middle Eastern countries were better suited to conduct these interrogations because of their cultural similarities with the suspects (Bonner, Van Natta Jr. and Waldman 2003; Priest and Gelman 2002).

Meanwhile, President Bush under his authority as Commander in Chief of the US armed forces issued a military order (Bush 2001a) that declared apprehended Al Qaeda members and supporters "enemy combatants" who could be detained, potentially indefinitely. The United States subsequently imprisoned over 600 enemy combatants in Cuba, Afghanistan, and elsewhere. President Bush issued a second military order that authorized the establishment of military tribunals to try non-United States citizens on charges that involve international terrorism or the harboring of international terrorists (Bush 2001b). These tribunals grant fewer procedural protections to defendants and critics attack them for encroaching upon civil liberties (Cole 2002; Heymann 2002; Katyal and Tribe 2002; Rutherglen 2002). The Bush administration disagrees and argues that relying upon the "regular" criminal justice system would hamper the war on terrorism and undermine American security (e.g., by revealing United States intelligence methods).

In October 2001, President Bush issued a directive that established a Foreign Terrorist Tracking Task Force, headed by the Attorney General, to prevent foreign terrorists from entering the United States (*Georgetown Immigration Law Journal* 2002). The Bush administration also relied upon the Material Witness Statute, 18 US Code Section 3144 (2000) to detain, without charge, over 40 individuals (most of whom were non-citizens) it suspected of involvement with terrorist organizations or having knowledge of information relevant to ongoing terrorist investigations. Under this provision, the government may arrest and hold individuals for grand jury testimony if a judge finds that the individual's testimony is critical, and the person is likely to flee. Critics maintain that the government misused this statute to justify preventive detention, and claim that it is another example of government overreaching in the post 9/11 environment. The government contends that unconventional measures are needed, however, to prevail in the war against Al Qaeda, which is different from any previous conflict (Akram and Johnson 2002; Fainaru and Williams 2002; McAllister 2003; Ting 2003).

President Bush and others have similarly justified the USA Patriot Act (2001) that became law on October 26, 2001. Provision 236(A)(a) of this statute allows mandatory detention of non-citizens if the Attorney General certifies there are reasonable grounds to believe the individual is a terrorist, a supporter of terrorist activities, or engaged in activities that endanger the United States. The Act encompasses membership and any "material support" of organizations designated as terrorist by the Secretary of State, groups which publicly laud acts of terrorism, and groups not designated as terrorist but in some fashion support it. The onus is on the suspect to prove that s/he did not intend to further terrorism (Germain 2002). Under this statute, individuals may be held without charge for up to seven days, after which the detainee must be charged with a crime, granted a removal hearing, or released. Importantly, the act allows the Attorney General to detain non-citizens for six months at a time upon certification that there are reasonable grounds to believe the individual poses both a danger to the national security of the United States and his/her removal is unlikely in the foreseeable future. These detainments must be reviewed every six months by the Attorney General and the detainees must be allowed to present evidence challenging their confinement.

Civil libertarians attack the Patriot Act for authorizing preventive detention and penalizing individuals under a guilty by association standard. They contend that the definition of terrorism is too broad and criminalizes the behaviors of individuals who contribute to peaceful charitable activities that may be run by terrorist groups (Cole 2002; Lebowitz and Podheiser 2002). Supporters of the act counter that since financial contributions are fungible, donations made to support the peaceful activities of terrorist groups could end up funding terrorist acts.

American Border Security, Visa Applications, Refugees and Asylum Seekers

In response to the 9/11 attacks, the United States improved security at its borders to guard against future terrorist acts. The Patriot Act tripled the number of agents guarding the borders and upgraded the technology (for example, "seismic meters, infrared devices, magnetic sensors and sophisticated software programs ... [and] state of the art video-surveillance system", Seper 2003: 2) employed at the border to screen entrants. In addition, the Defense Department patrolled the Canadian border during most of 2002, and customs officials currently vet non-citizens more carefully (Foster 2003; Holman 2001; Lebowitz and Podheiser 2002; Lester 2002).

The government also tightened the foreign visa application procedures. Presently, many tourists and business visitors to the United States are granted visas that limit their stay to 30 days. Immediately after the 9/11 attacks, the government delayed granting visas to males aged 16–45 from specified Middle Eastern countries for about 20 days to conduct background checks. Further, all male non-immigrant visa applicants aged 14–65, as well as applicants requested by consular officials, are required to complete an additional document that "solicits information on the applicant's previous travels, [and] military experience" (Fragomen Jr. and Gordon 2002: 183; see also Foster 2003; Lebowitz and Podheiser 2002).

The Patriot Act (Section 411) also increased the grounds for denying entry to non-citizens. Individuals, or their immediate families, who supported or endorsed terrorism, joined or supported groups that engaged in terrorism are barred from the United States (Cole 2002; Holman 2001). In addition, consular officials were granted the authority to bar individuals who "they know or have reason to know" will conduct sabotage or espionage activities during their stay. To protect the United States, the Patriot Act requires the State Department and immigration service to bar individuals listed as offenders on government-run crime-related data bases (Foster 2003; Holman 2001; Lebowitz and Podheiser 2002). The Border Security Act of 2002 similarly denies non-immigrant visas to individuals from seven countries listed as state sponsors of terrorism unless the Secretary of State rules otherwise (Otto 2002). Further, nations that are part of the Visa Waiver Program (whose citizens are not required to obtain a visa before entering the United States) must start issuing special passports that incorporate "biometric identifiers and tamper resistant identity features to determine if the passport is counterfeit or stolen" (Fragomen and Gordon 2002: 181; see also Lebowitz and Podheiser 2002; Lester 2002).

The United States policies toward refugees and asylum seekers also changed as a result of the war on terror. President Bush imposed a temporary moratorium on refugee admissions which affected thousands of already authorized refugees and also lowered the number of refugees admitted in 2002 (Germain 2002; Hill and Kerwin 2002). Similarly, in the spring of 2003 (as the United States prepared to attack Iraq), the government modified its regulations, and asylum seekers from Iraq and over 30 other mostly Middle-Eastern nations (where Al Qaeda had a presence) were detained while their applications were reviewed. Previously, asylum seekers had been detained on an individual basis (Drew and Liptak 2003).

American Internal Measures

The federal government initiated a wide-ranging internal investigation into the September 11 attacks. Hundreds of illegal immigrants, the majority in the New York City area, were rounded up. Many were held for months before being deported on non-serious immigration violations. A government report later criticized the government for subjecting some detainees to severe conditions that caused them financial and psychological harm (Akram and Johnson 2002; Cole 2002; Foster 2003; Lichtblau 2003; Murphy 2002; Silverman 2002; Ting 2003).

Chief Immigration Judge Creppy, in an effort to aid investigators and enhance public security, ordered that some immigration hearings be held in secret (Akram and Johnson 2002; Cole 2002; Germain 2002; Mantle 2003; Ting 2003). In addition, the immigration service doubled the amount of time a suspected alien may be held before charges must be filed from 24 to 48 hours (Federal Register 2001a; see also Cole 2002; Germain 2002; Hom 2002). The immigration courts also enacted an amendment that in some cases allowed aliens who were ordered to be released to be held an additional 10 days to allow the government to decide if it intended to appeal the decision (Federal Register 2001b; Hom 2002; see also Cole 2002). Finally, the Bush administration's Absconder Initiative focused on apprehending and deporting over 5,000 male illegal immigrants from Middle Eastern countries who appeared on a list of 300,000 names compiled by the FBI for the National Crime Information Data Center Database (Harris 2002; Hom 2002; Johnson K. 2002; Silverman 2002).

Other government measures included the increased monitoring of certain non-citizens legally inside the United States. In November 2001, Attorney General Ashcroft ordered federal officials to voluntarily interview thousands of selected individuals (from mostly Middle Eastern Countries) in the United States on student, tourist, or business visas. Ashcroft explained that the interviews were non-coercive and were designed to obtain information helpful to the war on terror. Critics argued that the "interviews" were inherently coercive however, and that they amounted to racial and religious profiling (Harris 2002; Heymann 2002; Murphy 2002; Silverman 2002). Although many interviews never took place, thousands were carried out and a few individuals were arrested on criminal or immigration charges.[3]

Because some of the 9/11 perpetrators legally entered the United States under student visas, Section 416 of the Patriot Act, and other federal statutes, calls for improved monitoring of foreign students studying in the United States. The Student and Exchange Visitor Information System is "designed to monitor students (F-1 visa holders), vocational students (M-1 visa holders), and exchange visitors (J-1 visa holders) at each and every milestone during their stay in the United States" (Foster 2003: 38). A single database is to be created that contains "the names, addresses, nationality, courses of study, and degree programs, credits completed each quarter and disciplinary violations" (Lebowitz and Podheiser 2002: 881) of each foreign student. Further, schools are required to notify the authorities within 30 days if an admitted foreign student does not enroll for classes[4] (Holman 2001; Lebowitz and Podheiser 2002; Mantle 2003; Ting 2003; Treyster 2003). Finally, the *Washington Post* reported that the FBI tried to improve its relations with college campus police forces to obtain information on foreign student communities and help in tracking potential terrorists. In some cases, college campus police officers were added to joint terrorism task forces and in a few situations the FBI requested lists of foreign students and faculty from colleges and universities.

3 Similarly, in the time period leading up to the war with Iraq, the FBI conducted voluntary interviews with thousands of Iraqi born individuals residing in the United States (Drew and Liptak 2003).

4 Both the registration system and the student information system had been authorized in earlier statutes but due to the complexity involved were not actually implemented until 2003 (Mantle 2003; Ting 2003; Treyster 2003).

In September 2002, as a precursor to a new computerized entry and exit data system, the government ordered temporary male visitors 16 years and older from specified (mainly Middle Eastern) countries, as well as requesting visitors from other countries, to "register". The National Security Entry-Exit Registration System required individuals to report to immigration authorities within 30 days of their entry into the United States, within 10 days of changing jobs, houses, or school and when they depart. Under this program, government clerks recorded the male visitors' parents, American contact names and residences, and questioned the visitor about terrorism, and their entrance into the United States. The clerks also fingerprinted and digitally photographed the visitors to determine if they appeared in criminal and immigration databases. Over 80,000 foreign visitors registered, and 10,000 alleged to be illegal immigrants were told to report for deportation hearings (Akram and Johnsonn 2002; Broder and Sachs 2002; Foster 2003; Fragomen Jr. and Gordon 2002; Lester 2002; Mantle 2003). The government canceled the program, in November 2003, however, in response to criticisms that the policy was biased against Arabs and Muslims (Swain 2003).

The National Security Entry-Exit Registration System was a preliminary step that built on the Patriot Act which mandated the Attorney General and the Secretary of State to implement an Integrated Entry and Exit Data System. Under this system "certain information is to be collected and an automated record created for every entry of foreign nationals at all ports. The person's presence in the United States is then tracked until a corresponding departure is entered" (Lester 2002: 14–15; see also Lebowitz and Podheiser 2002). On January 5, 2004, the government instituted the US Visitor and Immigrant Status Indicator Technology program (Operation VISIT) which required foreigners, except those from countries in the Visa Waiver Program, to have their fingerprints scanned and photographs taken. The fingerprints and photos are to be checked against government-run crime and immigration databases (Associated Press 2004).

The Patriot Act also contained provisions that benefited aliens, and their families, victimized by terrorism (such as the 9/11 attacks). The Responsible Cooperator Program permits the government to grant S-visas to non-citizens who aid the government in terrorist investigations and prosecutions (Demleitner 2002). Similarly, proposals have been put forward to shorten or eliminate the three years that aliens who serve in the US armed forces must currently wait before receiving citizenship. On the other hand, the 9/11 attacks negatively affected certain "pro immigration" measures. Proposals to provide amnesty to certain illegal immigrants or institute temporary worker programs were temporarily sidelined (Bellino 2002; Law and Rosario 2001; Meissner 2002). In addition, a few federal statutes, such as the Aviation and Security Act, required American citizenship for certain positions such as airport security (Akram and Johnson 2002). Finally, in March 2003, the Immigration and Naturalization Service was dissolved and immigration responsibility was transferred to the new Homeland Security Department and divided into three bureaus: border enforcement, interior enforcement, and immigration services.

Post 9/11 Canadian Legislative and Policy Responses to Non-Citizens

Canadian Operations Abroad

Although 9/11 occurred on US soil, over 25 Canadians also perished in the attacks. Canada supported the American operation against Al Qaeda and the Taliban in Afghanistan, and committed troops to this campaign. This cooperative spirit did not extend, however, to the American military strike against Iraq. The Canadian government vehemently opposed the war and engaged in sharp disputes with the Bush administration. Similarly, the Canadians, unlike the United States, did not conduct targeted operations in response to the 9/11 attacks (Jenkins 2003; Roach 2002).

Canadian Detainment and Treatment of Alleged Foreign Terrorists

The Canadian government engaged in only a single limited operation abroad, and therefore apprehended few foreign fighters or terrorists. Further, the Canadian government appeared to view its participation in Afghanistan as ancillary to the American role. In a few cases, that engendered controversy, Canada transferred enemy fighters it captured to American custody. Thus, except for a few isolated cases, the Canadians did not take custody of foreign terrorists or fighters. Finally, the United States added Canada to the United States Foreign Terrorist Tracking Task Force to promote greater cooperation between the two nations in combating terrorism.

Similar to the United States, the Canadians approved a major anti-terrorist legislation (Bill C-36 was passed in December 2001) in response to the 9/11 attacks. Although this law is designed to address terrorist acts, and is not an immigration statute, some sections affect non-citizens residing in Canada. The legislation (besides expanding the definition of terrorism, criminalizing participation, facilitation and contributions in/to terrorist groups) allows law enforcement in some circumstances to preventively arrest suspected terrorists and hold them on evidence that is withheld from their attorneys (Jenkins 2003; Roach 2002). While the law is directed at both Canadians and non-Canadians, some observers claim the bill will have a greater impact on non-citizens. Macklin (2002) argues that the Canadian government could rely upon the anti-terrorism law to gather evidence against foreigners and based upon the same secret evidence, employ immigration law to deport them as security risks. Adelman (2002) counters, however, that few individuals have been detained under the acts.

Under Bill C-36, foreigners found to pose a danger to Canadian security will be denied entry. The Act also requires individuals to testify during the fact-finding stages (before charges are filed) of terrorist investigations (Jenkins 2003). In other words, illegal immigrants who testify about such activities and aid terrorist investigations could find themselves subject to deportation if their illegal status becomes public since civil immunity is not granted to testifying witnesses (Millard

2002). Legal migrants may also be deported if they are indirectly linked to terrorism (e.g., by financing "any" aspect of terrorist-related activity), do not cooperate with the authorities, or fail to aid the investigation.

Canadian Border Security, Visa Applications, Refugees and Asylum Seekers

Canada tightened security and upgraded the infrastructure and technology used at the border (e.g., greater numbers of X ray machines, ion scanners, and detection equipment were employed). Further, digital fingerprint machines were installed in border offices to transfer fingerprints electronically to the Royal Canadian Mounted Police for security checks. In addition, Canada increased funding for law enforcement agencies that monitor immigration and intelligence and assigned more agents to guard the United States border. The Canadians also discussed requiring individuals who regularly cross the border to scan their retinas into a database to allow security personnel to check individuals at the border and facilitate their swift movement.

Besides increasing the number of its own security personnel at the border, Canada allowed American agents to be posted in Canadian ports of entry and departure (to conduct pre-clearance security checks on people and goods) and the two countries agreed to increase their intelligence sharing. While both nations weighed security and economic factors, each balanced these concerns differently. It appears that because Canada was not directly attacked, and its economy is more vulnerable to disruptions of trade with America, it is not as preoccupied with security concerns. Accordingly, in some instances Canadian importers are allowed to transport goods across the border *into Canada* without passing through pre-clearance checks. Conversely, goods crossing *into the United States* are subjected to greater security procedures which results in the destruction of greater numbers of perishable goods. Paradoxically, it seems as if it is easier to move people rather than goods across the border (Adelman 2002; Baldwin 2002; Daigle et al 2001; Goldfarb and Robson 2003).

While the United States Visa Waiver Program lists 29 countries, Canada's Temporary Entry Visa program originally consisted of 46 countries. In response to American pressure, Canada removed eight countries from its program. Soon after 9/11 Canada began requiring Saudi Arabian and Malaysian citizens to acquire visas before entering Canada. The Canadians are currently coordinating with the United States a common list of countries that are exempt from visas (Adelman 2002; Rekai 2002). Finally, both countries redoubled their efforts to harmonize their immigration policies to "ensure maximum possible compatibility of ... [their] customs, and procedures" (Adelman 2002: 21).

The Canadian government also instituted stricter procedures pertaining to refugees and asylum seekers. Even before the 9/11 attacks, Canada had considered increasing security in these areas. For instance, although Bill C-11, the Immigration and Refugee Protection Act, did not go into effect until June 2002 it was proposed before 9/11. Prior to 9/11 refugee claimants were interviewed, fingerprinted, and photographed before being released. Now refugee and asylum claimants as well as legal immigrants undergo more thorough security checks (such as having their names, photographs and fingerprints checked against security databases), more in-depth interviews (that verify the past activities of the claimant), and background checks before being allowed entry to Canada. Unlike pre- 9/11 when detentions were rare, refugee or asylum seekers are detained if they cannot verify their identity, or are found to be a terrorist or a war criminal.

The United States and Canada agreed to share information and intelligence on refugee claimants and individuals or groups that are engaged in terrorist activities, and also to complete negotiations on the Safe Third Party Agreement. After this agreement is finalized, claimants who travel through the United States to Canada to apply for asylum will be returned to the United States (and vice versa) (Adelman 2002; Rekai 2002). Finally, although a post 9/11 ruling by the Canadian Supreme Court prohibited Canada from deporting rejected refugee applicants to countries that might torture them, there is a narrow exception. Individuals who pose a serious criminal or security threat to Canada, such as suspected terrorists, may be deported to such countries even at a substantial risk of future torture.

Despite these initiatives, Canada has been criticized for not going far enough. The conservative *Washington Times*, in a series that focused on the US and Canadian border, reported that some American border agents believe that "Canada's lax immigration laws allow aliens from around the world – including those from Islamic nations that embrace terrorism – to enter that country with little or no scrutiny and to stay indefinitely" (Seper 2003: 3). Further, critics maintain that under Canada's revised refugee policy most claimants are still not detained, "even those with questionable backgrounds, [and therefore] more than 10,000 disappear into Canada's ethnic communities each year" (Seper 2003: 4). Finally, critics contend that Canada has not implemented strict screening processes for foreign students and workers (Rekai 2002).

Canadian Internal Measures

Canada instituted only a few internal changes in response to 9/11 and has not yet devised measures to monitor visitors better. On the other hand, one pre 9/11 policy that was fast tracked after the attacks requires new immigrants and refugee claimants to carry fraud-resistant identity cards. This proposal was partially instituted in response to reports that the Canadian government had lost track of 27,000 rejected refugee applicants who were required to leave the country. Finally, in the aftermath of 9/11, Canada devoted more attention to tracking, and deporting illegal immigrants with criminal backgrounds (Rekai 2002).

Post 9/11 Australian Legislative and Policy Responses to Non-Citizens

Australian Operations Abroad

Although Australia is far from the United States, its citizens also perished on 9/11 and the attacks influenced her foreign policy. The Howard administration diplomatically supported the wars in Afghanistan and Iraq, and committed troops to both campaigns (Beeson 2002). While the 2,000 Australian troops sent to Iraq was much lower than the number of American and British troops it was a significant percentage of Australia's standing (53,000 person) army. Although important symbolically, Australian troops did not engage in many operations or suffer large numbers of casualities. One reason for Australia's support of President Bush's policies was that Australia also suffered losses at the hands of terrorists. In fact, the bombing attack by Muslim extremists in Bali, Indonesia in October 2002 (that killed over 200 people including over a 180 Australians) is called Australia's 9/11 (Hugo E. 2002; Hugo G. 2002).

Australian Detainment and Treatment of Alleged Foreign Terrorists

Australia did not conduct large-scale operations abroad and therefore captured few foreign-born terrorists. Similar to Canada and the United States, however, Australia passed an anti-terrorism statute in response to the 9/11 attacks. The Security Legislation Amendment of 2002 allows the Australian Security Intelligence Organization (ASIO) to detain non-citizens, for questioning, under national security grounds for up to 48 hours (with continual roll-overs) without charging them. There is no obligation to grant the detainees access to counsel (Head 2002; Hocking 2003; Rogers and Ricketts 2002). The statute expanded the domain of who is a terrorist and which acts constitute terrorism, by potentially criminalizing "domestic political activists engaged in legitimate non-violent protests and conscientious acts of civil disobedience" (Rogers and Ricketts 2002: 150). Although the Act was on the face of it neutral, in practice it may have greater effects on non-citizens. Taylor (2002a, 2002b) argues that the Australian government could deport foreigners who qualify as terrorists under this statute as a national security threat. Finally, the constitutional immunity this statute usually grants Australian citizens, who may not be detained by the ASIO and other law enforcement agencies, does not extend to immigrants or asylum seekers (Head 2002).

Australian Border Security, Visa Applications, Refugees and Asylum Seekers

Post 9/11 Australia began requiring visa applicants for permanent residency to fill out a new form-1190 and answer a series of questions relating to military and weapons training experience. Further, visa applications for permanent and temporary residency are asked about prior deportations, war crimes, criminal charges and convictions, and whether any charges are pending against them. Individuals who respond incorrectly or falsely will be denied visas. In addition, the Australian Department of Immigration and Multicultural and Indigenous Affairs (DIMIA) scrutinizes more closely the police clearances of overseas applicants and cooperates with the FBI in conducting clearance checks on individuals seeking to migrate to Australia from the United States (Hugo E. 2002).

Although the terrorist attacks in the United States and Bali greatly impacted Australia, no issue has dominated Australian political life as much as the debate surrounding refugee and asylum seekers. Because of Australia's location (an island close to Asian countries with high poverty levels and varying degrees of political repression) and history, its immigration debate has focused less on economic matters and more on political persecution claims. These issues have assumed a greater role in political discourse than in other countries, even though refugees and asylum seekers make up a small percentage of all newcomers (Hugo G. 2002; McMaster 2002).

One major incident, the Tampa boat incident, occurred a month before the 9/11 attacks. On August 26, 2001 this boat, which held over 400 asylum seekers from Afghanistan and Indonesia, sank near Australian territory. While the Australian military offered aid and medical assistance to those on board, the Australians barred these individuals from Australia and instead transported them to the barren island of Nauru in the South Pacific to have their refugee claims heard. Ultimately, while some qualified as refugees, most had their claims rejected (Hugo E. 2002).

This incident, combined with 9/11, heightened anxiety among Australians and convinced many that additional measures were needed to safeguard Australian security and sovereignty from terrorists and unfettered migration. Previously, Australian immigration law had called for mandatory detention of individuals attempting to enter the country without a valid visa or permit. These individuals were usually detained inside Australia, in some cases for up to five years, while their claims were pending (Hugo E. 2002; McMaster 2002).

The Howard government responded aggressively to the Tampa and 9/11 incidents and sought to reassure the Australian public. The Security Legislation Amendment enhanced the powers of the ASIO. This organization now plays a role during the initial interview with asylum seekers and the DIMIA and provides input about security determinations during earlier stages in the process (Taylor 2002a, 2002b). Since a large number of asylum seekers entered Australian territory at the Christmas, Ashmore and Cartier islands, the Border Protection Bill designated these locations as equivalent to non-Australian territory. The bill also streamlined the process and made it easier for the Australian government to transfer the asylum seekers to the previously mentioned territories, process their claims, and deport them. Further, the bill calls for the mandatory detention of refugees until they successfully complete a medical exam, background investigation and satisfy refugee and national criteria (Hugo E. 2002; McMaster 2002). Finally, the companion statute the Border Protection Act granted the Australian navy the right to board and search foreign ships before they enter Australian territory if refugees are on board. The Australian navy is authorized to detain any ship, either inside or outside Australian territory, if there is a reasonable suspicion the ship violated, or attempted to violate, the Australian Migration Act (Fitzpatrick 2003; Hugo E. 2002; Hugo G. 2002; McMaster 2002).

Australian Internal Measures

Australia did not institute many internal changes in response to 9/11. Previously, the government relied upon the Migration Act to deport foreigners who had been convicted of a criminal charge and served at least a year in prison. Lately, however, the government has relied upon the section of the Act that denies and cancels visas based upon broader character grounds. Individuals who are untruthful with the DIMIA, have a serious criminal record, or violate the conditions of their visas will fail the character test and could be deported. Finally, Australia cracked down on illegal immigrants and redoubled its efforts to apprehend and deport these individuals (Hugo E. 2002).

Comparison and Discussion

It is clear that post 9/11 the United States pursued the most aggressive policies against terrorism and its non-citizens, and placed national security concerns ahead of economic matters. Australia embraced a middle-range policy, and Canada was the least aggressive. The United States was the only country which explicitly passed legislation that authorized the granting of citizenship (as a reward) to non-citizens who aided the campaign against terrorism. The United States also embarked upon two wars, detained hundreds of foreigners, rendered some to foreign governments for possible torture, and issued executive orders that authorized the confinement of enemy combatants and the use of military tribunals. Domestically, America rounded up hundreds of foreigners, enacted the Patriot Act, used the material witness statute, implemented the registration program, student tracking system, and the voluntary interview program, increased security at the border and tightened up visa requirements.

Overall, the United States placed security concerns ahead of individual liberties, economic concerns and other matters.[5] Australia also placed a greater priority on public safety as opposed to civil liberties and other concerns. Australia supported and contributed to the Iraq and Afghanistan wars (though it committed fewer troops than the United States), authorized preventive detention, and increased its border security to defend against terrorism and national sovereignty. Further, because of its unique location and history, Australia responded aggressively on the refugee and asylum seeker front. The Howard administration decided security and sovereignty should sometimes override the individual rights of non-citizens. Indeed, the issues of terrorism and immigration (which became conflated with Islamic fundamentalism) played a major role in the 2002 election campaign and aided Prime Minister Howard's re-election (Beeson 2002; Hugo E. 2002; Taylor 2002). Australia apparently did not, however, completely dismiss economic concerns. One report stated that Australia was recruiting foreign students who had been denied admission to the United

5 The Bush administration took foreign policy considerations into account, however, in the timing of the Iraq war and made sure to satisfy Great Britain's concerns.

States (under its stricter policies) to study in Australia to contribute to its economy (Associated Press 2003).

Canada's policies have been more nuanced. While Canada has been cognizant of security concerns (for example, the Suresh decision, the statute that authorized preventive detention, and its increased scrutiny of visas), it has also been concerned with economic factors. This makes sense since Canada's immigration policy has long been based upon economic concerns. The majority of its immigrants are "economic" as opposed to the United States where the majority of migrants enter under "family reunification" (Ting 2003). Further, since 86 percent of Canadian exports are destined to or pass through the USA (and traded goods worth $1.4 billion daily cross the border), Canada has acted to ensure that trade continues to flow unhindered through the shared border (Goldfarb and Robson 2003).

Canada has been criticized for not providing enough scrutiny of foreign students or workers (since they are still not screened prior to entering Canada), and for employing lax refugee (Canada does not generally detain asylum seekers while their claims are pending) and legal immigration policies. This may be because, as discussed, Canada's economy is more dependent on foreigners. Conversely, Macklin (2002) contends that many of the increased security measures at the United States–Canadian border are unnecessary. She notes that terrorists do not have to enter a country to attack its interests and could instead attack that country's embassies or assets abroad. Toope (2002) argues that Canada's legislation was passed too swiftly, and that the statutes are therefore vague and open to different interpretations. Canada's relations with the United States have been mixed. On the one hand, the two countries cooperated in fighting terrorism (e.g., Canada was added to the United States Terrorist Tracking Force), and collaboratively initiated some policies (such as increased security at the border, pre-clearance checks, and harmonization of visa and asylum policies). Canada also turned over to the United States foreign fighters it captured in Afghanistan. On the other hand, they disagreed sharply about the Iraq war.

The specific Australian, Canadian and American post 9/11 responses might be due to their different experiences with foreigners and terrorists. The 9/11 attacks occurred on American soil and the United States suffered the most in terms of casualties, trauma and financial costs. It is therefore not surprising that the United States responded forcefully. Although Australia was not directly attacked on 9/11, it was significantly affected by incidents involving foreigners and terrorism (the attack in Bali) and asylum claims (the Tampa case). Canada's more restrained approaches, and allegedly more lax immigration, refugee and legal immigration policies could be due the limited number of terrorist attacks perpetrated by foreigners on her soil in the last few years. Alternatively, it could be that Canada has avoided attacks precisely because of its lax policies. In other words, terrorist organizations might have decided to take advantage of Canada's policies and use it as a base for launching attacks elsewhere.

Another issue concerns the ideology of the ruling party in each country. It appears that conservatives were more likely than liberals to support aggressive actions.

Both President Bush in the United States and Prime Minister Howard in Australia campaigned on conservative issues. Indeed, Howard used the 9/11 and Tampa incidents to bolster his re-election campaign. Similarly, Canada, which did not agree with the American and Australian approach, was ruled by the leftist Liberal Party. This interpretation faces some problems however, when the actions of Great Britain are considered. Tony Blair, the head of the liberal Labour Party wholeheartedly supported President Bush's war on terror, and committed a significant number of troops to the Afghan and Iraq wars. Perhaps Great Britain's experiences with terrorism (from the IRA and other groups) along with its traditional support of an Anglo-based (i.e., pro-American) foreign policy, as opposed to a Euro-centric approach, made it more amenable to forceful responses. In any case, Blair's decision to attack Iraq initially received more support internally from conservatives, as opposed to liberals. Similarly, when Blair's internal standing weakened as the war in Iraq bogged down and weapons of mass destruction were not found, most of the criticism directed at him came from liberal members of his own party.

All three countries approved anti-terrorism statutes that criminalized aid to non-terrorist activities run by terrorist groups and widened the domain of what constitutes "supporting" terrorist activities. There are interesting differences, however, among the statutes. Canada and Australia's definitions refer to the political, ideological or religious motivation of the perpetrators (Head 2002; Jenkins 2003; Roach 2002), while the United States statute does not and instead mandates "some form of intimidation of the government or public" (Ramraj 2002: 2). It appears that Australia and Canada explicitly recognize the religious motivations (of radical Islamic groups like Al Qaeda) that underlie much of the current terrorist threat. In contrast, the United States statute (possibly because of the First Amendment's freedom of religion clause) does not. Roach (2002: 49) maintains that the Canadian statute "will make the politics and religion of the accused terrorists a central feature of their criminal charges" (but for an opposing view see Jenkins 2003). In addition, while the three countries appear to have approved some form of preventive detention the American Patriot Act as well as the Bush administration's use of the material witness statute appear more far-reaching than Canada's and Australia's laws and policies.

The Australian and Canadian statutes have been criticized for not incorporating explicit bans on religious and racial profiling.[6] Roach (2002: 13) writes that "the [Canadian] act provides no assurance to those in Canada who may feel they are targeted or suspected simply because they are perceived to be of the same race or religion of the September 11th terrorists". While the United States Patriot Act does contain such a section, it also includes an exception that allows profiling to protect national security. The United States has, in fact, been more likely to profile than either Canada or Australia. The voluntary interviews, visa changes, registration program, and absconder initiative, undertaken by the United States, were wholly or partly based upon country of origin (i.e., Middle Eastern), gender (i.e., male) and age (i.e., 16–45).

6 Jenkins (2003: 423) notes, however, that the Canadian act outlaws "hate propaganda on Internet sites and criminal mischief against a place of religious worship".

Although Canada and Australia made some visa changes based upon national origin[7] they did not implement initiatives which explicitly relied upon national, age and/or gender characteristics. Indeed, while all three countries announced crackdowns on illegal immigration and promised to speed up deportations, only the United States' absconder initiative was nationally profiled. Defenders of these policies point out, however, that:

> none of these initiatives discriminate on the basis of appearance, skin color, race, ethnicity, or religion. The individuals subject to these initiatives are certainly being profiled but the profiling is done on non invidious factors such as age, gender and the objective immigration documents presented i.e., passports from designated countries… no constitutional challenge has ever been sustained against such discrimination. (Ting 2003: 504)

Conclusion

The repercussions of 9/11 extended far beyond New York City and Washington DC, and affected nations all across the globe. The present study outlined and compared the legislative and policy responses of Australia, Canada and the United States toward non-citizens residing within and without their borders. Although much was learned, a great deal remains to be examined. Were the legislative and policy changes effective? Did they achieve the goals of their proponents? How did these changes impact on immigration and tourist decisions? Critics have attacked the Bush administration for instituting a series of draconian measures pertaining to legal immigrants, tourists, foreign students, and foreign workers. Treyster (2003: 527) claims, for example, that "the implementation of SEVIS will reduce the number of foreign students coming to study in the United States. The idea of treating people as potential terrorists is not welcoming. These students may choose to study in England or Australia or any other country that wants them." Did this in fact occur? Did the number of foreign students decrease in the United States and increase in Australia post 9/11?

Similarly, were the changes successful in reducing further terrorist attacks? Did they negatively impact upon the economy or not? In other words, did the post 9/11 initiatives have any effect on the public safety and the economies of these three nations? Further, where did the legislative and policy initiatives originate from? Were they novel proposals that had never been discussed before? Or were they longstanding proposals that had been previously debated, but not acted upon, and the changed post 9/11 context led to a renewed interest in them?

It would also be interesting to explore the deep controversies among political parties and the public as a whole that lay behind the legislative and policy actions taken by the American, Canadian and Australian governments. It appears that the

7 Canada removed some countries from its Visa Waiver program, and Australia "even before September 11 … [had] classified … countries … into high to low risk [categories]" (Hugo E. 2002: 8).

specific initiatives of each government were driven by home-grown concerns and longstanding local issues. The American and Australian contexts are especially intriguing since although Prime Minister Howard and President Bush were both denounced by many (including the media), they nonetheless retained public support. Indeed, both men were re-elected to office and their respective parties increased their majorities. A final point concerns asylum seekers and refugees. The post 9/11 attempts of these nations to improve their screening processes of refugees and asylum seekers, raises a far more controversial issue. What is a fair quota of refugees for each nation? How can this be determined? Could there ever be international agreement on such matters? Research is needed to answer these questions and to address the complicated issues of foreign policy, international relations and national security that underlie their solution.

References

Adelman, Howard (2002), "Canadian Borders and Immigration Post 9/11", *International Migration Review*, 36 (1): 15–27.

Akram, Susan M., and Kevin R. Johnson (2002), "Migration Regulation Goes Local: The Role of States in U.S. Immigration Policy: Race, Civil Rights, and Immigration Law after September 11, 2001: The Targeting of Arabs and Muslims", *New York University Annual Survey of American Law*, 58: 295–355.

Associated Press (2003), "International Student Enrollment Slows in U.S.", CNN, at http://www.cnn.com/2003/EDUCATION/11//03/foreign.students.ap/index.html (accessed December 3, 2003).

Associated Press (2004), "New Security Checks at U.S. Airports", Fox News, at www.foxnews.com (accessed January 5, 2004).

Baldwin, Fletcher (2002), "Organized Crime, Terrorism and Money Laundering in the Americas", *Florida Journal of International Law*, 15: 3–25.

Beeson, Mark (2002), "Issues in Australian Foreign Policy", *Australian Journal of Politics and History*, 48: 226–40.

Bellino, Adrienne R. (2002), "Changing Immigration for Arabs with Anti-Terrorism Legislation: September 11th Was Not the Catalyst", *Temple International and Comparative Law Journal*, 16: 123–46.

Bonner, Raymond, Dan Van Natta Jr., and Amy Waldman (2003), "Questioning Terrorism Suspects in a Dark and Surreal World", *New York Times*, March 9: A1.

Broder, John M., and Susan Sachs (2002), "Facing Registry Deadline, Men from Muslim Nations Swamp Immigration Offices", *New York Times*, December 17: A20.

Bush, George W. (2001a), Military Order of President George W. Bush, *Detention, Treatment, and Trial of Certain Non-Citizens in the War Against Terrorism & 3,66 Fed. Reg. 57,833, 57,834-35 (Nov 13, 2001).*

Bush, George W. (2001b). Military Order of President George W. Bush, *Detention, Treatment, and Trial of Certain Non-Citizens in the War Against Terrorism & 3,66 Fed. Reg. 57,833, 57,834-35 (Nov 13, 2001).*

Cole, David (2002), "Terrorizing Immigrants in the Name of Fighting Terrorism", *Human Rights*, 29: 11–22.

Cole, David (2003), "The New McCarthyism: Repeating History in the war on Terrorism", *Harvard Civil Rights-Civil Liberties Law Review*, 38: 1–30.

Daigle, Gilles, D. Saul, S. Heller, M. Opashinov, C. Curtiss, C. Forcese, C. and R. Mansell (2002), "Foreign Law Year in Review: 2001", *International Lawyer*, 36: 753–69.

Demleitner, Nora V. (2002), "Immigration Threats and Rewards: Effective Law Enforcement Tools in the War on Terrorism?", *Emory Law Journal*, 51: 1059–94.

Drew, Christopher, and Adam Liptak (2003), "Immigration Groups Fault Rule on Automatic Detention of Some Asylum Seekers", *New York Times*, March 31: B15.

Fainaru, Steve and Margot Williams (2002), "Material Witness Statute Has Many in Limbo: Nearly Half Held in War on Terror Have Not Testified", *Washington Post*: November 24, A1.

Federal Register (2001a), 66 Fed Reg 48,334-35, September 17, 2001.

Federal Register (2001b), 66 Fed. Reg. 54,909-12, October 31, 2001.

Fitzpatrick, Joan (2003), "Australia's Tampa Incident: The Convergence of International and Domestic Refugee and Maritime Law in the Pacific Rim", *Pacific Rim Law and Policy Journal*, 12: 1–8.

Foster, Charles (2003), "A Legal Perspective: Immigration Law", *Texas Bar Journal*, 66: 38–9.

Fragomen, Jr., T. Austin and Howard W. Gordon (2002), "Managing Change: Recent Legislation and Current Immigration Topics", *Practicing Law Institute: Corporate Law and Practice Course Handbook Series*, 1340: 173–98.

Galea, S., J. Ahewrn, H. Resnick, D. Kilpatrick, M. Buculvas and J. Gold (2002), "Psychological Sequelae of the September 11 Terrorist Attacks in New York City", *New England Journal of Medicine*, 346: 982–7.

Georgetown Immigration Law Journal (2002), "Current Development: Developments in the Executive Branch", *Georgetown Immigration Law Journal*, 16: 535–7.

Germain, Regina (2002), "Rushing to Judgment: The Unintended Consequences of the USA Patriot Act for Bona Fide Refugees", *Georgetown Immigration Law Journal*, 16: 505–30.

Goldfarb, Danielle and Robson, W. (2003), "Risky Business: U.S. Border Security and the Threat to Canadian Exports", *Commentary: The Border Papers*, 177.

Harris, David A. (2002), "Racial Profiling Revisited: Just Common Sense in the Fight Against Terror?", *Criminal Justice*, 17: 36–41, 59.

Head, Michael (2002), "Counter-Terrorism Laws: A Threat to Political Freedom, Civil Liberties, and Constitutional Rights", *Melbourne University Law Review*, 26: 666–89.

Heymann, Phillip B. (2002), "Law and the War on Terrorism Essay", *Harvard Journal of Law and Public Policy*, 25: 441–56.

Hill, Charles, and Donal Kerwin (2002), "International Legal Developments in Review: Public International Law", *International Lawyer*, 36: 527–47.

Hine, Barbara (2002), "So Near Yet so Far Away: The Effect of September 11th on Mexican Immigrants in the United States", *Texas Hispanic Journal of Law and Policy*, 8: 37–46.

Hocking, Jenny (2003), "Counter-Terrorism and the Criminalisation of Politics: Australia's New Security Powers of Detention, Proscription and Control", *Australian Journal of Politics and History*, 49: 355–71.

Holman, Lester A. (2001), "The Impact of September 11th on America's Laws, Policy, and Procedures", *Vermont Bar Journal*, 27: 17–20.

Hom, Howard (2002), "The Immigration Landscape in the Aftermath of September 11th: New Policies, and Regulations Present Challenges to Immigrants and their Counsel", *Los Angeles Lawyer*, 25: 23–6.

Hugo, Etienne de Villiers (2002), "The Effect of 11 September 2001 on International Immigration Policies, from an Australian Perspective", paper presented at the International Bar Foundation, Durban South Africa, October.

Hugo, Graeme (2002), "Australian Immigration Policy: The Significance of the Events of September 11", *International Migration Review*, 36(1): 37–40.

Jenkins, David (2003) "In Support of Canada's Anti-Terrorism Act: A Comparison of Canadian, British and American Anti-Terrorism Law", *Saskatchewan Law Review*, 66: 419–54.

Johnson, Kevin R. (2002), "Symposium: Beyond Belonging: Challenging the Boundaries of Nationality: Twelfth Annual Depaul Law Review Symposium: September 11 and Mexican Immigrants: Collateral Damage Comes Home", *DePaul Law Review*, 52: 849–70.

Johnson, Jr., James H. (2002), "U.S. Immigration Reform, Homeland Security, and Global Economic Competitiveness in the Aftermath of the September 11, 2001 Terrorist Attacks", *North Carolina Journal of International Law and Commercial Regulation, Inc*, 27: 419–64.

Katyal, Neal K., and Lawrence H. Tribe (2002), "Essay: Waging War, Deciding Guilt: Trying the Military Tribunals2, *Yale Law Journal*, 111: 1259–310.

Law, Tsiwen, and Enrique Rosario (2001), "Special Reports: A Changing America: The Immigration Backlash", *Pennsylvania Lawyer*, 23: 50–1.

Lebowitz, Lawrence M., and Ira L. Podheiser (2002), "A Summary of the Changes in Immigration Policies and Practices after the Terrorist Attacks of September 11, 2001: The USA Patriot Act and Other Measures", *University of Pittsburgh Law Review*, 63: 873–88.

Lester, George N. (2002), "Post 9/11 Changes in U.S. Immigration Law and Procedure", *Boston Bar Journal*, 46: 14–15.

Lichtblau, Drew (2003), "U.S. Report Faults the Roundup of Illegal Immigrants after 9/11", *New York Times*, June 3: A1.

Macklin, Audrey (2002), "Borderline Security", *University of Toronto Law Review*, www.utoronto.ca/ethnicstudies/BorderlineSecurity.pdf.

Mantle, D. Ray (2003), "What Foreign Students Fear: Homeland Security Measures and Closed Deportation Hearings", *Brigham Young University Education Law Journal*, 2003: 815–34.

McAllister, Stephen R. (2003) (Moderator), "The 2002 Tenth Circuit Judicial Conference Proceedings: Life After 9/11: Issues Affecting the Courts and the Nation", *University of Kansas Law Review*, 51: 219–47.

McMaster, Don (2002), "Asylum-Seekers and the Insecurity of a Nation", *Australian Journal of International Affairs*, 56(2): 279–94.

Meissner, Doris (2002), "Immigration Symposium: Immigration in the Post-11 Era", *Brandeis Law Journal*, 40: 851–59.

Millard, Jeremy (2002), "Special Notes on Bill C-36: Investigative Hearings Under the Anti-Terrorism Act", *University of Toronto Law Review*, 60: 79–86.

Motomura, Hiroshi (2003), "Symposium on Confronting Realities: The Legal, Moral, and Constitutional Issues Involving Diversity: Panel II: Immigration policy: Immigration and We the People after September 11", *Albany Law Review*, 66: 413–29.

Murphy, Sean D. (2002), "Contemporary Practice of the United States Relating to International Law Human Rights: U.S. Detention of Aliens in the Aftermath of September 11 Attacks", *American Journal of International Law*, 96: 470–5.

Otto, Catherine Etheridge (2002), "Tracking Immigrants in the United States: Proposed Tracking and Perceived Needs to Protect the Border of the United States", *North Carolina Journal of International Law and Commercial Review*, 28: 477–516.

Pantin, Hilda M., Seth J. Schwartz, Guillermo Prado, Daniel J. Feaster, and Jose Szapocznik (2003), "Posttraumatic Stress Disorder Symptoms in Hispanic Immigrants after the September 11th Attacks: Severity and Relationship to Previous Traumatic Exposure", *Hispanic Journal of Behavioral Sciences*, 25(1): 56–72.

Priest, Dana, and Barton Gellman (2002), "U.S. Decries Abuse but Defends Interrogations: Stress and Duress Tactics Used on Terrorism Suspects Held in Overseas Facilities", *Washington Post*, December 26: A1.

Ramraj, Victor V. (2002), "Special Feature: Terrorism, Security, and Rights: A New Dialogue", *Singapore Journal of Legal Studies*, 2002: 1–29.

Rekai, Peter (2002), "US and Canadian Immigration Policies: Marching Together to Different Tunes", *Commentary: The Border Papers*, 171.

Roach, Kent (2002), "Special Feature: Terrorism, Security and Rights: Canada's New Anti-Terrorism Law", *Singapore Journal of Legal Studies*, 2002: 122–48.

Rogers, Nicole, and Aidan Ricketts (2002), "Special Feature: Terrorism, Security, and Rights: Fear of Freedom: Anti-Terrorism Laws and the Challenge to Australian Democracy", *Singapore Journal of Legal Studies*, 2002: 149–75.

Romero, Victor C. (2003), "Symposium: Beyond Belonging: Challenging the Boundaries of Nationality; Twelfth Annual Depaul Law Review Symposium:

Proxies for Loyalty in Constitutional Immigration Law: Citizenship and Race after September 11", *DePaul Law Review*, 52: 871–91.

Rutherglen, George (2002), "Structural Uncertainty over Habeas Corpus and the Jurisdiction of Military Tribunals", *Green Bag*, 5: 397–406.

Seper, Jerry (2003), "Guarding America's Border: Part I: Controlling America's Northern Border in the New Age of Terrorism is a Daunting Task", *Washington Times*, at http://www.washingtontimes.com (accessed December 8, 2003).

Silverman, Henry (2002), "Effects of the American Response to the 9/11 Terrorist Attack on Civil Liberties", *Michigan State University-DCL Journal of International Law*, 10: 563–71.

Swain, Rachel L. (2003), "Special Registration for Arab Immigrants Will Reportedly Stop", *New York Times*, November 22: A16.

Taylor, Savitri (2002a), "Reconciling Australia's International Protection Obligations with the 'War on Terrorism'", *Pacific Review*, 14 (2): 121–40.

Taylor, Savitri (2002b), "Guarding the Enemy from Oppression: Asylum Seeker Rights Post September 11", *Melbourne University Law Review*, 26: 396–421.

Ting, Jan (2003), "Immigration Reform After 9/11: What Has Been Done and What Still Needs to Be Done", *Temple International and Comparative Law Journal*, 17: 503–21.

Toobin, Jeffrey (2002) (Moderator), "The USA-Patriot Act and the American Response to Terror: Can We Protect Civil Liberties After September 11?: A Panel Discussion with Congressman Barney Frank, Assistant Attorney General Michael Chertoff, Professor David Cole, Mr. Stuart Taylor, Jr., and Ms. Beth Wilkinson", *American Criminal Law Review*, 39: 1501–33.

Toope, Stephen (2002), "Fallout from '9–11': Will a Security Culture Undermine Human Rights?", *Saskatchewan Law Review*, 65: 281–97.

Treyster, David (2003), "Foreign Students v National Security: Will Denying Education Prevent Terrorism?", *New York Law Journal of International and Comparative Law*, 22: 497–527.

Vargas, Sylvia R. Lazos (2002), "Missouri, the War on Terrorism, and Immigrants: Legal Challenges Post 9/11", *Missouri Law Review*, 67: 775–827.

Wishnie, Michael J. (2002), "Migration Goes Local: The Role of States in U.S. Immigration Policy: Introduction: Immigration and Federalism", *New York University Annual Survey of American Law*, 58: 283–93.

PART II
Migration and Offending Issues

Chapter 5

Religiosity and Crime: Attitudes Towards Violence and Delinquent Behavior among Young Christians and Muslims in Germany

Katrin Brettfeld
University of Hamburg

Peter Wetzels
University of Hamburg

Introduction

Established criminological textbooks rarely discuss religion and religiosity in the context of the explanation of criminal behavior. This is exemplified by Morrison (1995: 5), who argued – "Criminology claims the status of the rational and scientific attempt to study the phenomenon of crime. It was born with the death of God". Cochran (2000: 321) indicates that in criminology religion is "a rather narrow area of scholarly interest".

However, important recent theories of crime rely on variables which are also strongly related to religion. This indicates that religiosity might be an important factor in the explanation of crime. On one hand, religion can bring people together and serve as an important source of social networks. It is but one of the possible sources of social capital which is strongly related to social integration and negatively associated with criminal behavior (Sampson, Raudenbush and Earls 1997). In addition, religious communities can be an important source of both informal and formal social control. One would therefore expect that religion in general and the individual commitment to religion in particular would be inversely related to crime on both the individual and aggregate levels (Cochran 2000). On the other hand, differing religious orientations and beliefs could also separate people. Historically, religion has been a major source of conflict and war. Even today different religious beliefs sometimes result in mutual marginalization and exclusion. Religious beliefs sometimes legitimize violence and enforce claims of religious predominance.

Therefore, religion might act to increase individual delinquent behavior and macro-level crime rates.

After the terrorist attacks of September 11 2001 the association between religion and religiosity and the inclination to commit violent acts became a hot topic in Western societies. For example, Huntington's (1996) controversial clash of civilizations thesis, particularly its focus on Islamic fundamentalism and the religiosity of Muslims and its relation to violence there, could possibly reinforce negative attitudes towards Muslims in Western society. This increases the possibility of the exclusion and stigmatization of this group. One common stereotype is that: "the more religious Muslims are – the more violent they are".

Literature Review

There are several theoretical approaches that incorporate religion into their explanations of criminal behavior. Hirschi's (1969) social control theory, for example, argues that beliefs play an important role in explaining why some people do not commit deviant behavior. Such beliefs are internalized moral norms and individually relevant ethical values which influence the behavior of people in social settings. Quite often these norms are based on religious values, e.g., the norm prohibiting murder can be found in nearly every monotheistic religion. The same is also true for the norm to be honest and not to cheat other members of society. The exceptions to these general norms are quite different, however, depending upon the particular religion. In addition, social control theory argues that involvement is related to less delinquency. Membership in religious communities should not only produce such involvement, but also increases one's attachment to others outside one's own family. Based upon this, social control theory would expect that increased social control would be negatively related to criminal behavior.

A second theoretical approach addresses the interpretation of adverse experiences and coping with strain. According to Agnew's (1992; 2001) general strain theory negative experiences or aversive behaviors of others could elicit negative emotions. One possible strategy of coping with such negative emotions is fighting and other aggressive and deviant behaviors. Whether people perceive incidents and situations as a kind of strain and how individuals react to such strains depends on internal and external factors. Religion can operate in two contradictory ways. On one hand, religion can be a source of strain and negative emotions if people are discriminated against because of their religion. On the other hand, religion can be a coping resource. Examples include the support offered by the members of the religious community and the reinterpretation of adverse incidents as fate, both of which might strengthen persons coping capacities and thereby prevent deviant behavior.

Religion has always played an important role in social science research. Most of this research was initiated by religion researchers or sociologists. For the most part, however they did not examine criminological issues such as the effect of religion on deviant behavior. Indeed, research on the effect of religiosity on criminal behavior is rare and in Germany such research is nearly non-existent.

Hirschi and Stark (1969) conducted one of the first classic studies in this area. This study investigated whether or not church attendance and the belief in supernatural sanctions had a deterrent effect and was positively associated with conforming behavior. Contrary to their expectations, no association was found between religion and crime. More recently Jang and Johnson (2003) examined general strain theory. Religiosity was conceptualized as a moderating factor in the relationship between negative emotions and deviant behavior. Jang and Johnson found that religiously committed people were both less likely to lose their temper and to engage in deviant coping but they were more likely to feel inner-directed negative emotions as reaction to personal problems. In sum, religiosity was found to have a negative effect on deviant behavior.

Baier and Wright (2001) published a meta-analysis of 60 American studies. The studies reviewed produced mixed results regarding the effects of religion on individual deviance and criminal behavior. While some studies found no effect at all (e.g., Hirschi and Stark 1969), some found a reducing effect at the bivariant level that disappeared after controlling for social background variables like socioeconomic status, age, and sex (Burkett and Warren 1987). Some studies, however found that religiosity was negatively associated with deviant behavior (Benda 1995). Overall, the meta-analysis found a moderate inverse effect of religiosity on delinquency.

One reason for these rather mixed results was the heterogeneity of measures of religiosity used. Frequent church attendance and/or the participation in religious events were used as the only indicators of religiosity. However, church attendance does not say anything about the strength of individual beliefs and religious commitment. It can simply be a result of social pressure and individual adaptation. More recent studies have employed more sophisticated measures of the individual religiosity. These studies focused on the content of religious convictions as well as on the individual relevance of religious norms, for example the longing for forgiveness and reconciliation (e.g., Benda 2002, Johnson et al 2001). Another explanation for the different results in prior studies could be that religion affects various kinds of delinquency differently. For example, some research indicates that religion more strongly affects behavior that is sanctioned by religious norms but not by social norms in everyday life – such as gambling and alcohol use.

Further, most of the studies used homogeneous samples with respect to religious affiliation. Nearly all American studies included only Christian people (Burkett 2000). If Muslims were interviewed, they usually were excluded from the analysis. In Germany a well-known study conducted by Heitmeyer, Müller and Schröder (1997) included only Muslims of Turkish origin. As a consequence, the results of this study are not representative of all Islamic juveniles living in Germany.

The extant research does not examine the effects of religiosity of different religions on crime. If religiosity has a crime reducing effect for Christians as most of the studies show, why should it be associated with an increase in crime for Muslims? Obviously terrorism and violence is not restricted to Muslims (Stern 2003).

Investigating the effects of religiosity on crime for different religious affiliations has to take into consideration another problem: Muslims living in Western societies are mostly migrants. Segregation, low socioeconomic status, lack of education and high unemployment rates are characteristics of their living conditions. These are variables which are also correlated with deviant behavior. Studies that investigate the different effects of particular religions, such as Christianity and Islam, on crime must control for these social structural conditions. Further, cultural differences between different ethnic groups could be associated with different ethical values which independent of religion might affect delinquent behavior.

Research Questions

The current study analyzed the effect of religious affiliation and individual religiosity on attitudes towards violence and delinquent behavior of juveniles and took into account the migration status and the social background of the study participants. We examined the following questions:

1. Does the degree of religiosity differ between different religious affiliations and ethnic groups?
2. Is there an effect of religiosity on violence-approving attitudes and delinquent behavior in general?
3. Do the effects of religiosity on attitudes and delinquent behavior differ between Christians and Muslims?
4. Is the effect of religiosity on delinquency the same for different types of offences?

Sample

In spring 2000 we conducted community-based regional-representative surveys on victimization and delinquency in four major cities and one rural district of Germany. The sample consists of a random sample of school classes (9th and 10th grade) stratified according to school type within each city and district. The juveniles were contacted in their classrooms where they anonymously filled in a written standardized questionnaire (Wetzels and Brettfeld 2003).

The total number of juveniles participating in the survey was 11,819. The participation rate was 84.5 percent and the sample is representative of 14 to 16-year-old juveniles who attend German schools. 13.6 percent of the sample had no German citizenship and an additional 10.9 percent who had German citizenship also had a migration background (repatriated or naturalized). Juveniles with German citizenship and no migration background were coded as autochthones (75.5 percent). Juveniles with migration background were coded as allochthones (24.5 percent). Males comprised 50.5 percent of the sample and the mean age was 15.3 years (SD=0.84). Table 5.1 shows the distribution of both ethnicity and religious affiliation.

Table 5.1 Religion by ethnicity

	Autochthones	Repatriated	Turkish	Naturalized (other)	Foreigners (former Yug)	Foreigners (south. Europe)	Foreigners (other)	Total
Christianity	4 894 (80.7%) [60.8%]	357 (5.9%) [86.2%]	7 (0.1%) [1.4%]	330 (5.4%) [58.8%]	174 (2.9%) [58.0%]	120 (2.0%) [85.7%]	185 (3.0%) [40.6%]	6 067 *[58.1%]*
Islam	25 (2.9%) [0.3%]		478 (55.1%) [93.4%]	93 (10.7%) [16.6%]	109 (12.6%) [36.3%]	7 (0.8%) [5.0%]	155 (17.9%) [34.0%]	867 *[8.3%]*
Other religion	156 (55.7%) [1.9%]	14 (5.0%) [3.4%]	13 (4.6%) [2.5%]	30 (10.7%) [5.3]	10 (3.6%) [3.3%]	12 (4.3%) [8.6%]	45 (16.1%) [9.9%]	280 *[2.7%]*
No religion	2 977 (92.4%) [37.0%]	43 (1.3%) [10.4%]	14 (0.4%) [2.7%]	108 (3.4%) [19.3%]	7 (0.2%) [2.3%]	1 (0.0%) [0.7%]	71 (2.2%) [15.6%]	3 221 *[30.9%]*

Proportions in () are row-percents; in [] are column-percents

Most of the sample are Christians (58.1 percent). Of the Christians, 80 percent were native Germans (autochthones). Just over eight percent of the respondents were young Muslims. While 55 percent of the Islamic respondents were Turkish over 90 percent of the Turkish were Islamic. The next highest proportion of Islamic affiliation is found among juveniles from the former Yugoslavia, North Africa and the Middle East. 31 percent of the sample reported no religion; mostly all of them are autochthone Germans. The distribution in Table 5.1 clearly show that the affiliation to a certain religion depends highly on the ethnic background of the juveniles (χ^2=6800.6; df=18; p<.0001).

To control for the effect of religion and migration simultaneously we created a nominal variable (migration/religion) that considered both migration background and religious affiliation. This variable differentiated between Christians and Muslims on the one hand and juveniles with and without migration background on the other hand. Juveniles with no religious affiliation, but with at least one religious parent were categorized according to the religious affiliations of their parents because their families had a religious background. The analyses were restricted to Christian and Muslim juveniles. Consequently in the following analyses we compared three groups: Islamic allochthones, Christian allochthones, and Christian autochthones (see Table 5.2).

Table 5.2 Distribution of the sample analysed (N=7,280)

	Migration	
Religion	Allochthone	Autochthone
Christianity	12.1%	75.8%
Islam	12.1%	--

Measures

Religiosity was measured by three items including institutional and individual aspects of religious behavior:

1. How often do you attend to church service?
2. How often do you pray? and
3. How important is religion for you in every day life?

The response format ranges from 1 = "daily"/"very important" to 6 = "never"/"not important at all". Juveniles without religious affiliation were coded with 0 and the scale scores range from 0 to 6, where high values correspond to high religiosity. Chronbach's Alpha = .77 indicating internal consistency of the scale.

Juvenile delinquency was measured using modified version of the DBS ("Delinquenzbelastungsskala"; Lösel 1975), a self-report measure of delinquency, comprising 12 specific criminal acts. The measure has two response formats: One for lifetime prevalence (yes/no) and the other for the frequency of having committed the respective act during the last 12 months (number of incidences). For the present analysis only assault, threat by weapon, extortion, robbery, vehicle theft, car burglary, burglary, and driving without license committed during the last 12 months are considered here. The first four are aggregated into an index of violent crime, the next three into an index of severe property crime. Driving without license is a simple measure. Because the number of criminal acts is highly skewed (zero inflated counts), an ordinal measure of incidence with five incidence classes was constructed: never, once, twice to four times, five to nine times, ten times and more. Alcohol use and illegal drug use were measured as an ordinal variable also with five incidence classes: once or twice, three to twelve times a year, sometimes a month, and weekly or daily.

Attitudes towards violence were assessed by an 11-item Likert scale (see Wetzels 2000). The response format ranges from 1 = "completely disagree" to 4 = "completely agree". It is a one-dimensional scale with an internal consistency (Cronbach's Alpha) in the current sample of .90 (see Appendix A). The test-retest reliability for this scale is .78 (Wetzels 2000: 67).

The social situation of the juveniles' families was assessed by two measures. The first used the ISEI (standard International Socio-Economic Index of occupational status, see Ganzeboom et al 1992), a measure of socioeconomic status based on information about the vocational training and the present occupation of the parents. The second is a binary variable indicating whether the head of the household was unemployed or whether the family was receiving social welfare benefits.

Victimization by parental corporal punishment in childhood (parental violence in childhood) was assessed by a German adaptation of the Conflict Tactics scales (Straus 1979). Respondents were asked to indicate whether they had experienced parental violence varying in intensity from mild forms of punishment like spanking to severe forms of maltreatment like kicks or blows with the fist before they had reached the age of twelve. Responses ranged from 1 = "never", 2 = "seldom", 3 = "sometimes" to 4 = "frequently" and were aggregated by weighting the items according to their intensity (see Wetzels 2000).

The "parental norms towards violence" variable measured the perception of juveniles regarding how their parents would react if they had committed a violent act in school. They were asked, separately for their father and their mother, whether such a violent act would be approved by them or not. The response format ranged from 1 = "not disapprove" to 5 = "strongly disapprove". The distribution of this measure is highly skewed, and we therefore used the reflected and inverted responses. The internal consistency (Cronbach's Alpha) of this scale was .76.

Parental supervision was measured by using five items on the parental concerns about the juveniles' friends and their activities during leisure time. The response format ranged from 1 = "completely disagree" to 4 = "completely agree". The scale has been shown to be one-dimensional. The internal consistency (Cronbach's Alpha) in the current sample was .70.

Traditional gender role orientation was measured by an eleven item Likert scale. The response format ranged again from 1 = "completely disagree" to 4 = "completely agree". This scale is one-dimensional with an internal consistency (Cronbach's Alpha) of .83 (see Appendix B).

Results

Figure 5.1 lists the distribution of religiosity for the three groups. To illustrate the interaction effect we used the median split at the midpoint of the scale of religiosity and displayed the category "not religious" separately.

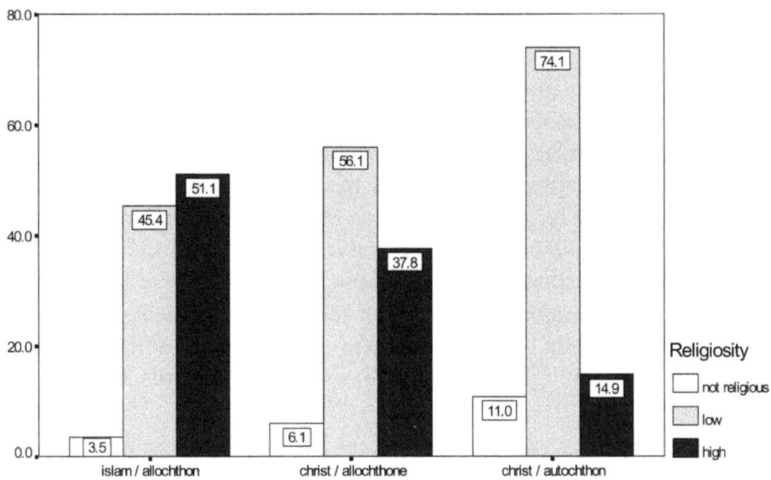

Figure 5.1 Religiosity by migration/religion

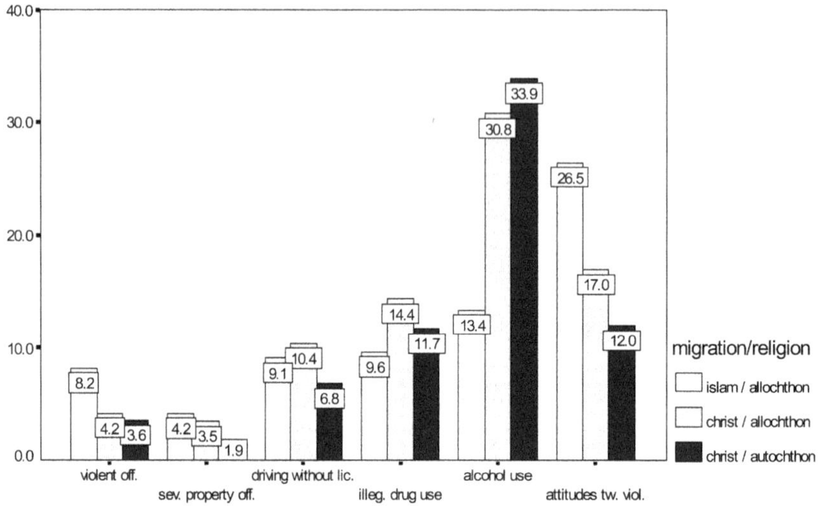

Figure 5.2 Prevalence of repeated deviant behavior, and positive attitudes towards violence by migration/religion (5 or more offences or at least monthly drug/alcohol use)

There is a statistically significant difference of religiosity among the three groups. The rate of high religiosity for the Islamic people was 51 percent while this rate was generally lower for Christians (38 percent for allochthones and only 15 percent for the native Germans). The rates of non-religious people and people with low religiosity was very small in the Islamic group compared to the Christians.[1] There were also statistically significant differences in the rate of self-reported delinquency. However, these differences were not homogeneous across different offences.

Figure 5.2 illustrates the different profiles of the groups. Islamic juveniles had clearly higher rates of violent offences and slightly higher rates of severe property offences, but the lowest rates of alcohol abuse and illegal drug use. This finding illustrates the importance of religion, because alcohol use is forbidden by the Koran. For violent offences, the Christians showed similarities independent of their migration background. For severe property offences the migration background seems to be more important than the religious affiliation. The same was true for driving without license. The last bars show the rates for positive attitudes towards violence. The bars illustrate that the proportion of people whose scores are above the absolute scale midpoint. The profile is rather similar to the self-reported violent offences, with the Islamic group showing the highest rates. With respect to the attitudinal domain we analyzed the effect of religiosity on positive attitudes towards violence applying

1 The rate would be even higher if we had included those German native juveniles because the rate of not religious juveniles where neither parent was a member of a religious group and where the children also indicated that they were not at all religious was 37 percent.

Table 5.3 Multiple linear regression of attitudes on religiosity, and migration/religion

	B	Beta	T	p
Main Effects :				
migration/ religion				
(0=Christianity/autochthones)				
Islam/allochthones	.177	.093	2.976	**
Christianity/allochthones	.114	.600	2.397	*
Religiosity	-.058	-.133	-9.037	***
Interaction Effects:				
religiosity*Islam/allochth.	.073	.146	4.415	***
religiosity*Christianity/allochth.	.017	.030	1.136	n.s.
(Constant)	1.903		123.186	***

Notes: Dependent variable was "attitudes toward violence"
R^2=.046 ; $F_{(5;7072)}$ = 68.925 ; p<.001

multiple regressions. In the first step we only included the group variable and the measure of religiosity.

The results show a significant main effect of the group variable, there were significant differences between the three groups in their positive attitudes toward violence. This difference was highest between autochthones and Islamic allochthones. Further, there was a significant negative main effect for religiosity, indicating that high levels of religiosity are associated with lower levels of violence-approving attitudes. In addition, we found a significant interaction effect for Islamic respondents, indicating that religiosity does not affect all groups in the same way. There was a difference between the Muslims and Christians, which was not found between the Christian allochthones and autochthones. These effects are illustrated

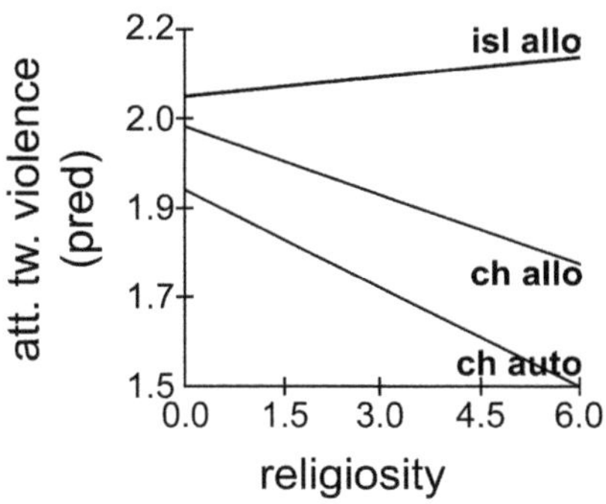

	B	p
Main Effects		
migration/ religion		
(0=christ / autochthones)		
islam / allochthones	.177	**
christ / allochthones	.114	*
religiosity	-.058	***
Interaction Effects:		
religiosity*islam / allochth.	.073	***
religiosity*christ / allochth.	.017	n.s.

Notes: R^2=.046 ; $F_{(5;7072)}$=68.925 ; p<.001

Figure 5.3 Multiple linear regression of attitudes towards violence on religiosity, and migration/religion (model 1)

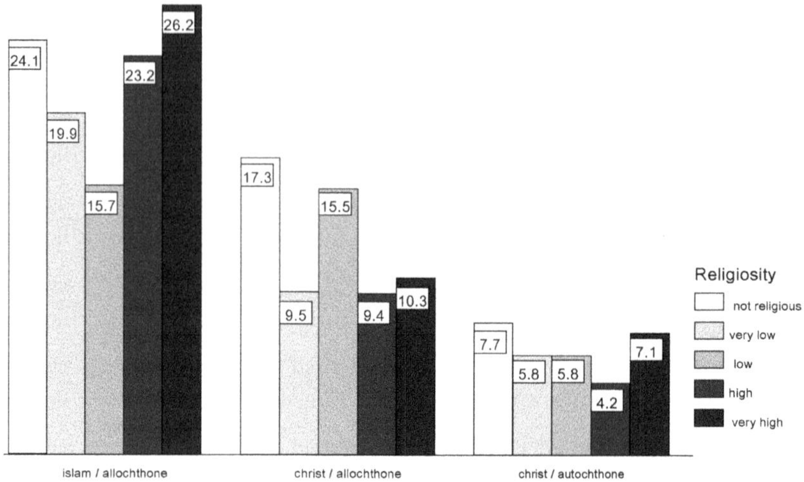

Figure 5.4 Victimization by severe parental maltreatment in childhood by religiosity and migration/religion

in Figure 5.3 that shows the moderate positive slope for the Islamic juveniles and negative slopes for the Christians.

Model 2 included the social background variables: socioeconomic status, employment/welfare dependency, school degree of the parents, and the statutory education level of the juveniles. After these variables were controlled for there were no longer significant main effects for the group variable. The groups were really different with respect to these social background factors. But the effect of religiosity and the interaction effect of religiosity and group membership remained significant.

The variables concerning family socialization experiences, like parental violence in childhood, parental supervision, and parental norms towards violence, were included in model 3. The prior analyses demonstrated that there were substantial differences among these different ethnic groups with respect to these variables (see Wetzels 2000). The bivariate association of victimization by parental violence and religiosity is illustrated in Figure 5.4.

Young Muslims posted the highest rate of victimization from severe parental maltreatment. Unlike the Christian group, the Islamic group shows a U-shaped distribution with the highest rates for very high values of religiosity. Because we assume that social norms inherent in religion are communicated, at least in part via the process of family socialization, we included these variables in model 3.

The interaction effect for the Islamic respondents in model 3 remained the same after controlling for the family socialization variables. That is surprising because the family socialization is the way by which religious commitment is translated into individual attitudes and behavior as well. But it could be explained by the result found in the bivariate analyses of parental violence and religiosity that for all groups the higher the parental violence, the higher the positive attitudes toward violence. While for Christians high religiosity was associated with lower parental violence, for

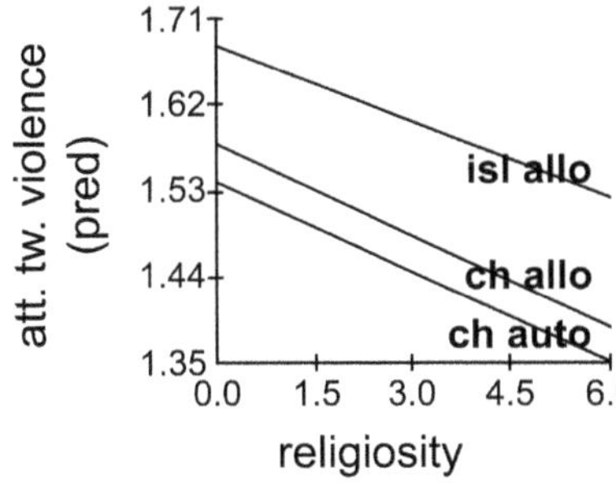

	B	p
Main Effects		
migration/ religion		
(0=christ / autochthones)		
islam / allochthones	.145	*
christ / allochthones	.043	n.s.
religiosity	-.030	***
Interaction Effects:		
religiosity*islam / allochth.	.004	n.s.
religiosity*christ / allochth.	-.002	n.s.

Notes: R^2=.331 ; $F_{(19 ;5929)}$=154.226 ; p<.001

Figure 5.5 Multiple linear regression of attitudes towards violence on religiosity, and migration/religion controlling for socio-economic situation, family socialization, and sex role orientation (model 4)

Islamic juveniles the opposite was true. The higher the religiosity, the more parental violence they experienced.

We also found a significant difference in the degree of traditional gender role orientations between Christian and Islamic respondents. In addition, more traditional gender role orientations were associated with higher approval of positive attitudes toward violence. Finally, according to our bivariate analyses there was a positive correlation of religiosity and traditional gender role orientations, which was particularly pronounced for Islamic juveniles (see Wetzels and Brettfeld 2003: 150). We therefore assumed that violence-approving attitudes might be a result of gender specific socialization which itself is influenced by gender specific religious norms. If this theoretical assumption holds empirically then the interaction effect of group membership and religiosity should disappear after controlling for gender role orientation. Including this variable in the final model 4 we found the following effect shown in Figure 5.5.

After controlling for traditional gender role orientations there was a significant main effect for the group variable. Islamic juveniles differ from both Christian groups, showing higher positive evaluation of violence. There was no difference between the allochthones and autochthones Christians, a negative main effect of religiosity on positive attitudes towards violence and there was no longer a significant interaction effect. It appears therefore that the Islamic religion is highly confounded with traditional gender role orientations and these orientations are highly correlated with positive attitudes towards violence. This corresponds to the results we found in the investigation of the role of masculinity for the explanation of violent behavior and ethnic group differences in the conception of masculinity (see Enzmann and Wetzels 2003).

We next analyzed the effect of religiosity on delinquent behavior. Because the incidence measure of self-reported delinquency is ordinal and highly skewed we applied ordinal logistic regression. The models tested are the same as those for the analyses on attitudes toward violence. In the first step we only analyzed violent delinquency. In contrast to the model for attitudes towards violence reported above,

Table 5.4 Hierarchical ordinal logistic regression of violent offences on religiosity, and migration/religion controlling for socioeconomic situation, family socialization, and sex role orientation (model 4)

	B	Exp(B)	p
Socioeconomic situation:			
unemployment/soc. welfare	.353	1.423	**
Socioeconomic-status (ISEI)	.006	1.006	*
school degree of parents *(0=grammar school)*			
without degree	.003	1.003	n.s.
secondary school (1)	.206	1.229	n.s.
secondary school (2)	.251	1.285	*
statutory education *(0=high)*			
low	.947	2.578	***
middle	.748	2.113	***
Family socialization:			
parental violence in childhood *(0=no violence)*			
mild corporal punishment	.235	1.265	**
severe corporal punishment	.321	1.379	**
occasional physical abuse	.549	1.732	**
frequent physical abuse	.820	2.270	***
Supervision	-.429	1.536^{-1}	***
parental norms towards violence	-1.248	3.483^{-1}	***
Traditional sex role orientation:			
sex role	.726	2.067	***
Religion:			
migration/religion *(0=christ / autochthones)*			
Islamic/allochthones	.865	2.375	**
Christian/allochthones	.145	1.156	n.s.
Religiosity	-.103	1.108^{-1}	**
Interaction effects:			
religiosity*Islamic/allochth.	-.081	1.084^{-1}	n.s.
religiosity*Christian/allochth.	.054	1.055	n.s.

Notes: Pseudo-R^2=.152; odds-ratios<1 are shown as 1/Exp(B)

on the behavioral level religiosity had a negative crime-reducing effect for all three groups. This indicates that for Islamic respondents there seems to be a difference between attitudes and behavior, which is not found for the other groups. In the next steps we included the same variables as in the former regressions on attitudes towards violence. The results of the final model 4 are presented in Table 5.4.

The results show that religiosity had a slight reducing effect on violent delinquency. Again, there was a significant effect of traditional gender role orientation. But with respect to behavior the results differ from our results on attitudes. Most importantly, there were no significant interaction effects.

Table 5.5 Odds-ratios of the effects of religiosity on indicators of deviance, controlling for socioeconomic situation

	Islam/ allochthone		Christianity/ allochthone		Christianity/ autochthone		total		interaction effect	
	Exp(B)	p	Exp(B)	p	Exp(B)	p	Exp(B)	p	rel*isl/allo	rel*ch/allo
Violent offenses	1.113^{-1}	n.s.	1.120^{-1}	n.s.	1.154^{-1}	***	1.158^{-1}	***	n.s.	n.s.
Severe property offenses	1.188^{-1}	n.s.	1.194^{-1}	*	1.105^{-1}	*	1.112^{-1}	*	n.s.	n.s.
Driving without license	1.024	n.s.	1.059^{-1}	n.s.	1.130^{-1}	***	1.132^{-1}	***	n.s.	n.s.
Illegal drug use	1.392^{-1}	***	1.297^{-1}	***	1.276^{-1}	***	1.278^{-1}	***	n.s.	n.s.
Alcohol use	1.685^{-1}	***	1.271^{-1}	***	1.147^{-1}	***	1.140^{-1}	***	1.484^{-1} ***	1.117^{-1} *

Notes: *odds-ratios<1 are shown as 1/Exp(B)*

To examine the question whether the effect of religiosity was the same for different kinds of offences, we applied this ordinal logistic regression approach separately for the three groups and the five types of offences with separate tests for interaction effects.

Table 5.5 shows odds-ratios and their levels of significance for the effect of religiosity on each kind of deviant behavior studied. We found that there were differences across both the three groups and the various offences. The highest negative effects (odds-ratios less than 1) were found for alcohol abuse and illegal drug use for all the three groups. The Islamic group in particular demonstrated no positive significant effects. The only significant results were the negative effects of religiosity on alcohol abuse and illegal drug use. Sometimes non-significant results are the most important ones. There was no increase in delinquency associated with higher religiosity among young Muslims.

Significant negative effects were found for the Christian autochthones for all kinds of deviance. However, these effects were rather small. The fact that they reached the level of significance was mainly due to the sample size. Interestingly we also found significant interactions effects for alcohol abuse. The highest effect of religiosity is found in the Islamic group. This was to be expected because alcohol use is particularly forbidden for Muslims. Therefore this result is not surprising but instead demonstrates the validity of the model. If we had found such an interaction effect the plausibility of our results might have been suspect.

Conclusion

This study found that the effect of religiosity on attitudes towards violence is negative for Christians but positive for young Muslims. These different effects could be explained by differences in parental education, parental supervision, and gender role orientation. While religiosity for Christians has a buffering effect on positive attitudes towards violence, this is not the case for the Islamic group. This greater acceptance of violence seems to be the result of specific gender role socialization that is more prevalent among young Muslims. Interestingly this higher proneness to violence among young Muslims is not acted out, as our results on the behavioral level show. This greater difference between attitudes and behavior among young Muslims might be due to an increased social control. We assume that highly religious young Muslims live in ethnically segregated communities with higher degrees of informal social control that preclude their uncontrolled acting out of these attitudes. This is only a tentative conclusion however. Further research is needed on this issue.

In sum, we reach the following conclusions:

1. While for young Muslims there is a positive association between religiosity and positive evaluations of violence (i.e. positive attitudes towards violence), for young Christians religiosity has a buffering effect which reduces the positive approval of violence. The difference between these two groups could be due to different gender role orientations, with young Muslims showing a more traditional concept of gender roles.
2. There is a low negative effect of religiosity on delinquent behavior in general. In contrast to the results reported for the attitudes, for young Muslims there is no increase in delinquency in cases of higher religiosity.
3. On the behavioral level a significant difference of the effects of religiosity on deviant behavior between Christians and Muslims juveniles was found for alcohol use only.
4. In sum, the common stereotype that "the more religious Muslims – the more violent and delinquent they are" is not supported empirically with respect to juvenile delinquency.
5. Finally, while the hypothesis of a positive association between juvenile delinquency and Muslim religiosity cannot be supported by our results there remain important open questions. This is particularly true with respect to family violence.

Our results indicate an increased level of family violence in the Muslim group which is significantly related to the religiosity in this group. This should be focused carefully in future cross-cultural criminological research.

References

Agnew, R. (1992), "Foundation for a General Strain Theory of Crime and Delinquency", *Criminology*, 30: 47–84.

Agnew, R. (2001), "An Overview of General Strain Theory", in Paternoster, R. and R. Bachman (eds), *Explaining Criminals and Crime*, Los Angeles: Roxburry Publishing.

Baier, C.J. and Wright, B.R.E. (2001), "'If You Love Me, Keep My Commandments': A Metaanalysis of the Effect of Religion on Crime", *Journal of Research in Crime and Delinquency*, 38(1): 3–21.

Benda, B.B. (1995), "The Effect of Religion on Adolescent Delinquency Revisited", *Journal of Research in Crime and Delinquency*, 32(4): 446–66.

Benda, B.B. (2002), "Religion and Violent Offenders in Boot Camp: A Structural Equation Model", *Journal of Research in Crime and Delinquency*, 39(1): 91–121.

Burkett, S.R. (2000), "Religion and Crime", in Bryant, C.D. et al (eds), *Encyclopedia of Criminology and Deviant Behavior*, Philadelphia: Roudledge, vol. 2.

Burkett, S.R. and B.O. Warren (1987), "Religiosity, Peer Associations, and Marijuana Use: A Panel Study of Underlying Causal Structures", *Criminology*, 25: 109–31.

Cochran, J.H. (2000), "Religion and Deviance", in Bryant, C.D. et al (eds), *Encyclopedia of Criminology and Deviant Behavior*, Philadelphia: Routledge, vol. 1.

Enzmann, D. and Wetzels, P. (2003), "Ethnic Differences in Juvenile Delinquency: The Role of Violence Legitimizing Norms of Masculinity", in Dünkel, F. and K. Drenkhahn (eds), *Youth Violence: New Patterns and Local Responses – Experiences in East and West*, Mönchengladbach: Forum.

Ganzeboom, H.B.G., P.M. De Graaf, D.J. Treimann and J. de Leeuw (1992), "A Standard International Socio-Economic Index of Occupational Status", *Social Science Research*, 21: 1–56.

Heitmeyer, W., J. Müller and H. Schröder (1997), *Verlockender Fundamentalismus*, Frankfurt am Main: Suhrkamp.

Hirschi, T. (1969), *Causes of Delinquency*, Berkley: University of California Press.

Hirschi, T. and R. Stark (1969), "Hellfire and Delinquency", *Social Problems*, 17: 202–13.

Huntington, S.P. (1996), *The Clash of Civilizations and the Remaking of World Order*, New York: Simon & Schuster.

Jang, S.J. and B.R. Johnson (2003), "Strain, Negative Emotions, and Deviant Coping Among African Americans: A Test of General Strain Theory", *Journal of Quantitative Criminology*, 19(1): 79–105.

Johnson, B.R., S.J. Jang, D.B. Larson and S.D. Li (2001), "Does Adolescent Religious Commitment Matter? A Reexamination of the Effects of Religiosity on Delinquency", *Journal of Research in Crime and Delinquency*, 38(1): 22–44.

Lösel, F. (1975), *Handlungskontrolle und Jugenddelinquenz*, Stuttgart: Enke.

Morrison, W. (1995), *Theoretical Criminology. From Modernity to Post-modernism*, London: Cavendish.

Sampson, R.J., S. Raudenbush and F. Earls (1997), "Neighborhoods and Violent Crime: A Multilevel Study of Collective Efficacy", *Science*, 277: 918–24.

Stern, J. (2003), *Terror in the Name of God*, New York: Harper Collins.

Straus, M.A. (1979), "Measuring Intrafamily Conflict and Violence: The Conflict Tactic (CT) Scales", *Journal of Marriage and the Family*, 41: 75–88.

Wetzels, P. (2000), "Ausländerfeindlichkeit und Ethnozentrismus bei Schülerinnen und Schülern: Ergebnisse repräsentativer Befragungen in Rostock und Delmenhorst", *Politisches Lernen*, 18(3–4): 50–73.

Wetzels, P. and K. Brettfeld (2003), "Auge um Auge, Zahn um Zahn?", in *Migration, Religion und Gewalt junger Menschen*, Münster: Lit.

Appendix A: Attitudes towards Violence

Item
To have fun a bit violence is simply part of the game.
You have to resort to violence because that is the only way to attract attention.
If someone attacks me I will strike back.
The strong have to prevail or else there will be no progress.
I am ready to exert violence if I feel the need to impress.
Without violence everything would be much more boring.
I quickly become violent if someone provokes me.
Juveniles get things clear by violent means, adults are merely havering.
I think it is quite normal for males to compete with each other in violent fights.
An eye for an eye, a tooth for a tooth, that's life.
Sometimes, when I am in the mood, I take part in roughing up others.

Appendix B: Traditional Sex Role Orientation

Item
It's enough for a woman to be housewife and mother.
A good vocational education is not as important for a woman as for a man.
A woman should be allowed go to a bar without her husband.
A man has to be strong and has to protect his family against mischief.
Men and women should share the household chores 50-50.
Only the woman should attend to the children.
A woman has to be decent and economical.
Primarily the man is responsible for the family subsistence.
The household is a matter for the wife.
A man should not cry.
A woman has to obey the man.

Chapter 6

Immigration and Juvenile Delinquency in Germany

Kerstin Reich
University of Tübingen

Introduction

In recent years Germany has become increasingly concerned about the increase of juvenile delinquency. In particular, there has been considerable discussion about violent crime levels which have risen since the beginning of the 1990s. In this context, one question – or rather a hypothesis – is repeatedly discussed. That is, whether or not young immigrants are responsible for the increase in delinquency. These assumptions seem to develop primarily in times of increased immigration and scarce economic resources. This situation leads to biased perceptions and attitudes of the host society towards foreigners.

The objective of this contribution is to put together the most comprehensive picture possible of the juvenile crime situation in Germany within the context of overall migratory processes. First, an overview of the main immigrant groups in Germany is presented. Second, the chapter will provide a view into the problems we face with the assessment and appraisal of the topic of immigration and crime. Then some developments of the crime situation together with some common explanations for these phenomena will be presented. Finally, some ideas about how to deal with the problem of immigration and juvenile delinquency will be discussed, both in terms of measures for integration and for crime prevention.

Immigrant Groups in Germany

In Germany we have a very specific situation since we have to differentiate between immigrants with a German passport and immigrants without a German passport. The reason is a rather unique phenomenon with immigration concerning the population of ethnic Germans who are born and socialized abroad but are owners of a German passport. Beside the German passport there are some more peculiarities within these immigrants, called "*Aussiedler*", which differentiate them from other immigrants.

Aussiedler constitute an immigrant group that has to be viewed from an historical perspective. Their ancestors emigrated more than 100 years ago from Germany

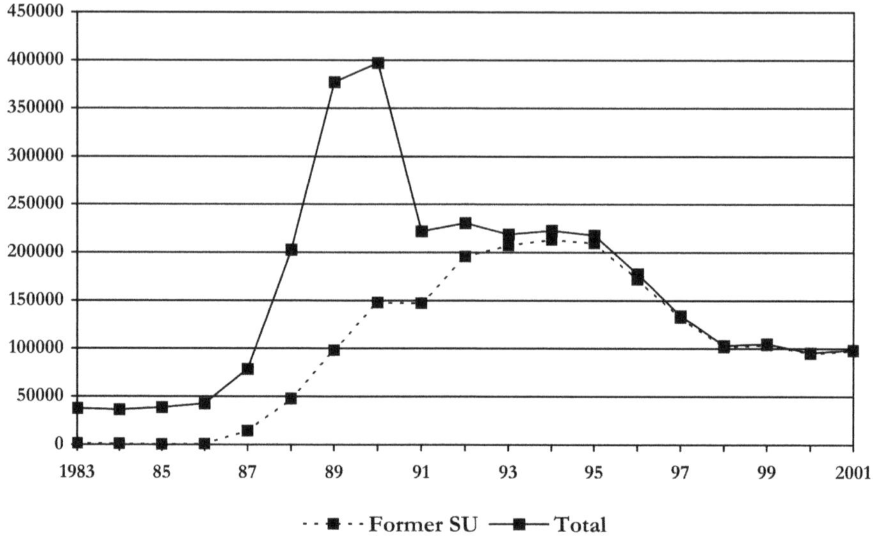

Figure 6.1 Immigration numbers of ethnic Germans (Aussiedler), 1983–2001

Source: Bundesverwaltungsamt, Referat VIII A 5.

to Russia. Aussiedler who migrate to Germany today have never lived within the borders of Germany. Despite this fact Aussiedler are, according to the principle of descent, the *ius sanguinis* which is valid in Germany and according to the Basic Law Art 116 considered as Germans. Therefore they are naturalized immediately upon their arrival in Germany and consequently they receive a German passport.

Additionally they enjoy – in contrast to other immigrant groups – extensive welfare support to smooth the hardship of migration and to provide support for integration at the same time. Although ethnic Germans from Eastern Europe certainly form a minority group distinct from other foreign populations, they face in many respects the same problems. For example, they largely lack equal societal participation compared to resident Germans. Aussiedler have been coming to Germany, increasingly since the late 1980s and the early 1990s, when the breakdown of the former Soviet Union resulted in the lessening of emigration restrictions.

Since 1950 about four million Aussiedler arrived in Germany, of which about three million came during the last 15 years (see Figure 6.1). The peak of the arrival of Aussiedler took place in 1991 with nearly 400,000 immigrants, most of them from the former Soviet Union. Since that time the state tried to reduce and to control the influx of Aussiedler with various regulations. Nevertheless, Aussiedler represent the largest group of immigrants in Germany accounting for about 5 percent of the overall resident population. But there are some other important immigrant groups which must be considered if one wants to provide an impression of the immigration situation in Germany. Immigrants without a German passport account for roughly

Table 6.1 Foreign residents in Germany

Nationality		Number	Percent
Europe		5,930,311	80.8
	Countries of the European Union	1,858,672	25.3
	France	107,191	1.5
	Greece	364,354	5.0
	Great Britain and Northern Ireland	113,487	1.5
	Italy	615,900	8.4
	Netherlands	110,519	1.5
	Austria	186,090	2.5
	Portugal	132,623	1.8
	Spain	129,893	1.8
	Non EU-Countries		
	Bosnia	167,690	2.3
	Yugoslavia	737,204	10.0
	Croatia	213,965	2.9
	Poland	291,673	4.0
	Turkey	2,053,564	28.0
Africa		300,611	4.1
	Morocco	81,450	1.1
America		205,373	2.8
Asia		823,092	11.2
	Iran	116,446	1.6
Australia		10,033	0.1
Total		**7,343,591**	

Source: *Central Registration of Foreigners.*

9 percent of the resident population in Germany. A breakdown of the specific proportion of immigrants is provided in Table 6.1.

Immigrants in Germany – like in most other countries – do not form a homogeneous group. About 7.3 million foreigners live in Germany, 1.2 million of them are refugees, including acknowledged asylum seekers and their relatives. The number of refugees corresponds to about 17 percent of all foreigners in Germany.

One out of four foreigners is a citizen of the European Union. Italians and Greeks comprise the largest portion. Their settlement is mainly the consequence of the recruitment of immigrant workers of the 1960s and 1970s. A substantial portion of the foreigner population comes from Turkey. Usually they are also guest-workers with their families. Another 10 percent of the non-Germans originate from the former Yugoslavia, 5 percent are from Croatia, Bosnia and Herzegovina. Every second foreigner has already lived in Germany for more than 10 years which indicates a non-transient immigrant population overall.

Over the last 20 years the ethnic composition of immigrants, the motivation for migration, and the perception of migration has changed significantly. First, the migrant workforce no longer originates predominantly from south-western European countries like Italy or Spain, but from south eastern European countries, especially Turkey and the former Yugoslavia. They currently account for almost half of the resident foreign population (Albrecht 1997). More recently, after the breakdown of socialist regimes, migration has begun to include Eastern European countries resulting in a wide range of ethnic and cultural diversity among the immigrant population.

A crucial factor for immigration and integration purposes, however, is not only the composition of the immigrant population but also the acceptance or rejection of the immigrants by the German society. In times where financial resources were low and unemployment rates were high, the public and political perception of immigrants and Aussiedler changed. No longer was immigration viewed as a solution to labor shortage or a humane task against the inhumane socialist political system. Rather the view became that of seeing immigration and immigrants as a social problem. In this context Tonry (1997: 10) convincingly argues, “In an era of rapid social and economic change, many people feel threatened and insecure, and minority or immigrant groups are often blamed for much of what seems wrong”.

Immigrants and Crime

In the Federal Republic of Germany, research on foreign and ethnic minorities has been stimulated mainly because of the so-called guest-workers who came to Germany in the early 1960s. Among the most important force providing information for an appraisal of the crime situation and shaping of the public perception of crime are police crime statistics (PCS). There are, however, some problems connected with this data pool especially when one wants to examine crime rates among immigrants. A first, more general, limitation of the PCS is that this annual report provides information about the number of offences which were reported to the police and the number of crime suspects recorded by the police. Thus, the PCS is not a mirror for actual crime but reflects the work and activities of the police.

Other problems emerge when one wants to analyze levels of crime of certain immigrant groups and wants to compare them with crime levels of Germans. For example, we are not able to obtain data about the particular group of Aussiedler. Although these ethnic Germans from Eastern Europe certainly form a minority group distinct from other foreign populations they have not attracted attention in terms of crime policy or criminological research. The reason for this is the fact that Aussiedler are Germans and immigrants at the same time. They do not become visible in police or criminal justice statistical figures because they are not registered separately but fall under the category of Germans. Other immigrants are separately registered as non-Germans in the PCS but the problem with respect to this “summarized” group is

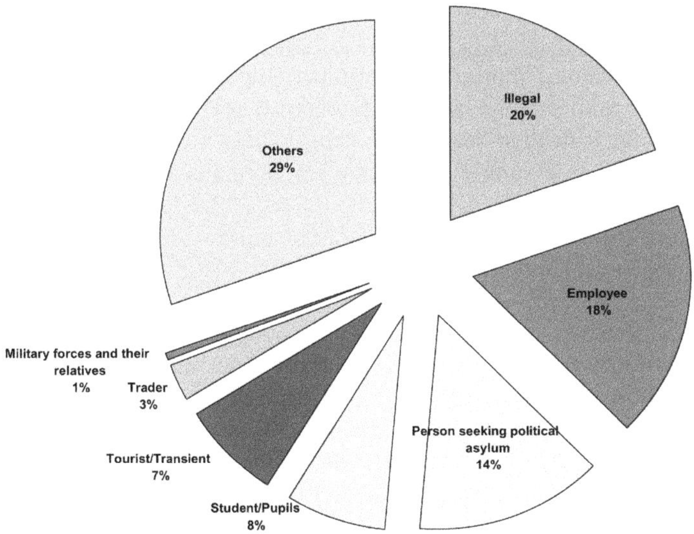

Figure 6.2 Non-German suspects, 2002
Source: Police Crime Statistics 2002.

that there are several factors which result in the overestimation of offending among non-German (immigrants). There are four primary reasons for this:

1. offenders are registered who are not represented in the resident population statistics;
2. registration of specific status offences (i.e., offences against the Foreigners Act);
3. insensitivity of social characteristics;
4. selective ethical reporting behavior.

In the following part each of these factors is briefly described. These should be considered when interpreting statistical crime figures from the PCS, especially for foreigners.

Registration of Offenders who are not Represented in the Resident Population Statistics

In the figures for crime suspects, tourists/illegal immigrants and "others" are included. What can be seen in Figure 6.2 is the large portion which those sub-groups of non-Germans have within the whole group of non-German suspects. But all these subgroups of non-Germans are not part of the resident population, because they did not register or do not need to register. They are, however, registered in the crime statistic. This creates methodological problems because it is impossible to calculate the number of crime suspects per 100,000 of the foreign population.

Registration of Specific Offences

The rate of crime among immigrants is also partially inflated due to the registration of non-Germans who commit and are prosecuted primarily for specific offences which have to do with their residential status. These are mostly offences against the Foreigners Act. It is simply impossible for Germans to be charged with these regulations.

Insensitivity of Social Characteristics

The PCS also does not provide data which account for different social situations. Immigrants without a German passport exhibit some differences in comparison to the German (resident) population. This is applicable too for immigrants with a German passport. In this respect Aussiedler have the same problems and experiences as other immigrants from distant countries and cultures.

Immigrants, on average are younger, with a higher proportion of men. This group of "male youngsters" is the most active with regard to criminal activity. They are less qualified for employment than Germans and most lack any form of professional training. A high percentage of them are unemployed and they tend to live more in urban rather than in rural areas. Accordingly, a high proportion of immigrants belong to a low social class (Bundesministerium des Innern 2001). Recently, the PISA Study (2002) demonstrated that social background is decisive for the possibilities of education. Children emerging from weak social positions have less of a chance to obtain higher education.

In short, the great majority of ethnic minorities living in Germany show various disadvantages in social and demographic characteristics. They differ sharply in terms of their composition with regard to age, sex and social standing. Because of these factors, a higher level of crime among the immigrant population is to be expected.

Selective Ethical Reporting Behavior

Self-report studies have found that the level of delinquency among immigrants is not higher than Germans who live in comparable social situations. The likelihood that offences are reported to the police, however, is much higher for immigrant people. Pfeiffer et al (1998) found that every second immigrant student who reported an offence was officially registered, compared to only every sixth German. The same variables which increase the likelihood of being involved in delinquency also heighten the likelihood of being reported to the police.

There are two major findings in this respect. First, on one hand ethnic minority offenders run a somewhat higher risk of being reported in cases of shoplifting or violent acts. This often has to do with their custom of spending their leisure time in public places such as playgrounds or street-corners. There they can be watched by the suspicious public. Second, minority victims of crime seem to be more reluctant to report an offence when the offender is of the same nationality or ethnic background than when the background of the offender is different from their own. Police crime data, then, may provide a distorted picture of criminal involvement of minorities. Findings from a comparative study of foreigners' crime illustrated the effects of demographic and other variables on rates of police recorded crime (Steffen 1992). Here it was shown how clearing procedures could help to obtain an estimate of the criminal involvement of foreigners which comes closer to reality.

The Steffen (1992) study found that the general offending rate among the immigrant population in Germany is 5.6-fold the offending rate in the German population. If the variable "place of residence" is controlled (and therefore only those foreigners are included who have a permanent place of residence in Germany), then the offending rate is reduced to 2.8-fold that of the German population. If offences against immigration laws are excluded, the offending rate is further reduced to 2.5 times that of the German population. If age and gender are controlled, then crime involvement of the male immigrant population aged 18 to 24 years drops to 2.2 times the crime involvement observed in the comparable age/gender segment of the German population.

These findings are also supported by self-reports of offending and by victimization surveys. A self-report study based on a large sample of pupils and students from the Criminological Research Institute of Lower Saxony showed that in general foreign juveniles were not more involved in overall delinquency than their German counterparts. The study did find, however, a significantly larger proportion of foreign juveniles – especially young Turks – reporting violent behavior.

The Crime Situation

Having discussed these limitations, there remains no reason to minimize youth criminality. There is a clear increase in rates of crime among both German and non-German juveniles.[1] In Figure 6.3 the numbers of suspects of crime increased in all groups but nevertheless the courses followed different trends especially in the last year. The numbers of suspects of crime for the German group – either the children or the juveniles show three times as many suspects in the year 2002 than at the beginning of the 1990s. The increase for the non-German children and juveniles is more modest. Accordingly, the rise of the graphs is much steeper within the German groups than those of the non-German children and juveniles. Additionally, the numbers of the later groups went down since 1998 whereas those of the Germans remained on a high level.

The Organization of German Police suggested that the increase in the crime rate among the German population, especially among German youth during the last few

1 The graphs which are shown are based on absolute numbers. The reason for this kind of presentation was already mentioned. It is only possible to calculate the numbers of crime suspects per 100,000 of the population for Germans, but this has not been feasible for immigrants without a German passport, because there are no exact numbers for the foreign resident population available.

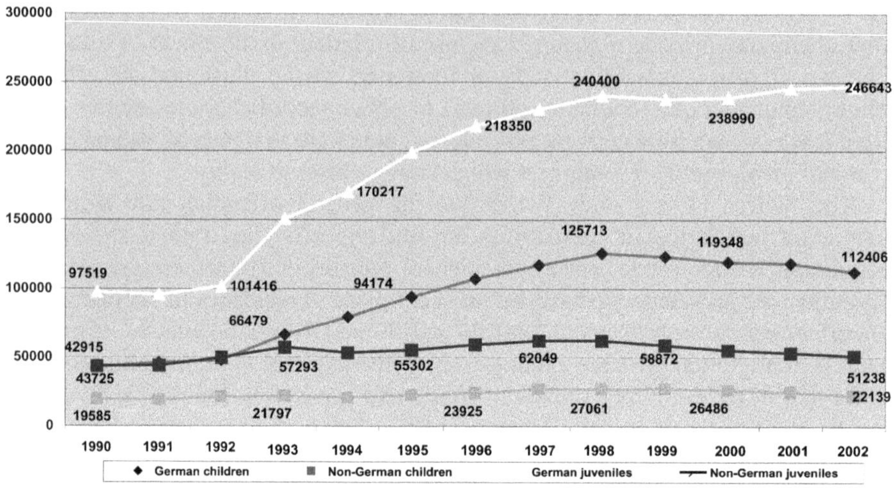

Figure 6.3 Development of suspects, 1990–2002

years, was due to heavy immigration of ethnic Germans from Eastern Europe. The number of German juvenile suspects has been on the increase since the beginning of the 1990s. Mostly male juveniles account for this, in particular those who belong to the last wave of ethnic Germans, meaning those who came to Germany from the mid-1990s onward. Additionally, prison data from the central youth correctional facility in Baden-Württemberg confirms the increasing involvement of young ethnic Germans in the criminal justice system.[2]

More important than the view of the development of the total crime picture is to examine what kind of criminal offences young immigrants commit, in order to understand what shapes the perception and the image that the host society has of the immigrant population. Recent studies have found that a lack of integration of young immigrants makes them more susceptible to acts of violence and property offences. In fact, the most common type of offence within the group of children and juveniles is shoplifting.

Analysis of offending patterns observed in groups of illegal immigrants (classified as tourists and foreigners seeking asylum) reveals that among this group petty offending is most common (see Figure 6. 4). Between 1988 and 1993 it was primarily shoplifting that drove the increase of the crime rate for this group. The increase was attributed in the first place to asylum seekers. Changes in the German constitution with regard to asylum took effect in July 1993, and had an immediate and strong effect on the total number of people applying for asylum. This in turn had immediate effects on the total number of crimes recorded for asylum seekers and consequently the crime rates for young foreign offenders.

2 The rate of prison admissions of young German offenders born abroad has increased from 2 percent in 1993 to 14 percent in 1998 (Grübl and Walter 1999).

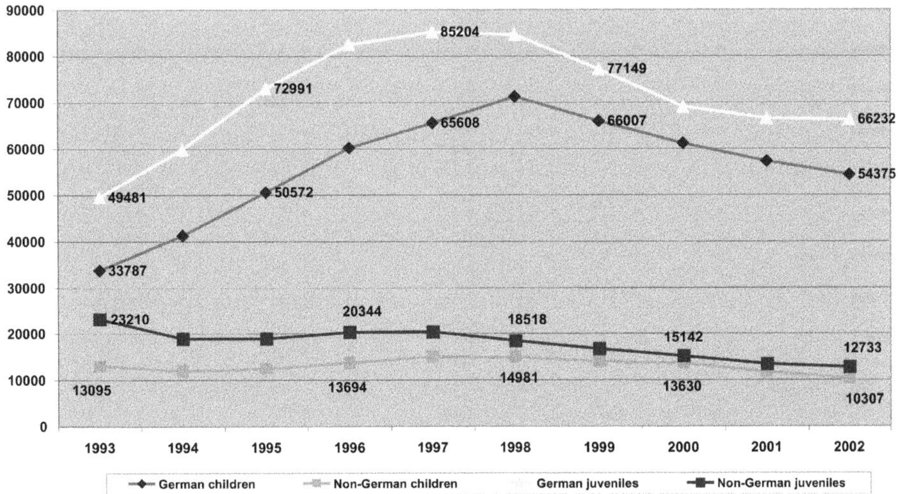

Figure 6.4 Development of shoplifting, 1993–2002

For the group of Aussiedler children and juveniles, shoplifting is also the most common delinquent activity. It is noticeable that above all shoplifting is the preferred delinquent behavior within the young group. Thus, 10–13-year-olds maintain levels of offending that are 3.4 times that of native Germans in this age group (Grundies 2000). What are the reasons for the differences in offending rates between juvenile and young adult Germans and the foreign population? The anomie theory offers a good approach for understanding this consistent finding and serves at the same time develop appropriate ways of remedy. That is, young immigrants are disproportionately affected by poverty and unemployment and are not able to obtain highly valued goods through legitimate means. When the youngsters realize that their requirements cannot be fulfilled with legitimate means it becomes more likely that they look for "innovative" solutions and use illegal ways to reach what is refused to them. It is possible that the marginal position of Turkish and other minorities with respect to income, socioeconomic status, housing conditions and education (PISA Study 2002) did not improve or in other words stayed on the same low level during the last decade.

In the public debate another type of offence that is of great interest is violent crime because the increase of violent behaviour is alarming within all three groups, the Germans, the non-Germans and the Aussiedler. One explanation for this is the traditional conceptions among young Turks and Aussiedlers regarding male power. These young immigrants are motivated to commit violent acts by their concept of honour and respect. The use of violence is a legitimate and approved means for demonstrating power and strength in order to protect the honor of the family and/or friends. In Germany they may suffer from conflicting expectations from their traditional views and the modern society.

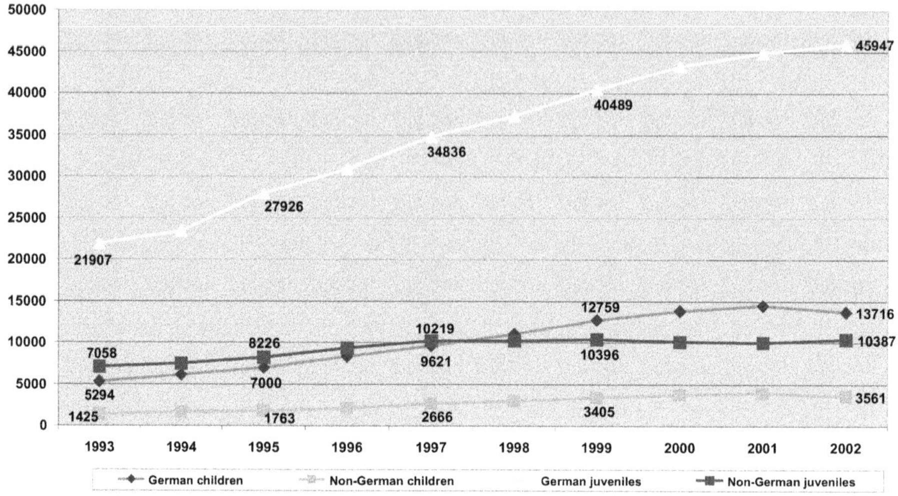

Figure 6.5 Development of bodily injury, 1993–2002

While non-Germans and Aussiedler are forced to interact with native Germans this also increases the risk of conflicts. The use of violence seems to be a mixture of a reaction to social rejection and traditional concepts of masculinity. What we found in our own study[3] that dealt with integration and desegregation processes of young male Aussiedler was, that the more young immigrants experience social rejection, the more they come back to familiar problem solving strategies, which derive from their home countries. One extract from of an interview with one young Aussiedler illustrates this concept of masculinity and honor:

> *Question: How is a fight judged in the group or gang?*
> In the past it was much worse. In my country of origin, when you did not engage yourself in fights, you were out.
>
> *Question: You were then considered to be a loser?*
> Much worse since nobody wanted to have anything to do with you. As a consequence you had to defend yourself at all times yourself, your girlfriend, gee, you had to protect everybody in order not to lose respect and honor. How is that said? All for one, one for all. That works for the group.

What is important in this context is the fact, that one solves conflicts based on macho culture and attitudes. Under this, one never goes to the police but solves problems amongst one another. Walter and Grübl (1999) reported that closely connected with the understanding of honor and masculinity is the fact that it is strongly frowned

3 This research was supported by grant WE 1445/6-1/6-2 from the German Research Foundation. Points of view or opinions expressed herein are our own and do not necessarily represent those of the German Research Foundation.

upon to regulate conflicts officially or involve official agents and their institutions in the solving process. The use of violence is thereby a legitimate means. They report the following statement by a Russian inmate of German descent which illustrates this point: "When you got to the police you are either a woman or an asshole". Consistent with this, one of our interviewees described his experience with the cultural discrepancies in problem-solving behavior:

> Here my first problem with the police was the following: I had a German friend and he was a very good friend of mine and we were together for about three to four years. He did then beat up my little brother and I told him: "Stop that and let me know what he did to you." However, he did beat him up again and I warned him a second time. At the third incident, I asked money from him. After my brother reported again beatings, I told him I would seriously beat him up in case it would happen again. He did beat my brother again and then I broke his jaw. He filed then charges against me with the police. Typically German!

If explanations are presented which argue that certain forms of criminal behavior especially violent crime are shaped by culture, then a further interesting question emerges. That is whether the values are imported or home-made, meaning that either the youngsters import their behavior from their native culture or they develop such behavioral strategies in response to migration-related problems. Some research in this area indicates that there is a close relationship between the duration of stay and the commitment of violent acts. Those who stay in the host country for longer periods of time or are born in Germany, show a higher likelihood of participating in violent crimes.

To the contrary, results of a school-based survey of self-reported crime (Pfeiffer et al 1998) found that the young Turks exhibit the highest rate of violent crime compared to their peers. In this respect, the in-patriated former foreigners had the second highest rate, closely followed by juveniles from Yugoslavia. These groups together with the group of Aussiedler maintain traditional conceptions of "maleness" which dictates their behavior patterns. As these immigrants arrived in Germany only recently (i.e., since the early 1990s), for these groups at least, it is likely that their violent behavior is both a product of a value system developed in their country of origin and an adaptation to marginalization in the host country. It could be, then, that "imported" criminality does not play such an important role but what should be kept in mind is that young males are susceptible to fall back on culturally shaped behavior patterns, especially in such situations where they have to defend their honor and masculinity.

Conclusion

What became clear in the last few years is that the increase of juvenile delinquency is not a statistical artifact but reality. Yet controversial discussion persists as to whether delinquency of young immigrants is the result of failed integration. There is a consensus, though, that juvenile crime is a warning signal indicative of problems faced by young immigrants. Many hold that crime more generally is a product of marginalization and socio-structural deficiencies in society and it is plausible that these same variables account for crime among immigrant groups. Many criminologists would agree that ethnicity and nationality are insufficient to understand crime among immigrant groups (Albrecht 2001, Steffen 1992).

The vast majority of immigrants feel strong bonds to their native culture and deny an acquisition of "German identity". These feelings correspond strongly to the observed or experienced rejection by German society. Consequently, we can observe that young immigrants build as a reaction to these migration-related problems homogeneous groups along ethnical lines which further impede the process of integration. Additionally, they rely on traditional strategies they are familiar with in order to solve conflicts, build their own identity and regain self worth. The incentive these groups offer is what the young immigrants are deprived of and miss most in their new environment – a sense of belonging, acknowledgment, respect and status.

The urgent question to which we have to find an answer is: how should we react to delinquency among young immigrants? The host country is obliged to enable young immigrants the opportunity to participate in every dimension of life. We do not have to leave the young people with their problems alone or with their own ethnic group. Integration is a task of the host society which has to take place in close cooperation with the young immigrants and their families. We have to enable young immigrants to lead a life without committing crimes. This may happen in different ways – through education, mutual appreciation and participation. An important contribution or even starting point for dealing with the challenges of immigration and integration would be to look not at the deficiencies, but at the abilities of young immigrants.

References

Albrecht, Hans-Jörg (1997), "Minorities, Crime, and Criminal Justice in the Federal Republic of Germany", in Haen Marshall, Ineke (ed.), *Minorities, Migrants, and Crime*, Thousand Oaks: Sage.

Albrecht, Hans-Jörg (2001), "Immigration, Kriminalität und Innere Sicherheit", in Albrecht, Günter, Otto Backes and Wolfgang Kühnel (eds), *Gewaltkriminalität zwischen Mythos und Realität*, Frankfurt am Main: Suhrkamp.

Bundesministerium des Innern (2001), *Erster Periodischer Sicherheitsbericht. Langfassung*, Berlin: Selbstverlag.

Geißler, Rainer (1995), "Das gefährliche Gerücht von der hohen Ausländerkriminalität" *Aus Politik und Zeitgeschichte*, 35: 30–9.

Grübl, Günter and Joachim Walter (1999), "'Russlanddeutsche' im Strafvollzug", *Bewährungshilfe*, 46(4): 360–74.

Grundies, Volker (2000), "Kriminalitätsbelastung junger Aussiedler, Ein Längsschnittvergleich mit in Deutschland geborenen jungen Menschen anhand polizeilicher Registrierungen", *Monatsschrift für Kriminologie und Strafrechtsreform*, 83(5): 290–305.

Pfeiffer, Christian, Ingo Delzer, Dirk Enzmann and Peter Wetzels (1998), *Ausgrenzung, Gewalt und Kriminalität im Leben junger Menschen, Kinder und Jugendliche als Opfer und Täter*, Hanover: DVJJ.

PISA-Studie (2002), at http://www.pisa.oecd.org.

Steffen, Wiebke (1992), *Ausländerkriminalität in Bayern. Eine Analyse der von 1983 bis 1990 polizeilich registrierten Kriminalität deutscher und ausländischer Tatverdächtiger*, Munich: Bayerisches Landeskriminalamt.

Steffen, Wiebke and E. Elsner (2000), "Kriminalität junger Ausländer", at http://www.polizei.bayern.de.

Tonry, Michael (1997), "Ethnicity, Crime, and Immigration", *Overcrowded Times*, 8(2): 1, 9–10.

Walter, Joachim and Walter Grübl (1999), "Junge Aussiedler im Jugendstrafvollzug", in Bade, Klaus J. and Jochen Oltmer (eds), *Aussiedler: deutsche Einwanderer aus Osteuropa*, Osnabrück: Rasch.

Chapter 7

The Prison Situation of Foreigners in Japan

Koichi Miyazawa
Keio University

Philipp Osten
Keio University

Introduction

Since the early 1990s, the number of foreigners in Japanese prisons increased rapidly. At that time, foreign prisoners were more or less concentrated in Fuchu. In one sector of the prison, which was built in a radial shape according to the Pennsylvanian model, signs and labels saying "Peking Times" or "No Pork" had been attached to the doors of some cells, indicating the Chinese, Indonesian, Pakistani or Iraqi nationality of the inmates. This was the first visible evidence, not only of an increase in foreigners, but also of a diversification of the nationalities of foreign prisoners in Japanese prisons.

Administration Issues

Currently, foreigners are detained in nearly all Japanese prisons. The knowledge of foreign languages, however, is not widespread in Japan. In particular, prison officers and wardens can barely communicate in English, often knowing no more than a few words. When it comes to Asian languages, the language barrier is even greater. Therefore, one could assume that the increase of foreigners caused a lot of administrative problems for the Japanese correctional institutions. However, this is only partially correct. The correctional institutions benefit greatly from the profits obtained through prison labor performed by foreign prisoners. Their workforce has by now become essential for most Japanese prisons. Even more than European or American prisons, penal institutions in Japan are increasingly encountering difficulties in sustaining a steady income source through prison labor. The Japanese Penal Code differentiates between two kinds of sanctions for criminal acts which can be imposed as forfeiture of freedom: imprisonment with and without hard labor. 97 percent of all prisoners are sentenced to imprisonment with hard labor. The Japanese

Ministry of Finance requires the prisons to ensure a yearly income of 9.1 billion Yen (70 million Euro) through prison work. Due to the fact that the average age of prisoners of Japanese nationality is over 35 years, however, their work ability with regard to "hard labor" is rather low. In contrast, the average age of foreigners in Japanese prisons is under 30 years, and in fact most foreign prisoners are in their late 20s. Japanese prisons rely to a large extent on the labor force of these young foreigners. Parenthetically, the top three placements in athletic competitions which take place in prisons in autumn and spring have in recent years always been won by foreign prisoners.

Asian Immigrants

The overwhelming majority of convicted foreign prisoners in Japan are Asian immigrant workers or professional criminals from neighboring Asian countries who entered the country with criminal intentions. Even though these foreigners face a variety of difficulties in adapting to the environment of Japanese prisons, such as the language problem, cultural differences and harsh treatment, most of them are for the most part content with their prison life. Their overall contentment is due to the fact that – compared to penal institutions in their respective countries of origin – Japanese prisons are clean and hygienic, the meals are nutritious, and, above all, gratifications (not wages) are paid for their prison labor amounting to an average of 5,000 Yen (40 Euro) per month. This average monthly gratification is tantamount to two-thirds of the monthly income of an average worker in China, and to half a year's income of a worker in Bangladesh.

Foreign convicted prisoners who require a fundamentally different treatment compared to Japanese convicts due to their specific cultural background are registered as "F-Category Prisoners". Even though their total number is rather low (1,304 prisoners in the year 2002, making up one-third of the total number of foreign convicts), their integration presents a great problem to many Japanese prison administrations.

Juveniles

Juvenile delinquents in Japan are dealt with under a separate legal code. A criminal offense committed by a person less than 20 years of age is, as a rule, dealt with according to the Juvenile Code, not the Penal Code. Forfeiture of freedom as defined by the Juvenile Code is executed in Juvenile Training Schools (comparable to juvenile prisons in European countries). Therefore, juvenile convicts under the age of 20 are rarely found in regular Japanese prisons: out of approximately 20,000 to 30,000 newly admitted prisoners each year, less than 50 are juvenile offenders. An average of 5,000 to 6,000 new juvenile delinquents enter the Juvenile Training Schools around the country every year, with an average custody period of 1.5 years.

Table 7.1 Convicted prisoners (non-resident foreigners) by gender (on December 31 of each year)

Year	Total	Male	Female
1997	1132	1065	67
1998	1391	1311	80
1999	1925	1718	207
2000	2178	2039	139
2001	2476	2316	160
2002	2854	2648	206

Source: White Paper on Crime (Research and Training Institute of the Ministry of Justice), Tokyo, 1997–2002; Statistical Bulletin of Corrections (Ministry of Justice), No. 99–104, Tokyo, 1997–2002; Annual Report of Statistics on Correction (Ministry of Justice), Tokyo, 1997–2002.

Legal Status of Prisoners

As mentioned, the total number of foreign prisoners in Japan has increased rapidly in the past ten years. Compared to 1987 (with only 1914 foreign inmates), an increase of more than 250 percent has taken place in the past 15 years. This increase is mainly due to crimes committed by *non-resident* foreigners, as opposed to long-term or permanently resident foreigners. As is apparent from the statistical data presented in Tables 7.1, 7.2 and 7.3, exact and detailed figures for the correctional situation of foreigners in Japan are only available from the year 1997 onwards.

At the end of 2002, the total number of foreign *inmates* in Japanese penal institutions was 5,092, or 8.9 percent of the total number of inmates. Most of the

Table 7.2 Numbers of convicted non-resident foreigner male prisoners by nationality (on December 31 of each year)

Nationality	1997	1998	1999	2000	2001	2002
Korea (N/S)	82	75	208	203	153	223
China	289	408	614	845	1054	1125
Iran	243	297	301	280	322	369
Philippines	62	69	75	75	69	64
Vietnam	27	65	74	65	77	84
Brazil	23	34	81	139	189	250
Peru	52	41	47	53	55	70
Others	287	322	318	379	397	463
Total	1065	1311	1718	2039	2316	2648

Source: White Paper on Crime (Research and Training Institute of the Ministry of Justice), Tokyo, 1997–2002; Statistical Bulletin of Corrections (Ministry of Justice), No. 99–104, Tokyo, 1997–2002; Annual Report of Statistics on Correction (Ministry of Justice), Tokyo, 1997–2002.

Table 7.3 Newly admitted convicted prisoners who were non-resident foreigners by nationality (per annum)

Nationality	1997	1998	1999	2000	2001	2002
Korea (N/S)	31	43	77	92	81	92
China	178	213	317	521	616	548
Iran	102	116	106	101	142	161
Philippines	26	28	26	29	41	35
Vietnam	23	18	37	31	54	66
Brazil	13	13	41	81	105	136
Peru	24	12	17	22	20	42
Others	101	105	141	193	217	230
Total	498	548	762	1070	1276	1310

Source: White Paper on Crime (Research and Training Institute of the Ministry of Justice), Tokyo, 1997–2002; Statistical Bulletin of Corrections (Ministry of Justice), No. 99–104, Tokyo, 1997–2002; Annual Report of Statistics on Correction (Ministry of Justice), Tokyo, 1997–2002.

foreign inmates, namely 3,892, are *convicted prisoners*, representing 6.8 percent of the total number of 56,959 convicted prisoners in Japan. The remainder consists of foreign inmates are awaiting trial, i.e., defendants or suspects. More than two-thirds of the convicted foreign prisoners are non-resident foreigners who entered Japan illegally or on short-term visas/residence permits (n = 2,854). The small remainder consists of convicted foreign prisoners who are long-term or permanent residents of Japan.

In terms of international comparisons, the percentage of foreigners among convicted prisoners in Japanese prisons (6.8 percent) is still quite low. According to the statistical records of the European Council for the year 1998, the percentage of foreigners among convicted prisoners in Switzerland was 61.3 percent, in Luxemburg 54 percent, in Belgium 36.3 percent, in Germany 34.1 percent, in Austria 28.2 percent and in France 26.8 percent. In the USA, convicted prisoners of African and Hispanic origin (not nationality) make up approximately 80 percent of all prison inmates.

Offense Types

Of all the registered criminal offenses committed by foreigners in Japan, offenses against the Penal Code make up less than half of all crimes, and half of these offenses against the Penal Code consist of theft-related crimes. The greater part of all crimes committed by foreigners consist of offences against other supplementary penal provisions regulated outside the Penal Code, for the most part being offenses against the Immigration Act (e.g., illegal entry/stay/residence), which account for 60–80 percent of the offenses against supplementary penal law; the remainder mainly consists of offenses against the Narcotics Act. However, as offenses against the Penal Code are generally prosecuted and punished more severely, the majority (approximately two-thirds) of foreign prisoners are convicted and sentenced to prison because of such offenses.

Chinese Nationals

The general increase in the number of non-resident foreigners among convicted prisoners in Japan and their predominance among foreign convicts is mainly caused by Chinese nationals who enter the country on short-term visas and/or stay in the country illegally after the expiration of their residence permit. They far outnumber Korean (North and South) prisoners. This is not only due to the fact that China by far has a greater population than Korea. In recent years, the South Korean economy has been recovering visibly, leading to a rise in gross national income. Therefore, the attractiveness and incentive of working in Japan has decreased for Koreans. On the other hand, with regards to China, even though the national economic situation has improved, the gap in average incomes compared to Japan is still extraordinarily large. It is still extremely profitable therefore for many Chinese to migrate to Japan for work opportunities. Further, in the past few years organized criminal groups like the infamous "Snake Head" gang from China have increased their activities in Japan, especially in the fields of drug trafficking, trafficking of human beings, larceny and burglary. This has also led to an increase in the number of Chinese inmates in Japanese penal institutions.

Brazilian Nationals

Another prominent group of inmates in the Japanese prison system are Brazilian nationals. The increase in the number of Brazilians in Japanese prisons may partially result from the disastrous immigration policy of the Japanese government in the 1980s and 1990s. At that time, the booming Japanese economy was facing a lack of manpower. Thus, Brazilians of Japanese origin (whose families had emigrated from Japan to Brazil at the beginning of the 20th century driven by poverty) were invited to come to Japan as a source of cheap labor. However, the Japanese government failed to provide measures for integrating these Brazilians into Japanese society, considering them as being more or less "Japanese". This proved to be a false assumption. Above all, the integration of their children (i.e., Brazilians of Japanese origin in the second or third generation) who were raised as Brazilians and could not speak Japanese, failed. They did not acculturate or adapt to Japanese society. Young Brazilians now make up the biggest group among foreigners in Japanese penal institutions for juveniles (Juvenile Training Schools).

Rehabilitation

Finally, the rehabilitation of foreign prisoners in Japan also presents a problem. In general, the correction of perpetrators is considered as one of the basic aims of their imprisonment. While living and working according to the prison rules, prisoners are supposed to be prepared for a later life in society after their release. This, at the same time, is conceived as a means to prevent recidivism. However, this kind of rehabilitation is only feasible in the case of foreign prisoners who are (legal) long-term or permanent residents of Japan. In contrast, convicted prisoners who are non-resident foreigners – which are by far the majority – are usually taken into custody prior to their deportation by the Immigration Office as soon as they are released from prison. The custody facilities run by the Immigration Office are located close to the international airports in Tokyo and Osaka to enable a quick and smooth deportation to the respective countries of origin. With regard to these foreigners, correction and rehabilitation by means of imprisonment cannot be achieved. Their punishment and imprisonment can only be regarded as a form of isolation from Japanese society and as a means of deterrence, thus serving "negative general prevention."

Chapter 8

Media, Evil and Society: Media Use and its Impacts on Crime Perception, Sentencing Attitudes and Crime Policy in Germany

Christian Pfeiffer
Minister of Justice, Lower Saxony

Michael Windzio
Criminal Research Institute of Lower Saxony

Matthias Kleimann
Criminal Research Institute of Lower Saxony

Introduction

In democratic societies, crime policy and its management by legislatures and ministries largely depend on crime trends. If, over a prolonged period, the media reports large upward trends in the number of crimes committed and if the public debate on crime focuses on spectacular, serious crimes, policy makers come under heavy pressure to increase statutory punishments and tighten the rules of procedure for criminal prosecutions.[1] The courts in turn feel duty bound to hand out tougher sentences[2] – passed in the name of the people – and their sentences are meant to reflect public opinion.[3] The question thus arises as to whether long periods of either

1 A topical example in Germany is the debate about increasing juvenile violence and the proposals adopted by a majority in the Bundesrat (upper house of parliament) to toughen the criminal law in response to crimes committed by offenders aged 14 to 21; see Bundesrats-Drucksache 15/1472 (Bundesrat bill based on motion 2138/04 brought by the states of Saxony, Bavaria, Hessen, Lower Saxony and Thuringia).

2 From a recent example in *Hannoversche Allgemeine Zeitung* May 26, 2004 p. 4.

3 See the interview with Professor Winfried Hassemer, Vice President of the German Federal Constitutional Court, in *Zeitschrift für Rechtspolitik* (2004: 93–4). He stresses that one purpose of sentencing is to "accommodate popular sentencing demands" and, further, that "the state does well to watch" such demands. He qualifies this sweeping statement later on,

decreasing or stable crime figures allow policymakers and the courts to soften punishments for specific offenses and to consider, for example, the alternatives of offender–victim compensation and offender re-socialization.

There is thus every reason to examine the relationship between the media and perceptions of crime. The German Police Crime Statistics for the last 10 years indicate that there is a strong downward trend in the number of crimes that people perceive as very threatening or generally worrying. There has also been a 45 percent reduction in both the number of break-ins at private homes and in bank robberies. In the past 10 years, the number of murders has dropped by around 41 percent, and car thefts are down by as much as 70 percent. While other offenses like fraud have increased, overall there has been a slight reduction in the number of crimes recorded since 1993.[4] This is unsurprising in light of the aging of German society. In the past decade, the 18 to 30 age group – a group which in 1993 made up almost half of all crime suspects – has shrunk from 9.4 to 7 percent of the population. Conversely, there has been a large increase (from 20.4 to 24.4 percent) in the number of people aged 60 and over – a group that accounts for less than 3 percent of all violent crime suspects. Germany's aging society is evidently good for domestic security.

Another significant preventive effect is the stabilization of migration rates since 1993. This is largely a result of the asylum compromise reached in 1992, the end of the civil war in the former Yugoslavia and the phased reduction in the repatriation of ethnic Germans from the former Soviet Union.[5] Accordingly, the number of foreigners involved in crimes investigated by the police during the period 1993 to 2003 dropped from 26.7 to 19.0 percent.[6] Another aspect to be considered is the marked rise in the likelihood of a crime being detected. The police success rate in solving most types of crime has increased significantly over the past decade, from 43.8 to 53.1 percent overall. This could also be viewed as a causal factor of the reduction in crime.[7]

Positive trends of the type indicated for the last 10 years may, of course, only influence crime policy if they shape the public debate on crime and are publicized

---

however: "Judges should not mirror public opinion, of course, but they must be mindful of it" Dreher (1967: 42 ff.) justifies such a stance and argues that: "Judges, bound up in the spirit of the times, are meant to prevent mob rule and lynch justice by channelling and taming public sentencing demands"; see also Streng (2002: 14).

4 See German Federal Criminal Police Office (Bundeskriminalamt), Police Crime Statistics 2004.

5 See Pfeiffer, Kleimann et al (2004: 24 ff.).

6 Crimes under Section 92 of the Aliens Act (AuslG) or under the Asylum Procedures Act (AsylVfG) are not included in these percentages because they are almost all committed by non-Germans.

7 Considering the amount of PR about it from the German Interior Ministry and police, it is safe to assume that many potential offenders will be aware of the increased success rate. The success rate thus becomes a considerable deterrent; see Pfeiffer 1990: 88 ff. for a discussion and summary of the numerous empirical studies on this point in the USA and European countries.

to most of the population. But this is not always the case. Whether or not crime is increasing or decreasing is not usually something most people are aware of. Unlike the rise and fall of gas prices that we all observe at local stations, crime is a social phenomenon that often occurs outside the public view. Even when crime occurs in public (e.g., graffiti spraying on the walls of buildings, drug dealing in open spaces, and mass hooliganism among drunken football fans), those who regularly observe such events can at best estimate its frequency based upon their personal experiences. The limited geographical scope of their personal experience does not allow them to make a reliable assessment of trends in the occurrence and the gravity of such offenses. This is certainly the case for serious crimes that occur less frequently. In assessing the situation, members of the general public must rely entirely on what is reported by the mass media. The question arises, therefore, as to how people perceive current trends in crime and what role the media plays in influencing their judgment.

Public Perceptions of Crime Trends

At the beginning of January 2004, the Criminological Research Institute of Lower Saxony (KFN) commissioned social scientists from TSN Infratest to conduct a representative survey of 2,000 people in Germany on their perceptions of crime trends. After respondents viewed the 1993 Police Crime Statistics, they were asked how many crimes overall they thought had been committed in 2003 and what their views were regarding specific crime trends. In addition, respondents were asked if they felt personally threatened by crime and what measures they took to protect themselves. The survey also looked at what sources people received their information on crime and how they thought crime should be punished.

The left-hand side of Table 8.1 shows trends in selected crimes and groups of identified crimes by comparing the Police Crime Statistics for 1993 and 2003. The right-hand side of the table lists the figures estimated by survey respondents. We have omitted the top and bottom 1 percent of the statistical distribution of responses to eliminate distortions due to a small number of extreme results.[8] The second column from the right lists respondents' estimates for the percentage increase in each crime. The far right column shows by how many percentage points these estimates exceed or fall short of the actual crime statistics.

Table 8.1 indicates that the respondents believe that there has been a large crime increase across the board. The only crimes for which their estimates come close to the police statistics are fraud and bodily harm. For these two they are in fact only slightly lower than the actual increase. With all other crimes, the respondents' estimates were incorrect and in some cases extremely off the mark. For example, respondents put the number of domestic burglaries at two-and-a-half times the actual

8 For an earlier article by Pfeiffer, *Dämonisierung des Bösen* ("The Demonization of Evil") published in *Frankfurter Allgemeine Zeitung* on March 5, 2004, we used the overall mean values; it was only upon checking the extremes at a later date that we discovered these resulted in exaggerated values for the means.

Table 8.1 Crime trends 1993–2003 (selected crimes) according to German police crime statistics and respondents' estimates

Crime	PCS 1993	PCS 2003	Δ%	2003 (mean estimate)	Δ% (mean estimate)	Percentage over/ underestimate
All crimes total [a]	6 750 613	6 572 135	-2.6%	7 962 506	+17%	+21%
Fraud [b]	419 834	700 013	+66.7%	622 026	+48%	-11%
Bodily harm	295 005	467 944	+58.6%	451 660	+51%	-3,5%
Domestic burglary	227 090	123 280	-45.7%	316 049	+39%	156%
Motor vehicle theft	214 836	63 240	-70.5%	316 070	+47%	400%
Handbag theft	7 916	5 986	-24.3%	9 495	+20%	59%
Murder	666	394	-40.8%	842	+27%	114%
Sexual murder	32	20	-37.5%	115	+260%	475%

[a] *Excluding road traffic offences; stimulus: 5 800 000*
[b] *Excluding fare-dodging*

figure recorded in 2003. They estimated that there had been twice as many murders, five times as many motor vehicle thefts and nearly six times as many sexual murders as were actually recorded.[9] Their 21 percent overestimate for the overall crime total was relatively moderate in comparison. This was partly due to a typing error, however, since respondents were told the 1993 figure had been 5.8 instead of 6.8 million. Based on the figure they actually had before them, respondents estimated the 10-year increase in all recorded crimes to have been 37 percent and not the 17 percent listed in Table 8.1.

In recognition of the fact that many people find it hard to give a numeric estimate, in Table 8.2 we also allowed respondents to rank their assessment of crime trends verbally on a predefined ordinal scale. We added four more offenses and one more group of offenses to the questionnaire: bank robbery, murder and robbery, sexual abuse of children, and the total for all crimes involving theft.

The right-hand side of Table 8.2 lists the percentage distributions of assumed crime frequency changes on a seven-point ordinal scale. The distributions are heavily skewed to the right; that is, a large majority of respondents assumed that there had been a large or very large increase in the crime rates. Of the added crimes, answers were mostly accurate only for drug dealing. Only 2 percent of the population correctly responded that there had been a marked decrease in bank robberies over the last decade, and only 1 percent guessed the downward trend in theft indicated by the police statistics. Overall, fewer than 10 percent of respondents identified the correct trend in the seven selected examples of decreasing crime rates.

Another representative survey of 1,500 respondents conducted by KFN with the help of TNS Infratest in early 2004, clearly demonstrates that most of the blame for the imagined crime increase is apportioned to foreigners. On average, people estimate that the percentage of foreigners among police-registered suspects has

9 See Reuband (1998: 144).

Table 8.2 Respondents' assessment of trends in selected crimes for the period 1993–2003, as percentages of all respondents

	Recorded trend			Respondents' answers							
Crime	PCS 1993	PCS 2003	Δ%	Very large increase	Large increase	Slight increase	No change	Slight decrease	Large decrease	Very large decrease	N
Total crimes	6 750 613	6 572 135	-2.6%	27%	39%	25%	7%	2%	0%	0%	1977
Fraud	419 834	700 013	+66.7%	30%	38%	21%	10%	1%	0%	0%	1980
Bodily harm	295 005	467 944	+58.6%	26%	36%	25%	11%	2%	0%	0%	1988
Domestic burglary	227 090	123 280	-45.7%	18%	35%	27%	16%	4%	0%	0%	1989
Motor vehicle theft	214 836	63 240	-70.5%	25%	34%	21%	11%	7%	2%	0%	1982
Handbag theft	7 916	5 986	-24.3%	22%	30%	24%	21%	3%	0%	0%	1985
Murder	666	394	-40.8%	16%	24%	27%	28%	5%	1%	0%	1874
Sexual murder	32	20	-37.5%	19%	26%	28%	23%	4%	1%	0%	1988
Total theft	4 151 087	3 029 390	-27.0%	29%	37%	22%	8%	1%	0%	0%	1980
Bank robbery	1 624	903	-44.4%	13%	22%	25%	29%	10%	2%	0%	1983
Drug dealing	37 212	68 701	+84.6%	37%	31%	18%	11%	3%	0%	0%	1977
Murder and robbery	140	74	-47.1%	12%	25%	27%	29%	7%	1%	0%	1977
Sexual abuse of children	15 430	15 430	0%	40%	31%	18%	10%	1%	0%	0%	1844

Table 8.3 Mean estimate of percentage change in the frequency of selected crime over the period 1993–2003

	Sex		Region		Education[a]		Hours TV per week (mean: 22h)		Age	
	Female	Male	East	West	High	Low	Low	High	≤ 45	> 45
All crimes	39.9	34.2	45.7	35.0	32.5	39.5	31.1	43.9	38.0	36.5
Bodily harm	55.3	45.0	52.0	50.1	38.2	56.3	46.9	54.7	57.4	43.5
Sexual murder	317.4	195.9	249.9	263.1	179.1	299.0	205.0	316.1	278.5	242.2
Domestic burglary	44.1	33.7	30.4	41.6	31.0	43.2	38.6	40.1	35.3	43.1

[a] High: Abitur (upper secondary school leaving qualification) and above

increased from 26.7 percent to 36.5 percent over the last 10 years.[10] In fact, as previously mentioned, the figure has actually fallen to 19.0 percent. In Table 8.3 we return to the estimated figures presented in Table 8.1, broken down this time by membership in selected groups.

Women are much more likely to assume that crime has increased, especially with regard to sexual murder. This finding is consistent with empirical studies that have established a link between vulnerability and fear of crime (Reuband 1992: 349). The fact that younger respondents are much more likely than their elders to think crime has increased can be interpreted along similar lines. Younger people are indeed far more likely to be affected by such crimes.[11] The data do not demonstrate any other uniform trend by age category or between east and west. It is interesting that respondents in the lower education and higher television watching categories believe there has been a larger increase in crime across the board.

The discrepancy between the public's perception of crime trends and the actual police figures raises two questions. How come such a large majority of people guess so incorrectly? How do these incorrect perceptions affect attitudes toward sentencing, crime policy, and the police and prosecution systems?

Crime in the Media

Studies from the USA and Canada whose starting point is the observation that people incorrectly believe that crime has risen despite the reality of falling crime rates (Roberts 1992: 116-117; Roberts and Stalans 1998) usually link this misconception to mass media representations of crime. Morris (1997: 108 ff.) media study similarly found that while there was a slight decrease in the number of serious crimes in the USA over the period 1991 to 1995 inclusive, an analysis of the evening news broadcast by all major television stations, on the other hand, indicated that the number of televised reports of spectacular violent crimes increased four-fold.

10 See Pfeiffer et al (2004: 6 ff.).

11 See Bundesministerium des Inneren and Bundesministerium der Justice (2001: 53).

Table 8.4 Crime-related programming as a proportion of all listed programming for selected television stations[a] and as a proportion of all programming

Station Year	ARD (n =31 broadcasts) Share (%)	ZDF (n =37 broadcasts) Share (%)	RTL (n=44 broadcasts) Share (%)	SAT.1 (n=50 broadcasts) Share (%)	PRO7 (n=31 broadcasts) Share (%)	All programming (N=309 broadcasts) Share (%)
1985	4.7	8.5	3.6	–	–	3.5
1995	11.3	8.5	13.1	11.4	32.9	15.4
2003	9.0	12.3	18.7	19.5	2.4	11.0

[a] *The following German television stations were coded and included in the "all programming" figure in addition to the stations shown: NDR, MDR, arte, 3Sat, RTL2, SuperRTL, Kabel1, VOX, 9Live*

As media research indicates, the selection, presentation and even the construction of what is deemed newsworthy are subject to certain rules. News and other information about human society is marketed according to its "news value" (Reuband 2000: 51). "Crime is not just a stable of general news reporting, but ... [is] also a conscious choice of subject for the purpose of competing with other media" (Reuband 2000: 43). For the consumer, news is not only there to provide information, but also excitement and entertainment (Schulze 1992). A factor in Germany might also be the increase nationwide since the mid-1980s of private television stations funded entirely by advertising. These stations are more dependent than public television on the kind of news, including crime news, which increase ratings.

To investigate this question we conducted an analysis – in conjunction with the Department of Journalism and Communication Research at Hanover University of Music and Drama – of the television listings published in a German tabloid newspaper, *Bild*. The analysis covered the second week of October in 1985, 1995 and 2003. Table 8.4 demonstrates how the relative shares of fiction and non-fiction programming featuring crime, investigation and prosecution changed over the three sampling periods.

The period 1985 to 1995 saw a marked increase in crime broadcasts as a share of all programming. The increase from 3.5 to 15.4 percent is primarily due to the fact that from the time private television began in the mid-1980s, private stations initially focused on the broadcasting of American fiction programming (feature films and series). There was a slight overall reduction in crime programming during the period 1995 to 2003. This was by no means a uniform trend, however. The two private stations with the largest audience, RTL and Sat.1, and also one of the main public stations, ZDF, further increased their share of crime programming from 1995 to 2003. As the other major public station, ARD, only reduced its crime share slightly from 11.3 to 9.0 percent, the overall decrease in crime broadcasts as a share of all programming is primarily due to a reduction at the smaller (by market share) public and private television stations. Another interesting trend is a shift in crime presentation from fictional (crime series and feature films) to non-fiction genres (court shows and "docu-soaps" showing the police at work).[12] That is, genres which give the viewer the impression that they represent a realistic picture of crime, crime investigation and prosecution.

An analysis conducted for ARD and ZDF since 1985[13] that employed a different methodology reported the proportion of all programming featuring crime for five major German television stations – ARD, ZDF, RTL, Sat.1 and Pro7 – from 1997 onwards. Three trends emerge for the last few years: First, there is a consistent tendency for crime to feature significantly more strongly on private than on public television (Krüger 1999: 322–39, 2000: 278–96). Second, a marked tabloid television has emerged during the same period (Krüger 1996: 362–74, 2000: 278–96; Krüger and Zapf-Schramm 2001: 326–44). Private television stations are incorporating tabloid elements into the style and content of their reporting (content: more "human interest" topics, plus reporting on spectacular crimes; style: emotion-ridden, dramatized and personalized reporting). In short, crime is dramatized as the face of evil. These findings are consistent with studies conducted by Medien Tenor, a Bonn media research center that has undertaken precise surveys of changes in news content for many years. The Medien Tenor surveys indicate that private television stations tend to present crime in a dramatized setting. Also, private television stations account for at least 70 percent of crime reporting in the context of news broadcasts (Stock 2004: 33). Finally, the third trend described by the authors of the ARD-ZDF analysis is a growing tendency for public television stations to match their reporting to that of private stations (Krüger and Zapf-Schramm 2003: 534–48).

These findings clearly demonstrate that the increasingly competitive television market since the mid-1980s has witnessed significantly more air time allocated both to the crime in the news and entertainment genres. There may have been a similar trend in newspapers, although no long-term studies have been done yet in this sector.[14] This described trend is similar to findings from news value and news selection research, according to which negative information in a news item is a key factor in its being preferred over other news items (Galtung and Ruge 1965). There is therefore a growing amount of air time dedicated to entertainment genres that combine apparent realism with a strong element of suspense (such as court shows), where crime often provides a background for playing out interpersonal conflicts. This has further raised the profile of crime in the media. The question arises whether this shift is a cause of or at least a factor in the popular misconceptions about crime rates. We use a multiple regression model to obtain some preliminary answers.[15]

---

12 The air time (in hours per day) for fictional programs featuring crime changed as follows: 1985 11.8h, 1995 149.2h and 2003 100.7h; for non-fiction programs: 1985 3.6h, 1995 8.5h and 2003 58.3h.

13 For an overview see Gerhard (1999: 340–4) and Krüger and Zapf-Schramm (2003).

14 Two studies for 1988 (Derwein 1995) and 1996 (Scharf, Mühlenfeld and Stockmann 1999: 445–62) found, however, that violent crime was highly over-represented in reporting on crime during the years in question.

15 To investigate the effect of media-use patterns on crime trend perceptions (step 1) and of crime trend perceptions on sentencing attitudes (step 2), ordinal logistic regressions

Table 8.5 Factor analysis of media use and factor weightings

Factor 1	Wt.	Factor 2	Wt.	Factor 3	Wt.
6:30 pm Sat.1 news	.86	Magazine programmes	.81	ZDF news programmes	.91
RTL Aktuell news	.80	Evening reportage	.79	ARD news programmes	.89
Pro 7 news	.77	Crime investigation	.58		
Tabloid magazines	.59				
Court shows	.58				

Source: KFN survey of crime and sentencing 2003; own calculations, N=1903.

The Use of Crime in the Media and its Consequences

In the "media" part of the KFN study, the 2,000 respondents were given a set of stimuli comprising a number of programs, from various broadcasters with the categories of Shows, Series, Feature Films and News, along with the explanation that their subject matter includes crime. Based on a six-point scale, they were asked to give their subjective ranking of how often they watched the named programs.[16] The analysis of dimensions of media use was restricted to programs that report on real-world affairs or at least claim proximity to the real world. Purely fictional genres like crime, horror and action films were excluded from the analysis, as were print media.

Table 8.5 indicates that it is possible to derive three dimensions or three scales of media use that are readily interpreted from the 10 items.[17] Factor 1 comprises consumption of private news broadcasts together with tabloid magazines and court

are estimated in the empirical part of the study. In these regression models, the probability that dependent variable y falls within category m of the ordinal scale is found by subtracting the probability of exceeding the empirically estimated threshold τm from the probability of attaining the next lower threshold τm-1, where the distance between the thresholds is permitted to vary. Formally, the model is of the form

$$\Pr(y_i = m|x_i) = \Lambda(\tau_m - x_i\beta) - \Lambda(\tau_{m-1} - x_i\beta), \text{ where } \Lambda(\varepsilon) = \frac{\exp(\varepsilon)}{1 + \exp(\varepsilon)}$$

is the logistic error distribution (Long 1997: 121), x a vector of explanatory variables and β a vector of regression coefficients. Unlike a multinomial logistic regression, however, the ordinal models are based on the assumption of proportional odds, which means the effects of the explanatory variables for threshold τm must be as close as possible to the effects for threshold τm+1. A suitable test (Long 1997: 143) was used to ensure that this assumption is met.

16 The possible answers were "(almost) every day", "several times a week", "once a week", "several times a month", "once a month or less frequently" and "never".

17 Incorporating the use of print media in the analysis makes for a poorer factor solution overall. Only the reading of local newspapers would weight one factor together with the ARD and ZDF public service television news programs, while reading the *Bild* newspaper and other tabloid magazines does not show a sufficient weighting on any factor. Because the recoding necessitated by including print media would also have meant a loss of information, only television programs were incorporated in the analysis.

Table 8.6 Determinants of crime perception: Ordinal logistic regressions

Dependent variable	Perceived change in frequency[a] between 1992 and 2003, by type of crime:				
	Domestic burglary	Murdery and robbery	Sexual murder	All crimes total	Bodily harm
τ_1	-2.73	-2.58	-3.86	-3.71	-3.77
τ_2	-.77	-.38	-1.54	-2.18	-1.79
τ_3	.72	.88	-.21	-.35	-.22
τ_4	2.63	2.38	1.09	1.47	1.46
Realschule/POS year 10[b] (Yes 1, No 0)	-0.338**	-0.414**	-0.566**	-0.238*	-0.121
[lower secondary school]	(2.91)	(3.58)	(4.91)	(2.02)	(1.01)
(Fach-)Abitur[b] (Yes 1, No 0)	-0.389*	-0.436**	-0.580**	-0.451**	-0.392**
[upper secondary school]	(2.38)	(2.72)	(3.67)	(2.81)	(2.67)
(Fach-)Hochschule[b] (Yes 1, No 0)	-0.579**	-0.731**	-0.999**	-0.872**	-0.595**
[tertiary education]	(3.18)	(3.94)	(5.43)	(4.71)	(3.81)
Child under 14 at home (Yes 1, No 0)	0.116	0.250*	0.026	0.032	0.190
	(1.09)	(2.34)	(0.24)	(0.29)	(1.74)
Age	0.024**	0.006	-0.009*	0.009*	0.002
	(6.68)	(1.72)	(2.42)	(2.39)	(0.44)
Female (Yes 1, No 0)	0.109	0.210*	0.158	0.180	0.221*
	(1.07)	(2.07)	(1.57)	(1.77)	(2.13)
Former East Germany (Yes 1, No 0)	-0.567**	-0.062	-0.007	0.018	-0.039
	(4.81)	(0.53)	(0.06)	(0.15)	(0.33)
Hours television per week	-0.001	0.003	0.011**	0.005	0.011**
	(0.19)	(0.77)	(2.75)	(1.35)	(2.68)
Private television	0.252**	0.261**	0.087	0.257**	0.251**
	(4.73)	(4.98)	(1.67)	(4.74)	(4.66)
Reportage	0.096*	0.094*	0.056	0.060	0.055
	(2.01)	(1.98)	(1.20)	(1.25)	(1.11)
Public service	0.135**	0.082	0.059	-0.038	-0.063
	(2.65)	(1.60)	(1.16)	(0.75)	(1.19)
Fear of crime:	0.236**	0.288**	0.301**	0.263**	0.237**
Precautions taken	(4.40)	(5.35)	(5.59)	(4.88)	(4.39)
Observations	1572	1570	1577	1571	1592
LR Chi-sq (df=12)	266.02	183.99	148.78	167.96	166.29

Absolute z values in brackets

[a] *"I think there has been..."*
1 = a slight/large/very large decrease 2 = no change 3 = a slight increase
4 = a large increase 5 = a very large increase
"... in such crimes over the last 10 years".

[b] *Reference category: No school leaving certificate, Hauptschulabschluss/ Volksschulabschluss/POS year 8/9 (lower secondary education)*

* *Significant at 5%;* ** *Significant at 1%*

Source: KFN survey of crime and sentencing 2003; own calculations.

shows, which are likewise dominated by private television. This dimension is accordingly named *Private Television*. The second factor is referred to as *Reportage*, and the third as *Public Service*. The original seven-point criminal perception items (see Table 8.2) had to be reduced to a five-point scale by merging the little-used "Slight Decrease", "Large Decrease" and "Very Large Decrease" into a single category.

Table 8.6 demonstrates that the multiple ordinal logistic regression model tends to corroborate the descriptive findings presented above. The probability of a respondent assuming that crime rates have risen declines with increasing education. At least in respect of murder and robbery and bodily harm, this probability is significantly higher for women than for men. With regard to age and east–west differences, the trend is similarly non-uniform to that identified based upon the descriptive analyses in Table 8.3. The likelihood of a respondent believing that there has been an increase in all types of crime also increases with fear of crime as measured on the subdimension of precautionary measures.

Table 8.6 also indicates that the choice of programming makes a difference. Each of the three media use patterns has a significant positive correlation with the perceived change in frequency for the "domestic burglary" crime category, with the "private television" viewing pattern exerting by far the strongest effect. Apart from sexual murders, whose perceived frequency change correlates with the amount of television (in hours) watched each week but not with the choice of programming, there is a positive correlation at the 1 percent significance level between media use corresponding to the "private television" viewing pattern and the perceived change in frequency of all types of crime.

The coefficients in Table 8.6 can only be interpreted as to sign and significance, however, as they represent the change in the log-odds [ln(P/(1-P))] of the threshold to the next category being exceeded. A more useful result can be obtained by converting the change associated with the "private television" variable to probabilities of belonging to the categories used for the dependent variables. To illustrate this point we will consider middle-aged men (aged 46) with average general education, average weekly television viewing time (24 hours) and average values for the "reportage" and "public service" media use patterns. Figures 8.1 and 8.2 indicate that the probabilities for the 10 percent of this group who view the least and the 10 percent who view the most private television.[18]

The two figures illustrate the effect on the perceived change in the crime rate for all crimes and in the crime rate for murder and robbery offenses. The 10 percent who view the *least* private television have a 15 percent probability of thinking there has been a very large increase in all types of crime (Figure 8.1). For the 10 percent who view the *most* private television, this probability is no less than 30 percent – twice the figure for the former group. Finally, the same effect is evident with murder and

18 Strictly speaking, the "private television" and "hours of television per week" ought to be varied simultaneously in the forecast to make the differences even more pronounced.

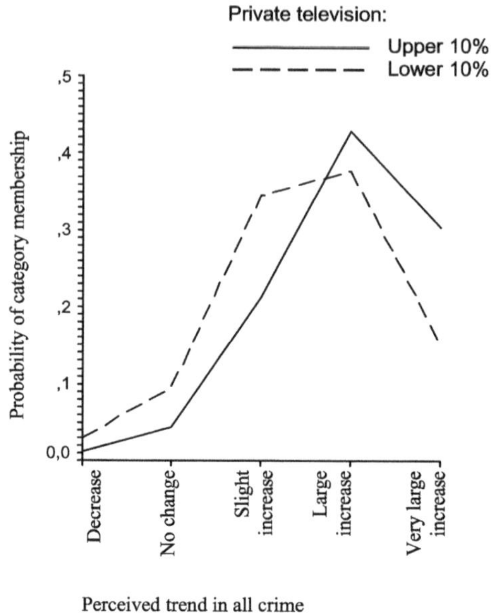

Figure 8.1 Effect of private television viewing on perceived crime trends: All crime

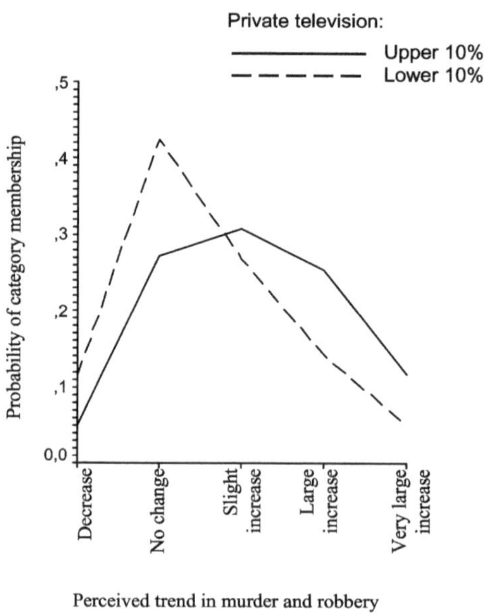

Figure 8.2 Effect of private television viewing on perceived crime trends: Murder and robbery

robbery, where the probabilities are 5 and 12 percent for the bottom and top 10 percent of television users respectively.

Crime Perception and Sentencing Attitudes

The strong influence of private television on perceived crime trends led us to enquire whether the same distorted public perceptions are behind harsher sentencing attitudes. This avenue of enquiry is supported by the findings of two representative surveys conducted by KFN in 1992 and 2004 that again examined sentencing attitudes. Comparison of the data reveals a marked increase in the proportion of respondents calling for tougher sentences. For instance, the mean approval ranking for the statement "Harsh sentences are needed in order to deter others from committing crimes" was 4.25 on a six-point scale in the 1992 sample and 4.83 in the 2004 sample.[19] Streng's continuous study of punitivity and preferences as to the purpose of sentencing among first-year law students produced very similar findings. Apparently, the period 1989 to 1999 saw a marked change in the attitudes of lawyers-to-be. They are much less likely to consider offender resocialization as the purpose of sentencing, and increasingly likely to prefer harsh punishments and a toughening of criminal law (Streng 2000: 422 ff.).

Streng also associates the increasing rigidity of prospective lawyers with the dramatization of crime in the media and in politics. But he rightly raises another possibility. The relatively stable 1980s were followed in Germany by a decade of growing poverty and unemployment, a surge in immigration that many found threatening, the unification of Germany with the vast problems that it produced, and the acts of terror perpetrated by Al Qaeda. It is possible that many people are unsettled by these changes and wish for a strong state capable of employing a hard line on law and order.

In view of these findings, respondents' sentencing attitudes were made the dependent variable in the analysis phase of our study, to be explained among other things by subjectively perceived crime trends. Table 8.7 lists the estimated factors affecting indicators of sentencing attitudes, i.e., affecting stated opinions regarding the appropriateness of the sentences generally handed down for each type of crime.

The strongest factor affecting sentencing attitudes overall proves to be the perceived trend in each crime. This predictor was incorporated in the model as a dummy variable, where 1 corresponds to "very large increase" or "large increase" and 0 corresponds to all other categories. For example, assuming there to have

---

19 Ranging from 1 for "not true at all" to 6 for "very true". Strictly speaking this is an ordinally scaled variable. The Mann/Whitney U-test that is appropriate for this scale level gives a highly significant z value of 13.57 for the difference. Based on three items for sentencing attitude contained in both the 1992 and the 2003 survey it is possible to form a 16-rank total index to accommodate the construct of sentencing attitude. The higher the index, the more punitive the attitude. Once again, both the means and the middle ranks of the index differ quite significantly (10.33 for 1992 versus 11.83 for 2003).

Table 8.7 Determinants of sentencing attitudes: Ordinal logistic regressions

Dependent variable	Sentencing attitudes[a] by type of crime: Thefts/ break-ins	All crimes total	Rape/sexual assault	Bodily injury
τ_1	0.56	-1.85	-3.74	-0.64
τ_2	1.58	-.13	-2.74	0.95
τ_3	2.52	1.26	-1.42	2.20
Realschule/POS year 10[b] (Yes 1, No 0)	-0.151	-0.362**	-0.238	-0.026
[lower secondary school]	(1.27)	(3.05)	(1.53)	(0.23)
(Fach-)Abitur[b] (Yes 1, No 0)	-0.104	-0.495**	-0.520**	-0.118
[upper secondary school]	(0.63)	(3.11)	(2.62)	(0.76)
(Fach-)Hochschule[b] (Yes 1, No 0)	-0.052	-1.096**	-1.029**	-0.048
[tertiary education]	(0.29)	(6.08)	(4.99)	(0.27)
Child under 14 at home (Yes 1, No 0)	-0.083	0.221*	-0.064	0.081
	(0.76)	(2.04)	(0.45)	(0.77)
Age	0.017**	0.011**	-0.008	0.020**
	(5.08)	(3.42)	(1.83)	(6.20)
Female (Yes 1, No 0)	-0.549**	-0.227*	-0.236	-0.231*
	(5.26)	(2.18)	(1.75)	(2.29)
Former East Germany (Yes 1, No 0)	0.181	0.437**	0.437**	0.062
	(1.60)	(3.80)	(2.80)	(0.55)
Fear of crime:	0.273**	0.329**	0.337**	0.382**
Precautions taken	(4.89)	(5.94)	(4.64)	(7.04)
Perception of crime trend[c]:	0.825**	0.861**	1.099**	0.611**
"large/very large increase" (Yes 1, No 0)	(8.14)	(8.30)	(8.13)	(6.35)
Observations	1597	1600	1603	1605
LR Chi-sq (df=9)	219.12	254.04	160.48	195.86

Absolute z values in brackets

[a] *"I think the sentences handed down for ... are generally..."*

1 = far too harsh to appropriate 2 = somewhat lax 3 = lax 4 = far too lax

[b] *Reference category: No school leaving certificate, Hauptschulabschluss/ Volksschulabschluss/POS year 8/9 (lower secondary education)*

The proportionality assumption is not met for the independent variable "perception of crime trend" in the "thefts/break-ins" model. However, a binary logistic regression (DV: lax/far too lax = 1, otherwise 0) produces almost identical results.

[c] *With the DV "sexual assault/rape" the IV is the perceived frequency of sexual murder.*

** Significant at 5%; ** Significant at 1%*

Source: KFN survey of crime and sentencing 2003; own calculations.

been a large or very large increase in all crimes over the last 10 years raises the odds of the sentencing attitudes shifting to the next higher category by 136 percent [exp(0.861)–1×100]. This is better illustrated by examining the effect on the probability of each category. We therefore focus on men in the former East Germany with lower secondary education and an average age of 46, one child under 14 living in the household and average fear of crime. Of this group, those who think there has been a strong or very strong increase in crime are 60 percent likely to consider sentencing to be too lax. For those who think crime has risen only moderately or not at all, this probability falls to 39 percent.

Because these empirical findings were not obtained by the ideal method of direct experiment, analysis of the causal relations between the various constructs requires further research. For example, it would be necessary to investigate in greater detail the factors that influence preferences for different types of television programming. It may be assumed that other unobserved personality traits are linked with viewing frequency for each genre and that these traits are not fully subsumed under fear of crime. They may themselves correlate with subjective perceptions of crime trends and with punitivity. All the same, the findings must be taken as a clear indication that widespread perceptions of crime trends are significantly affected by media reporting.

Changes in Crime Policy, Investigation and Prosecution Since 1990

These findings raise the question of how popular calls for tougher sentencing have affected crime policy. Schott recently surveyed criminal law enacted over the last two decades (Schott et al 2004). He found that the last example of a substantial reduction in criminal law penalties was in 1990, when the Bundestag enacted a Juvenile Courts Act (*Jugendgerichtsgesetz*) that increased the scope for alternatives to incarceration, abolishing open-ended sentences and restricted the use of remand for juvenile offenders. Subsequently, apart from certain minor adjustments, the five reform acts passed since 1992 brought nothing but tougher penalties. In sum, the legislature has significantly raised the penalties for some 40 offenses over the last 12 years.

Comparing the genesis of these five pieces of criminal law legislation with criminal law reforms adopted during the three decades that preceded them reveals one key difference: As Maelicke (1999) and Albrecht (2004) emphasize, there is now less of a tendency to consult academics.[20] Albrecht (2004: 491 ff.), in his discerning analysis of the links between crime policy and public opinion, rightly emphasizes a

20 The official preamble to the first criminal law reform act of 1969 (Bundestags-Drucksache V/4094), for example, still draws upon crime policy ideas culled from practical experience in law enforcement, and consequently argues along the lines of treatment and desired treatment outcomes. According to Maelicke (1999: 73) there was a broad consensus in the 1970s between academics, enforcement practitioners and policymakers. Since the early 1990s, however, there has been a power shift within the crime policy arena, "Policy makers are increasingly reluctant to seek advice from industry with its preference for restraint and caution. They are driven by the media ... constrained by the tightening of laws and by the room for maneuver available to the courts, and bring their influence to bear on practitioners with the aim of bringing about a shift in priorities: Safety is gaining in importance and maybe even priority relative to treatment and reintegration" (Maelicke 1999: 74).

change in the underlying focus of crime policy, which "has become more responsive to feelings of uncertainty and is being co-opted as a way of establishing a sense of security" (Albrecht 2004: 496; see also Sack 2003: 3 ff.). Formerly, policy makers' efforts centered on the quest for a rationale that could be communicated; they were required to supply verifiable arguments and provide empirical support for their proposals based upon extensive practical experience and clear research findings. Today, however, there is less demand for academically well-founded knowledge on crime trends, offenders and the effects of prosecution strategies. Increasingly, expert reports are being replaced by opinion polls designed to test the water and see what goes down best with the public. Politicians are increasingly likely to sprout populist demands, and to present themselves as warriors in the fight against evil.[21] David Garland arrives at similar conclusions in his in-depth study of crime policy trends in the UK and the USA (2001).[22]

Given the significant hardening of sentencing attitudes among the German population and the changes in crime policy described above, it comes as no surprise that German courts are handing down harsher sentences. We will use the example of actual and grievous bodily harm to illustrate this trend. According to the sentencing statistics, the share of tried suspects given an unsuspended prison or juvenile detention sentence for such crimes rose from 5.7 to 6.9 percent during the period 1990 to 2002. The average sentence also grew by almost a third, from 1.10 to 1.45 years.[23] Both trends together increased the total sentence handed down by the courts from 6.2 to 10 years per 100 tried suspects between 1990 and 2002 – an increase of about three-fifths.

The change in sentencing would be understandable if the average severity of such offenses had also increased over the period. In fact, the opposite appears to be true. This is the conclusion of two case analyses on juvenile sentencing performed at the Criminological Research Institute of Lower Saxony (Delzer 2004; Schott et al 2004). Comparisons of sentencing by selected courts for 1990 and 1996 and in two German *Länder* for 1991 and 1997 show a marked decline in the number of such

---

21 Chancellor Schröder provided a typical example in a 2001 interview for *Bild am Sonntag*, with his suggestion of what do with sex offenders: "Lock them away – for good!" (*Bild am Sonntag*, July 8, 2001).

22 Garland reports a similar loss of influence for practitioners and researchers in the UK and the USA, and that crime policy initiatives there are increasingly driven by public opinion and by calls for tougher statutory penalties from the mass media in response to spectacular individual crimes (2001: 13 and 151 ff.).

23 Where the sentencing statistics present sentence durations in class intervals, we arrived at the averages by adding 0.33 times the interval to the lower value for each class. Sentences from two to under three years, for example, were assumed to average 2.33. The factor of 0.33 is based on an analysis of cases from 1991 to 1997; see Schott et al (2004). It is conceivable that there has been an increase here in line with the generally observed trend in sentencing. In the absence of new data, however, we opted to keep the assumption that the average corresponded to the lower one-third point for the entire study period rather than changing to the mid-point.

crimes resulting in hospitalization of the victim. Conversely, there was an increase in the percentage of cases where the victim did not obtain any medical assistance. At least here, then, the average severity of offenses has tended to decrease.[24]

Based on these data, we calculated the total number of prison years that would have been imposed had court sentencing practices remained at their 1990 level of 6.2 years per 100 suspects tried for actual or grievous bodily harm. The comparison shows that, as a result of the change in sentencing over the 12-year period, 7,945 more years' prison were handed down than would have been under 1990 conditions. This has major implications for Western German prison budgets. Taking €80 as the daily cost of accommodating an offender in prison,[25] the additional cost over the 12 years was €232 million.

We also investigated the change in the number of years' prison per 100 suspects tried for all types of crime. There was an increase of close to 40 percent, from 5.2 years in 1990 to 7.3 in 2002.[26] This accords with data from the *Länder* penal statistics. In the former West Germany, prisoner numbers swelled from 37,468 to 51,881 between 1991 and 2003, an increase of 38.5 percent, yet the number of tried suspects had increased by only 1.7 percent between 1990 and 2002.[27] Again assuming a cost of €80 per day, the states comprising former West Germany had to allocate some €421 million more to finance their penal systems in 2003 than they did only 12 years earlier. In addition, a nationwide construction program begun in 2000 will create 12,000 new cells at a cost, according to research by Suhling and Schott (2001: 27), of €1.4 billion.

---

24 These findings cannot be reliably applied to the whole of Germany. They do, however, demonstrate that the widespread assumption of an increase in the brutality as well as the frequency of crimes involving bodily harm should be viewed with caution. In view of the fact that penalties for actual and grievous bodily harm were increased in 1998, it appears more likely that the observed rise in the number of years' prison per 100 tried suspects is a result of tougher sentencing.

25 This is the average value for the last 10 years based on calculations for the state of Lower Saxony.

26 Based on these data, comparing actual sentencing in 1990 with sentencing over the 12 ensuing years indicate an increase totalling some 154,000 years' extra prison as a result of the courts raising the frequency and duration of prison sentences rather than staying with 1990 sentencing levels. These hypothetical figures are subject to major uncertainties, however. For example, our method of calculation, under which class interval averages in sentencing statistics are assumed to be at the lower one-third point rather than the mid-point of each class, may underestimate the extent of the increase in sentencing. Conversely, it is conceivable that there has been a change in the average severity of offenses – something that is ultimately only verifiable from case analysis. Lacking such specific information on offense severity, we will refrain from repeating for all crimes the hypothetical cost calculation presented for actual and grievous bodily harm.

27 We intentionally used the data for one year later when comparing penal statistics. The average prison sentence of 1.1 to 1.5 years means there is a corresponding delay before any change in sentencing practices affect the prison population figures.

Even if the available data do not allow us to calculate the precise extent to which this added expense is due to harder penalties imposed by legislation, it is clear that, influenced by the media dramatization of crime, the need for a cost-benefit analysis has taken a back seat in crime policy over the last 12 years. Politicians have largely met the calls for tougher sentencing in order to calm the waters rather than objectively asking what benefit to society there was to be had from the sharp rise in costs.

There is one further issue that should be briefly examined. In a study on behalf of the German government's Immigration Council we investigated who took the main brunt of the described trend in crime policy and sentencing. This was occasioned by the following data: From 1993 to 2002, the number of foreign citizens charged in former West Germany declined by 20.6 percent.[28] This figure stands in sharp contrast to the fact that the number of foreign prisoners increased from 7,526 to 12,865 between the prison censuses taken in March 1993 and March 2004, an increase of 70.9 percent. Theoretically, this contrary trend could at least partly be explained by a sharp increase in the severity of crimes committed by foreigners, but no evidence for this is provided either by a long-term analysis of trial cases performed at KFN in the 1990s (Schott et al 2004) or by a systematic investigation of sentencing practices based on individual data records from sentencing statistics (Pfeiffer et al 2004). Instead, the two studies provide evidence for the assumption that non-German offenders are being handed down increasingly harsher sentences compared with their German counterparts. Other studies have produced similar findings (Delzer 2004; Ludwig-Mayerhofer and Niemann 1997). The evidence thus far gives grounds to suspect that the courts are working on the false assumption that they need to take a hard line as a general deterrent in the face of a rising wave of foreigner-committed crime. Again, more in-depth research would be needed to investigate this hypothesis.

Discussion and Conclusion

The crime policy trend described in the foregoing section is not restricted to Germany. In some countries it is even more pronounced. For example, the prison population in England and Wales rose from 44,552 to 74,468 between 1993 and 2004, an increase of 67.1 percent, and that was after a 12-year period of relatively stable numbers (Council of Europe 2004; Home Office 2004; ICPS 2004). Like the German situation, the primary reason is a marked increase in both the average duration and the frequency of prison sentences.[29] In the USA, the corresponding trend towards harsher sentences began as early as the end of the 1970s, and prisoner

---

28 The reduction from 237,867 to 188,962 foreign subjects charged relates to former West Germany excluding the states of Hessen and Saarland, for which separate sentencing statistics for sentenced non-German offenders are not available.

29 See page 6 onwards of the Home Office Annual Report 2004, which notes that the trend change coincided with the Bulger murder that shook the nation in 1993, following which a series of legislative initiatives led to a lasting increase in penalties.

numbers increased from 503,586 to 2,078,570 between 1980 and mid-2003, or no less than 412.8 percent (Glaze and Palla 2004).

Garland, too, in his analysis of crime policy and sentencing in the UK and the USA, considers crime reporting by the mass media and in particular by television as a factor that has significantly altered social perceptions of crime (2001: 156). For Garland, the emotive force of images of spectacular crimes abolishes the distance with which the middle classes used to view criminal developments. Garland nevertheless argues that the mass media played only a marginal role in recent changes in crime policy and sentencing practices. He ascribes central importance to other factors, which we outline below:

- The radical change from a system based on "penal welfarism" (Garland 2001: 35 ff.) to the other extreme of courts following strict sentencing guidelines (Garland 2001: 53 ff.).
- Processes of social change (individualization, the disintegration of the family due to rising divorce rates, growing workplace risks, the thinning of social networks and a decrease in informal social control), which have triggered increasing insecurity among many people and which fuel the desire for a strong state able to take a hard line on law and order (Garland 2001: 154 ff.).
- Growing identification with victims of crime and an increasing willingness to have the criminal law consider their needs and wishes to see the offender punished (Garland 2001: 11, 142 ff., 180 ff.).
- A growing fear of crime among the middle classes, who are increasingly the victims of crime themselves and therefore now more supportive of tougher sentencing policies (Garland 2001: 153).
- A society of growing social contrasts in which the state no longer responds to the needs of the social underclass with welfare schemes, but increasingly relies on prison as an instrument of discipline (Garland 2001: 82 ff., 178 ff.).

We do not dispute that these factors are of considerable importance to the described changes in crime policy in the USA. We think, however, that Garland has considerably underestimated the importance of the mass media in the genesis and amplification of these trends. This applies especially to the tendency, also lamented by Garland, of crime policy to be shaped by television reports of spectacular individual crimes and the associated populist calls for a toughening of criminal law. The identification with victims of crime that Garland himself rightly highlights is largely due to emotive reporting of individual victims' fates. Garland also neglects the fact, substantiated by American studies in media science, that reporting of spectacular crimes, especially on television, has continued to rise in intensity and frequency despite the falling crime rates since 1991 (Morris 1997). Marketing of the media commodity known as crime is primarily based on its entertainment value, not its frequency of occurrence in real life.

Developments in the UK and Germany also differ considerably from what Garland reports about the USA. Neither German nor English criminal law has undergone the same radical change from the one extreme of "penal welfarism" to the other of rigid sentencing guidelines. The changes in both countries have been slower and more gradual. For this reason, a marked rise in prisoner numbers did not begin in Germany until 1991 and in Britain until as late as 1993. Garland neglects this in his analysis of UK crime policy just as he neglects the country's current crime trends. Contrary to his proposition that a toughening of criminal law sanctions is to be expected when the middle classes are themselves exposed to increasing risk of crime, the new crime policies in England took hold at a time when the middle classes were living in increasing safety. The number of crimes recorded by the British police fell continuously from 1992 until a new method of counting was introduced in 1998 and has remained broadly constant ever since. More significantly, however, the British Crime Survey, a representative victim survey conducted on a regular basis in the English and Welsh population, demonstrates a continuous, marked decline over the last nine years in the risk of becoming a crime victim (a reduction of 39 percent; see Dodd et al. 2004). The victimization rate in England and Wales for 2003/2004 was thus at its lowest level since 1981. A similar trend is also observed in the USA since 1974 for crimes against property and since 1994 for violent crimes (Rennison and Rand 2003).[30]

There are no such longitudinal data for unreported crime in Germany. As the Police Crime Statistics we quoted earlier indicate, however, the German situation also does not support Garland's proposition that increased exposure to crime among the middle classes is a factor in calls for tougher sentencing and in the consequent tightening of the criminal law and sentencing practice. Instead, we have preliminary evidence that the large majority of people, under the influence of sensationalist reporting by the media, perceive an increase in crime that is simply not reflected in the data. And we can demonstrate that this has significantly hardened their attitudes on criminal sentencing.

The analysis presented here, however, does not adequately demonstrate how media reporting of crime by the various television stations and other media has changed in detail. In view of the key importance of this question for crime policy, it is necessary to subject it to a more in-depth analysis. In this regard, we see good prospects for the joint research being conducted with the Medien Tenor research institute in Bonn, which has been collecting data on how the mass media report on selected topics since the mid-1990s. A continuation of the analysis presented here is also desirable because a number of additional questions have not yet been adequately examined. For example, it is not yet known to what extent the rise in punitivity identified in Germany is due to other factors such as those named by Streng and Garland in their analyses. There is a need for more in-depth research into the specific route by which popular calls for tougher sentencing in general are taken

30 According to Rennison and Rand, the victimization rate for violent crime fell by 54.6 in the USA from 1993 to 2002, and the victimisation rate for crimes against property fell by 50.1 percent over the same period. Crimes against property have in fact declined by 345 percent since 1975 (Rennison and Rand 2003).

into account in crime policy and sentencing practice, and why the groups that seem to be most affected, such as violent criminals, sex offenders and foreign suspects, tend to be those that attract the most media attention.

Finally, further attention should be paid to one aspect that emerged from the British example above but which is also evident in the USA: The fact that police statistics and representative surveys of victims both show violent crimes and crimes against property have been declining steeply since 1993 and 1995 respectively, at a time when prison populations were fast increasing. The question arises whether this trend is partly due to the criminal justice system in both countries putting significantly more people behind bars than were released from prison each year, and that over a period of some years. In the short term, an imprisonment strategy of this kind can indeed contribute to domestic security because, for a time at least, a growing share of a country's high-risk population is temporarily incapacitated from committing any crimes. But what happens after some time has passed, when the very rapidly increasing cost of detention can no longer be met and the political opposition to this crime policy grows stronger? If the country then returns to moderate penal sanctioning, it faces a dilemma. For a period of many years, the number of releases will substantially exceed the number newly sentenced to prison. This gives rise to considerable crime risks, however, since it is well known that a stay in prison often tears people away from their prior social surroundings. This problem is already acknowledged in the USA, where a broad-based and very expensive reintegration program has been embarked upon to counter it (Travis, Solomon and Waul 2001). It remains to be seen whether Europe will learn from the American experience or whether the policy of ever-harsher sentencing will be allowed to continue unchecked.

References

Albrecht, Hans-Jörg (2004), "Öffentliche Meinung, Kriminalpolitik und Kriminaljustiz", in Michael Walter, Kania, Harald and Albrecht, Hans-Jörg, *Alltagsvorstellungen von Kriminalität. Individuelle und gesellschaftliche Bedeutung von Kriminalitätsbildern für die Lebensgestaltung*, Münster: LIT.

Bundesministerium des Inneren & Bundesministerium der Justiz (2001), *Erster Periodischer Sicherheitsbericht der Mundesregierung*, Berlin: Bundesministerium des Inneren

Council of Europe (2004), *Space I: Council of Europe Annual Penal Statistics*, Strasbourg: Council of Europe.

Delzer, Ingo (2005), *Jugendgewalt vor Gericht. Eine Analyse der staatsanwaltschaftlichen und gerichtlichen Erledigungspraxis gegenüber jugendlichen und heranwachsenden Beschuldigten von Raub- und qualifizierten Körperverletzungsdelikten in Hannover, Hamburg, Leipzig und Stuttgart*, Hanover: KFN.

Derwein, Christof (1995), "Wie wird Kriminalität in der Presse dargestellt, ist die Darstellung wirklichkeitsfremd und gibt es Entsprechungen im Vorstellungsbild der Bevölkerung?", doctoral thesis in law. University of Frankfurt am Main.

Ditton, Jason, Derek Chadee, Stephen Farrall, Elizabeth Gilchrist and Jon Bannister (2004), "From Imitation to Intimidation: A Note on the Curious and Changing Relationship Between the Media, Crime and Fear of Crime", *British Journal of Criminology*, 44: 595–610.

Dodd, Tricua, Sian Nicholas, David Povey and Alison Walker (2004), *Crime in England and Wales 2003/2004*, London: Secretary of State for the Home Department by Command of Her Majesty.

Dreher, Eduard (1967), "Zur Spielraumtheorie als der Grundlage der Strafzumessungslehre des Bundesgerichtshofes", *Juristenzeitung*, 22: 41–6.

Galtung, Johan and Marie H. Ruge (1965), "The Structure of Foreign News: The Presentation of the Congo, Cuba and Cyprus Crisis in Four Norwegian Newspapers", *Journal of Peace Research*, 2: 64–91.

Garland, David (2001), *The Culture of Control: Crime and Social Order in Contemporary Society*, Oxford: Oxford University Press.

Gerhard, Heinz (1999), "Programmanalysen im Vergleich. Anmerkungen zu Unterschieden in Methode, Aufgabenstellung und Ergebnissen", *Media Perspektiven*, 7: 340–4.

German Federal Criminal Police Office (Bundeskriminalamt) (2005) *Police Crime Statistics 2004*, Wiesbaden: Bundeskriminalmt.

Glaze, Lauren E. and Seri Palla (2004), *Probation and Parole in the United States, 2003*, Washington DC: US Department of Justice, Bureau of Justice Statistics.

Hassemer, Winfried and Rudolf Gerhardt (2004), "ZRP-Rechtsgespräch – Der Staat muss das Strafbedürfnis der Bevölkerung beachten: Aber einer nur symbolischen Kriminalpolitik verbessert den Schutz der Rechtsgüter nicht", *Zeitschrift für Rechspolitik*, 37(3): 93–4.

Home Office (2004), *Prison Statistics England and Wales 2002*, London: Secretary of State for the Home Department by Command of Her Majesty.

International Center for Prison Studies (2004), "Prison Brief for United Kingdom: England and Wales", at http://www.kcl.ac.uk/depsta/rel/icps/worldbrief/europe_records.php?code=168.

Krüger, U. Michael (1996), "Boulevardisierum der Information im Privatfernsehen", *Media Perspektiven*, July: 362–74.

Krüger, U. Michael (1999), "Stabile Programmstukturen trotz besonderer Fernsehereignisse", *Media Perspektiven*, July: 322–9.

Krüger, U. Michael (2000), "Unterschiedliches Informationsverständnis im öffentlich-rechtlichen und privaten Fernsehen", *Media Perspektiven*, 7: 278–96.

Krüger, U. Michael and Thomas Zapf-Schramm (2001), "Die Boulevardisierungskluft im deutschen Fernsehen", *Media Perspektiven*, 7: 326–44.

Krüger, U. Michael and Thomas Zapf-Schramm (2003), "Inhalte und Gestaltung öffentlich-rechtlicher und privater Informationsangebote im Fernsehen", *Media Perspektiven*, 12: 534–48.

Long, J. Scott (1997), *Regression Models for Categorical and Limited Dependent Variables*, London: Sage.

Ludwig-Mayerhofer, Wolfgang and Heike Niemann (1997), "Gleiches (Straf-)Recht für alle? Neue Ergebnisse zur Ungleichbehandlung ausländischer Jugendlicher im Strafrecht der Bundesrepublik", *Zeitschrift für Soziologie*, 35–52.

Maelicke, Bernd (1999), "Der Strafvollzug und die Neue Wirklichkeit", *Zeitschrift für Strafvollzug und Straffälligenhilfe*, 48: 73–7.

Morris, Norval (1997), *Crime, the Media and our Public Discourse, Perspectives on Crime and Justice: 1996–1997 Lecture Series*, Washington DC: US Department of Justice.

Pfeiffer, Christian (1983), *Kriminalprävention im Jugendgerichtsverfahren*, Cologne: Heymanns.

Pfeiffer, Christian (1990), "Doch eine 'Sogwirkung' leerer Zellen? Die Strafverfolgungsstatistik 1988 gibt Anlaß zu kritischen Fragen", *DVJJ-Journal*, 132.

Pfeiffer, Christian (2004), "Dämonisierung des Bösen", *Frankfurter Allgemeine Zeitung*, March 5, 2004: 9.

Pfeiffer, Christian, Matthias Kleimann, Tillmann Schott and Sven Petersen (2005), *Migration und Kriminalität. Ein Gutachten für den Zuwanderungsrat der Bundesregierung*, Baden- Baden: Nomos.

Rennison, Marie C. and Michael R. Rand (2003), *Criminal Victimization, 2002*, Washington DC: US Department of Justice, Bureau of Justice Statistics.

Reuband, Karl-Heinz (1992), "Objektive und subjektive Bedrohung durch Kriminalität. Ein Vergleich der Kriminalitätsfurcht in der Bundesrepublik Deutschland und den USA 1965–1990", *Kölner Zeitschrift für Soziologie und Sozialpsychologie*, 44: 341–53.

Reuband, Karl-Heinz (1998), "Kriminalität in den Medien. Erscheinungsformen, Nutzungsstruktur und Auswirkungen auf die Kriminalitätsfurcht", *Soziale Probleme*, 9: 126–53.

Reuband, Karl Heinz (2000), "Kriminalität als Thema ostdeutscher Massenmedien vor und nach der Wende. Eine Analyse Dresdner Tageszeitungen 1988–1994", *Kriminologisches Journal*, 32: 43–55.

Roberts, Julian V. (1992), "Public Opinon, Crime, and Criminal Justice", *Crime and Justice*, 16: 99–180.

Roberts, Julian V. and Anthony N. Doob (1990), "News Media Influences on Public Views of Sentencing", *Law and Human Behavior*, 14: 451–68.

Roberts, Julian V. and Loretta J. Stalans (1998), "Crime, Criminal Justice, and Public Opinion", in Michael Torny (ed.), *The Handbook of Crime and Punishment*, Oxford: Oxford University Press.

Sack, Fritz (2003), "Governing through crime?", paper presented at a symposium held by Arbeitskreises Junger Kriminologen (AJK), September 11–13.

Scharf, Wilfried, Hans-Ullrich Mühlenfeld and Ralf Stockmann (1999), "Zur Kriminalitätsberichterstattung in der Presse", *Publizistik*, 44(4): 445–62.

Schott, Tillmann, Rebecca Loebmann, Thomas Goergen, Stefan Suhling and Christian Pfeiffer (2004), "Der Anstieg der Gefangenzahlen in Niedersachsen und Schleswig Holstein – Folge der Kriminalitätsentwicklung oder unterschiedlicher Strafhärte?", unpublished final report, Hanover: KFN.

Schulze, Gerhard (1992), *Die Erlebnisgesellschaft*, Frankfurt am Main: Campus.

Stock, Wolfgang (2004) (ed.), "Hoher Preis der Sensationsgier: Wie uns Medien in Angst und Schrecken versetzen", *Medien Tenor Forschungsbericht*, 143, April.

Streng, Franz (2000), "Die heranwachsende Juristengeneration und die Aufgabe des Strafrechts", *Bewährungshilfe*, 4: 422–35.

Streng, Franz (2002), *Strafechtlicht Santionen. Die Strafzumessung und ihre Grundlagen*, Stuttgart: Kohlhammer.

Suhling, Stefan and Tilmann Schott (2001), "Ansatzpunkte zur Erklärung der gestiegenen Gefangenenzahlen in Deutschland", in Bereswill, Mechthild and Werner Greve, *Forschungsthema Strafvollzug*, Baden-Baden: Nomos.

Travis, Jeremy, Amy L. Solomon and Michelle Waul (2001), *From Prison to Home: The Dimensions and Consequences of Prisoner Reentry*, Washington DC: Urban Institute.

PART III
Organized Crime, Trafficking and Refugees

Chapter 9

The United Nations Global Program Against Trafficking in Human Beings: Results from Phase I of "Coalitions Against Trafficking in Human Beings in the Philippines"

Alexis A. Aronowitz[1]
University of Utrecht

Introduction

In March 1999, the former United Nations Centre for International Crime Prevention (CICP), now the United Nations Office on Drugs and Crime (UNODC), and the United Nations Interregional Crime and Justice Research Institute (UNICRI) launched the Global Program Against Trafficking in Human Beings (GPAT). Projects carried out within the framework of this program consist of an integrated package of policy-oriented research and assessment (bringing to the foreground the involvement of organized crime groups in the smuggling and trafficking of human beings) and targeted technical co-operation projects[2] to promote the development of effective criminal justice responses to trafficking (UNODCCP, 1999). There are currently about a dozen technical cooperation projects ongoing and several others are under preparation.[3] The GPAT project activity budget amounts to approximately

1 The author was a research expert at UNICRI and responsible for the project "Coalitions against Trafficking in Human Beings in the Philippines – Phase 1". All positions, statement of fact, opinion and analysis expressed in this chapter are those of the author and do not necessarily represent the position or views held by the United Nations Office on Drugs and Crime or the United Nations Interregional Crime and Justice Research Institute.

2 The program aims to achieve a number of objectives including providing advice on drafting and revising relevant legislation, providing advice and assistance on establishing and strengthening anti-trafficking offices and units, training law enforcement officers, prosecutors and judges, while strengthening victim and witness support and promoting awareness raising.

3 Projects in various stages of development in different regions of the world include: West Africa (Benin, Nigeria and Togo), Eastern Europe (the Czech Republic and Poland, and

US$3.5 million in 2003/2004. The assessment and research component of the pilot project, "Coalitions Against Trafficking in Human Beings in the Philippines – Phase 1" was completed in the spring of 2002, and this chapter presents its findings.

The reader will first be introduced to definitions of trafficking in human beings, smuggling of migrants and organized criminal groups (according to the definitions presented in the UN Convention against Transnational Organized Crime and its two protocols on trafficking and smuggling). Trafficking and smuggling will be placed within the larger context of illegal migration. The remainder of the chapter will focus briefly on the survey instruments and methodology and will follow with a discussion of the findings from the pilot project in the Philippines.

Defining the Phenomena

On September 29, 2003, the United Nations Convention against Transnational Organized Crime, the first international instrument of its kind against transnational organized crime, entered into force.[4] Supplementing it are the Protocol to Suppress and Punish Trafficking in Persons Especially Women and Children and the Protocol against the Smuggling of Migrants by Land, Sea and Air.[5] In line with the proposed definitions in the Convention and two Protocols, the UN GPAT uses the following definitions:

- *Organized criminal group* shall mean a structured group of three or more persons existing for a period of time and acting in concert with the aim of committing one or more serious crimes or offenses established in accordance with this Convention,[6] to obtain, directly, or indirectly, a financial or other material benefit.

Slovakia), South America (Brazil) and Asia (the Philippines and Vietnam). Projects are also under preparation in, among others, Lebanon and Columbia.

4 The Convention, adopted by the United Nations General Assembly at its Millennium meeting in November 2000 and entered into force on September 29, 2003, spells out how countries can improve cooperation on such matters as extradition, mutual legal assistance, transfer of proceedings and joint investigations. It contains provisions for victim and witness protection and shielding legal markets from infiltration by organized criminal groups. Parties to the treaty would also provide technical assistance to developing countries to help them take the necessary measures and upgrade their capacities for dealing with organized crime. The UN Convention and both protocols can be downloaded from the web at http://www.unodc.org/unodc/en/crime_cicp_signatures.html.

5 All three international instruments have entered into force. As of January 3, 2004, 147 countries had signed and 94 had ratified the Convention (entered into force on September 29 2003), 117 had signed and 76 had ratified the trafficking protocol (entered into force on December 25, 2003) and 112 had signed and 64 had ratified the smuggling protocol (entered into force on January 28, 2004).

6 "Serious crime" shall mean conduct constituting an offense punishable by a maximum deprivation of liberty of at least four years or a more serious penalty. "Structured group" shall

- *Smuggling of migrants* shall mean the procurement, in order to obtain, directly or indirectly, a financial or other material benefit, of the illegal entry of a person into a State Party of which the person is not a national or a permanent resident.
- *Trafficking in persons* shall mean the recruitment, transportation, transfer, harboring or receipt of persons, by means of the threat or use of force or other forms of coercion, of abduction, of fraud, of deception, of the abuse of power or of a position of vulnerability or of the giving or receiving of payments or benefits to achieve the consent of a person having control over another person, for the purpose of exploitation. Exploitation shall include, at a minimum, the exploitation of the prostitution of others or other forms of sexual exploitation, forced labor or services, slavery or practices similar to slavery, servitude or the removal of organs.

The trafficking definition, or the criminal act of trafficking contains three separate elements: an *action* (i.e., the recruitment, transportation, transfer, harboring or reception of persons), the *means used to commit these acts* (i.e., by threat or use of force, coercion, abduction, fraud, deception, abuse of power or vulnerability, or giving payments or benefits to a person in control of the victim), and *goals* (i.e., exploitation or for the purpose of exploitation, which includes exploiting the prostitution of others, other forms of sexual exploitation, forced labor or services, slavery or similar practices, and the removal of organs). At least one element from each of these three groups is required before the definition applies. The consent of a victim of trafficking in persons to the intended exploitation shall be irrelevant where any of the means set forth (in the definition) have been used. Further, the recruitment, transportation, transfer, harboring or receipt of a child for the purpose of exploitation shall be considered "trafficking in persons" even if this does not involve any of the means set forth in the definition.

In essence, smuggling involves the illegal movement of migrants across international borders whereas human trafficking may, but does not necessarily involve crossing international borders but by definition, *must* involve a form of coercion or deception *and* exploitation. At the core of the trafficking issue is the exploitation of the victim during the trafficking process which violates human rights doctrine. Much of the worldwide trafficking and exploitation of persons occur both within communities and countries (O'Briain 2002) as well as across country borders. It has been estimated that internal trafficking occurs with more frequency than international trafficking. As the United Nations aims to promote cooperative working relations between countries, and views internal trafficking as a serious, yet

---

mean a group that is not randomly formed for the immediate commission of an offense and that does not need to have formally defined roles for its members, continuity of its membership or a developed structure.

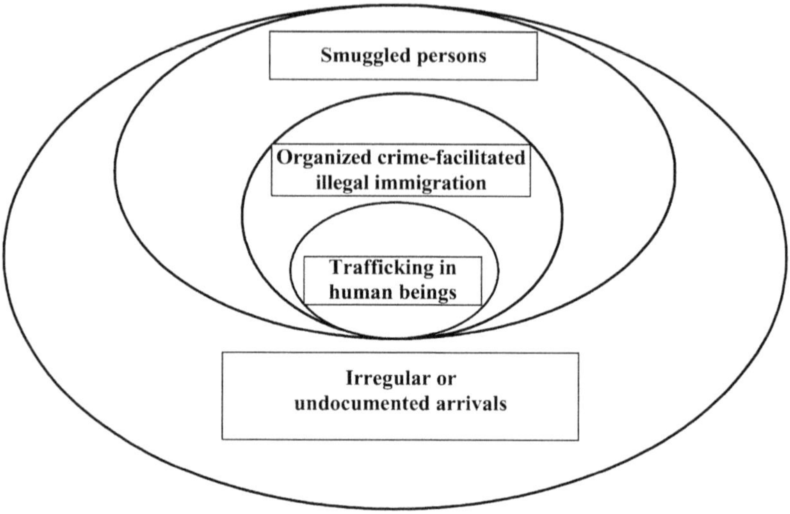

Figure 9.1 The relationship between smuggling, trafficking and the role of organized criminal groups in these activities

domestic problem, the UN GPAT is concerned with the phenomenon of cross-border trafficking.[7]

While smuggling and trafficking share some similarities, there are distinct differences.[8] Figure 9.1 illustrates how these two offenses are related with respect to illegal migration. Within the broader realm of irregular or undocumented arrivals, persons may enter a country either with fraudulent documentation or have been smuggled into the country with no documentation whatsoever. Migrants entering a country illegally sometimes may be aided by individuals, relatives or acquaintances, whereas in other instances organized criminal groups may be active in the smuggling of migrants into destination countries. A percentage of those having entered a country illegally aided by organized criminal groups are trafficked. When one examines the group of trafficked victims, a large part of this group is aided, or exploited by organized criminal groups from the point of recruitment in the source country to exploitation in the transit and destination country.

There are cases reported of men who recruit "wives" either personally or through marriage bureaus and who later force these women into prostitution. If they are operating alone, they would fall outside the realm of organized criminal trafficking. A percentage of trafficked victims also enter the destination country legally on a tourist, study or spousal visa procured or aided by (organized) traffickers who

7 An important element is the involvement of transnational organized crime groups in this offense. The UN seeks to promote working relationships between countries to fight organized crime's involvement in transnational offenses.

8 For a more in-depth discussion on trafficking in persons and smuggling of migrants see Aronowitz (2001).

promise jobs. Despite their legal entry into the country, they are still under the control of organized criminal groups and must pay off a debt incurred prior to departure. When the legitimate visa expires, their illegal status is used against them as leverage making them susceptible to exploitation. The relationships between and among illegal migration, smuggling, organized criminal groups' facilitation of illegal migration and trafficking in human beings is portrayed in Figure 9.1.

The UN GPAT Pilot Project: "Coalitions Against Trafficking in Human Beings in the Philippines – Phase 1"

This study comprises six research projects carried out in the Philippines, Japan, Malaysia, Italy and Australia.[9] Researchers interviewed victims, representatives from NGOs and criminal justice experts. Case files and government data were analyzed in the Philippines and Italy. The objective of the study is to improve the existing level of information on trafficking in human beings from the Philippines for the purpose of providing a tool for better policy planning and action. The aims of the study are five-fold:

1. identify the trafficking flows from the Philippines to various destination countries;
2. describe trafficking patterns to include *modus operandi* of recruitment, use of fraudulent documents, costs and debt, transportation, deception, coercion and exploitation;
3. provide information on the involvement of organized crime groups in the trafficking of human beings from the Philippines;
4. provide information on victims' reporting patterns and (their assessment of) government responses; and
5. identify NGO services to trafficked victims and their assessment of what further measures must be taken.

Research Methodology and Samples

UNICRI, with the assistance of local research teams and researchers from the Australian Institute of Criminology, designed four survey instruments: a victim survey, a questionnaire for criminal justice and government experts, a checklist for

---

9 Two studies were carried out in the Philippines – one involving NGOs (non-governmental organizations) and trafficked victims, the other examining government experts and case files. In Japan and Malaysia researchers conducted victim interviews and obtained information and data from government officials. Studies were more limited in Italy and Australia where researchers provided government statistics on illegal entrants and trafficked Filipinos (Australia) and analyzed Philippine government data on illegal migration and the contents of Italian prosecution department data of an extensive international smuggling ring from the Philippines to Italy.

the analysis of case files, and an NGO survey. As much as possible, the questionnaires contained closed-ended questions to facilitate coding and analysis. In almost all questions the option "other" allowed respondents to give answers that were not provided in the categories offered. The research instruments were used with varying degrees of success in different countries (see Aronowitz 2002 for more information on the methodology and problems encountered during data collection).

Trafficking victims in the Philippines and Japan were initially identified by and approached with the assistance of NGOs and shelters, which in turn constituted the sample for the NGO survey in the Philippines. In Malaysia, owing to the fact that there are no NGOs servicing migrants or trafficked victims in Sabah, the researchers relied upon key informants working in an entertainment center employing Filipinas, who facilitated contact with the women. In total, 77 persons were interviewed (Philippines n=29, Japan n=19, Malaysia n=29). The data from three women who made multiple trips were recorded into seven incidents, bringing the number of trafficking incidents to 85. In addition, researchers in all three countries conducted formal and informal interviews with 34 criminal justice and government experts. Researchers in Italy (n=1) and the Philippines (n=32) conducted evaluations on 33 case files, and case file data in the Philippines provided limited data on an additional 123 victims. Information was also obtained on 20 NGOs providing services to migrants and trafficked victims in the Philippines.

Findings

Demographics of Trafficked Victims

Of the 75 persons interviewed in the Philippines, Japan and Malaysia, all but two were women; this may be attributed to the fact that the study largely focused on exploitation in the sex industry.[10] Another possibility is that women are more willing than men to seek the assistance of NGOs.[11] While the age at the time of interview varied widely, most women at the time of their first departure to work abroad were in their early 20s (21–2 years). The Philippines, Japan and Malaysia studies indicated that eight girls were under the age of 18 at the time they first left the Philippines to work abroad.

The Philippines and Japan victim data demonstrate that women make multiple trips abroad and generally stay for short periods of time. Of the 48 women in Japan

10 Had research activities been extended to labor exploitation in factories, farms or other sectors in which men are more commonly employed, there may have been a higher percentage of male trafficked victims identified. In fact, the two male trafficked victims were exploited as farm workers.

11 Statistics involving smuggled persons show more of a gender balance, as was substantiated by the case files provided by the "District Anti-Mafia Investigation Division" of the Trieste Prosecution office.

and the Philippines sample, 29 (60 percent) had traveled abroad more than once.[12] 17 women (22 percent of the sample) had made three or more trips abroad (one respondent traveled abroad seven times, one traveled abroad eight times). The Malaysia sample, however, deviated from this pattern. At the time of the interview in Malaysia, all victims had been abroad only once, and were, on average, younger than the victims in the Philippines and Japan sample.

An examination of the entire sample of 85 responses indicates that in 57 cases (67 percent), victims spent between one and 11 months abroad. It appears that this short time frame, often as short as three to four months, is linked to the work contract. When the contract is finished, the women return to the Philippines. However, it must also be noted that 11 persons (13 percent) had spent more than 48 months in the destination country. Of these, the large majority (8) were still in Japan.

Recruitment Practices

All of the victims in the study left the Philippines willingly. Violence or kidnapping was never associated with departure from the Philippines. Contact with the recruiters was often facilitated through intermediaries known to the victim. A large majority in both the Philippines victim and Japan study (n=43 or 77 percent) were contacted through intermediaries that included family members, friends and/or acquaintances known to the respondent or the family.[13] This was often accomplished through word of mouth. In both studies a large number (n=15) were also contacted through job agencies, and a small number were recruited by formerly smuggled or trafficked persons. Of the 56 respondents (in the Philippines victim and Japan studies), almost half (n=27) were recruited at home or within the vicinity of the neighborhood/ community. Some (n=12) were recruited in their place of work, while others were recruited at a bar/restaurant/hotel (n=10). The recruitment stage is thus a crucial point in the trafficking/smuggling process in that it reflects the extent to which the victim trusts the recruiter, and this is certainly the case when family members, friends or acquaintances facilitate the contact.

The majority (n=68 or 80 percent) of the 85 instances of recruitment (in the Philippines victim survey and the studies in Japan and Malaysia), stated that they were sought out by the recruiter. In 14 other instances, the respondents sought out the recruiter; and in Malaysia, 3 women responded to advertisements. Criminal justice experts in the Philippines reported that the recruiters are often women. The initial recruitment is often done by Filipinos or in some cases married couples where the recruiter is a Filipina and the husband, a national of the country to which the women will eventually be sent. The final selection is often done by nationals who run the clubs and travel to the Philippines for the selection of the women.

---

12 These statistics are roughly the same if one examines the number of multiple trips made by the Japan and Philippines samples separately.

13 15 of 19 respondents in Japan and 28 of 37 responses in the Philippines victim survey. Data was not provided in the Malaysia study.

Routes and Experiences During the Travel

According to government experts in the Philippines, about 71 percent of smuggled and trafficked persons are transported by air, through regular commercial flights, and 29 percent by sea, ranging from big sea vessels to small fishing boats. On average, trips by air, from point of departure in the Philippines to arrival in the destination country, lasted a matter of hours and were generally restricted to the flight and possible transportation by car or van if the final destination was a city or town other than the point of arrival. Victims were not exposed to dangerous situations, other than the risk of getting caught with fraudulent documentation. The same cannot be said of those persons traveling by small boat via the "Southern Backdoor" to Malaysia, who, on occasion, experienced dangerous situations.

Data from Philippine government case files and victim surveys in the Philippines on 160 persons, indicate that Korea is the top destination country (n=87 or 54 percent of the sample), followed by Malaysia (n=26 or 16 percent), Japan (n=23 or 14 percent), Nigeria (n=10 or 6 percent) and Abidjan, Côte d'Ivoire (n=5 or 3 percent). The remaining 9 persons in the Philippines victims survey traveled to: Hong Kong (3), Saudi Arabia (2), Saipan (2), Bahrain (1) and Kuwait (1).

Little information on transit countries is available as many of the victims flew directly to Japan or traveled directly to Malaysia by plane or boat. The Japan, Malaysia and Philippine victim studies indicate that there were no long stays, abuse or exploitation in the transit countries. The amount of time spent in a country indicates that the "transit countries" were stopovers on a long flight. There is no indication that the women spent any significant amount of time in the countries, as the women were often traveling with a work contract. According to government experts in the Philippines, the most commonly used transit points for those exiting the Philippines are Bangkok, Hong Kong, and Kuala Lumpur. According to the government case files in the Philippines, those traveling to Korea often pass through Bangkok or Hong Kong before going to Korea.

There appears to be internal movement (often from the place of recruitment to the place of departure) and longer stays within the Philippines prior to departure. This varies from a few days to weeks. This may have to do with the "training" that women often undergo prior to departure.[14] Safe houses are sometimes used in the Philippines during the training session and in the destination country once the women have arrived and begun their employment. While in transit, women often stay in (luxury) hotels. Once in the destination country, a different pattern emerges and women are often controlled and guarded in their residences. In the Japan study, three women were kept in safe houses in the Philippines only, while six were kept in safe houses in both the Philippines and Japan. An additional four were kept in safe houses in Japan only. All 26 women working in the entertainment center in Sabah, Malaysia were guarded in their quarters and escorted to and from work.

14 The training often involves lessons in singing and dancing, leading the women to believe that they will be employed as entertainers in the destination country.

Use of Fraudulent Documents

Philippine government experts were able to provide estimated costs for the procurement of various (fraudulent) documents to specific destinations. For a passport, visa and related documentary requirements, the purchaser could expect to pay:[15] USA (US$3,000–6,000), Europe (Schengen visa) (US$4,000), Italy (residence permit) (US$5,000), Japan (US$3,000), Korea (US$400). Australian experts also provided data on the cost of fraudulent documents. A visitor visa application with a package of false documents may range from PhP50,000 (US$1,000) to PhP200,000 (US$4,000) (including airfare); a fraudulent Filipino passport (photo-substituted) may sell for between US$2,000 and US$4,000; counterfeit passports from other countries are more expensive, e.g., US$10,000-US$20,000. Filipinas trafficked to Japan paid varying amounts for the fraudulent documents, but generally the price ranged between US$300 and US$2,000.[16]

Of the total number of trips abroad (n=56) in the Japan and Philippines victim survey, a large majority of the sample (n=40 or 71 percent) reported using false documentation.[17] As persons sometimes reported using more than one form of fraudulent documentation (passport as well as supporting documentation to obtain the passport), the number of fraudulent documents used (n=51) exceeds the number of individuals claiming to have used them. Two persons reported using fake passports, while the majority (n=28) reported using tampered passports. The remainder (n=23) used various forms of supporting documentation that included tampered birth certificates, false marriage certificates, and police/National Bureau of Intelligence clearance or legal capacity to marry. It is unclear whether persons claimed to use a false passport because the passport was based on false documentation.[18]

While the data, with respect to the use of fraudulent documents was sometimes difficult to interpret, it is clear from this research that forged and tampered documents are being used to generate huge profits for the networks that produce them. Recognizing this, the Philippine government Department of Foreign Affairs

---

15 Figures are approximations and were provided in Philippine pesos. The peso is valued at approximately PhP50 to US$1.

16 According to a Filipino community worker from an NGO in Japan, there is substantial illicit trade in passports. A "low interest loan" scam has been designed to secure passports. Tagalog advertisements have been placed in the Filipino community newspaper in Japan, advertising "low interest" loans. To secure a loan, applicants must leave their passport with the lender, and advise them of the approximate amount of time it will take to repay the loan. The community worker suggested that the loan scheme is run by the Yakuza, and that while the passports are held, they are used to get Filipino women into Japan, and to assist over-stayers to leave. Japanese immigration officials also believe this to be the case.

17 Some individuals used legitimate documentation to enter the country, while others, traveling to Malaysia from the Southern Philippines did not use any type of documentation.

18 It may be that the passports are legal and legitimate but incorrect because they are based upon inaccurate information in the supporting documents.

has pursued a rigorous campaign against passport irregularities and has introduced the use of machine-readable passports and visas (Paredes-Maceda 2000).

Costs and Debts

Most of the respondents incurred a debt to the recruiter or smuggler. Of the total (n=85) number of incidents in the three victim studies, 74 persons (87 percent) incurred a debt to the smugglers/traffickers, while 8 "paid everything upfront", 1 incurred a debt to the family and 2 did not incur a debt in the Japan study, but were subjected to other forms of leverage which prevented them from leaving. Debts and upfront fees varied considerably. One of the determining factors is the destination country. Government officials in the Philippines report that cost for travel or recruitment services to developed countries are higher than to developing ones. Costs also vary according to distance, and payment for travel/job placement in Europe is much higher than that in Asian countries. Costs per selected country (which often includes procurement of fraudulent travel documents, passport and entry visas) are estimated at: USA and Canada (US$4,000–8,000), Australia, Italy (US$2,000–5,000), other European destinations (US$2,000–6,000), Japan (US$1,000–3,000), Korea (US$400–2,000), Malaysia (US$20–160).

In the Malaysia study, trafficked victims paid approximately RM4,500 (US$1,185 for the cost of transportation and job placement, and this was then deducted from the monthly salary of the women after they assumed work. The three women who were smuggled into Sabah from the Southern Philippines paid between PhP7,000 (US$140) and PhP9,900 (US$200). A senior law enforcement officer in Sabah estimated, based on investigations involving 2,710 women that, in general, Filipino women were indebted by between RM3,300 (US$870) and RM4,500 (US$1,185) for their travel and job placement. The difference between that paid "only" to be smuggled, and the debt incurred when a woman is promised a job is clearly seen in these figures.

It is difficult to determine exactly what this debt comprises. Prices may fluctuate due to cash advances made to the victim's family, the procurement of fraudulent documents or payments for safe houses or hotels. Other additional costs are arbitrary. It is therefore difficult to determine exactly how much money is paid separately for fraudulent documents since the price quoted is often for the "entire package" and includes both airfare and work placement. Further, it is also unclear exactly when debts are paid and women are free to leave. After the initial debt has been paid, the women are often charged additional costs for housing, transportation, drug use (often forced upon the victims) or payment to corrupt police officials.

Deception and Exploitation

Victims of trafficking are deceived about a number of things prior to their departure from the Philippines. These include deception in terms of the nature and conditions of work, living conditions, salary and allowances and debt. Government case file analysis in the Philippines reveal that 117 persons (95 percent) complained of being deceived about the nature of the work, such as being told that they would perform as entertainers or work as hotel chambermaids, in restaurants or bars, when in reality they ended up working in the sex industry. Similarly, over 97 percent of the sample (n=120) were deceived about their working conditions, such as having to maintain a quota of customers and drinks, work long hours, clean up the club after work, pay bar fines and work when they were sick.

Half complained of deception with regards to salary and allowances (i.e., no salary, salary less that what was promised or paid late, extensive deductions), while a small percentage (12 percent) complained of inadequate living conditions (inadequate food supply, small space, etc.) and other human rights violations (locked up, guarded, no medication when sick). The government case file data is supported by the victim studies as well. In Japan, 15 women (80 percent of the sample) complained about being deceived about the nature of the work, while 14 complained about deception involving the conditions of work. Other complaints involved deception about the destination countries (n=4), immigration rules in destination countries (n=3) or living conditions in destination countries (n=3).

Analysis of government case files in the Philippines indicates that of 123 cases involving victims, 15 persons were promised work which did not materialize, two women were forced to become hostesses, and the remaining 115 women were promised jobs, many as waitresses and entertainers, but ended up in a position which often required nudity or forced prostitution. Similarly, the Japanese study revealed that while a large number of the women (11) were promised jobs in restaurants or bars, the majority (17) ended up working as sex workers. In addition, all 26 victims working as sex workers in the club in Sabah, Malaysia were promised jobs as cashiers in supermarkets. The picture was similar in the Philippines victims' survey. Women were offered jobs in the "entertainment" sector (as dancers, singers, strippers) and many were forced into sexual contacts with customers. Only two women in the Philippine victim survey reported knowing that they would work as prostitutes prior to departure from the Philippines.

Coercion and Violence

Coercion, similar to deception, took on a number of forms. This varied from threats to stop payment to the victim's family, threats to report the victims to immigration officials, the seizure of the victim's documents, non-payment of wages, to threats against the victim's family, threats and the use of physical and sexual violence against the victim. Exploitation and coercion invariably occurred in the destination country, although victims' movements were sometimes restricted in the Philippines prior to departure.

Physical violence was directed solely against the women, and never at their families. In a limited number of cases, however, threats were made against the victim's family. In the Japan study, threats were made to withhold payments to the victims' families (n=4). In two cases, the women reported that their husbands threatened to take away their children. Coercion against the victim ranged from moderate, involving the confiscation of passports and travel documents (reported by most victims in the Philippines, Japan and Malaysia studies), to more severe forms.

In the Philippines victim study, 23 women were the victims of actual physical or sexual violence, while four more were the victims of threats and seven were restrained against their will. It is not clear from the interviews whether or not the women were victimized by traffickers, club owners or customers. Women in the Japan study (n=12) reported being threatened with violence by smugglers/traffickers in Japan. Eight reported that their smugglers/traffickers had been physically violent, while seven reported sexual violence by their smugglers/traffickers. Five reported restricted movement and reported restricted communication and confinement. Employers in Japan exercised the most frequent use of physical violence against the victims. 13 women reported having experienced physical violence while five respondents reported having been the victim of sexual violence (four of these were also victims of physical violence). Physical violence was not used to control the women in Malaysia, however, their freedom of movement was restricted and they lived in constant fear of being reported to immigration authorities.

It is clear from this study that women are held, manipulated, controlled, threatened and physically and sexually harmed during at least their initial period in the destination country. This period is directly tied to the debt that they incur for the journey to the destination country and the work provided. It appears from the Japan, Malaysia and Philippines victim surveys that original debts are usually paid off within three to six months. After that period, many restrictions are lifted and some of the women are free to leave, while others are further exploited and indebted (for drugs they may have been forced to use at the club, forced payment to police officers to avoid arrest and deportation, rent, food, housing, etc.) and must continue working for the club. This is perhaps the pivotal point between women who continue to remain in debt bondage as trafficked victims and those who are free to leave but choose to continue working, albeit under inhumane and exploitative conditions, to support their families back in the Philippines.

Involvement of Organized Crime

Based upon the definition put forth in the United Nations Convention against Transnational Organized Crime and the Philippines, Japanese, Malaysian and Italian studies, organized crime groups have been involved in the smuggling and trafficking of Filipinos to these destination countries. Since a large majority of those interviewed report that foreigners are working together with Filipinos in the recruitment process it appears that the trafficking groups are multi-ethnic and international. These foreigners are generally from the destination country. However, it is not uncommon for other foreign nationals, to also work together with those from and in the destination country. This was documented in the Philippines, Malaysia, Japan and Italy studies.

In the Japan study, in 12 of 17 cases (70 percent), Filipinos worked closely with Japanese in the Philippines.[19] This data, supported by the data from the Philippines victim study shows that once in Japan, it was more common for the Japanese to work predominantly with other Japanese. In a few cases, the Japanese worked with Filipinos or more often with Koreans. When they were joined by other ethnic groups, these were Chinese, Taiwanese and in one instance, American. In the majority of trafficking cases to Malaysia, those working in Malaysia were Malaysian-Chinese or Indonesians working together with Chinese. Two victims in Malaysia claimed that they were exploited by Filipinos (only) but this seems to be the exception rather than the rule.

According to the Australian study, facilitators in the Philippines appear to exist as loose networks of individuals, who have some level of association and may refer clients to each other for particular services, but who do not work as closely linked groups. The Italy and Malaysia study, as well as information provided by Philippines criminal justice experts categorize these groups as small networks comprised of fewer than 10 persons. At most stages of the process (recruitment, documentation, transport and settlement), the majority of individuals (in the Philippine victim survey) came into contact with only one to two persons.

In the Japan study, the majority of victims came into contact at different stages of the trafficking process with a group of three to five persons. When victims came into contact with a larger group of more than five persons, it was always at the settlement phase. The criminal justice expert in Japan claims that the Yakuza operate regionally, prefecturally or even smaller, however most Yakuza groups are somehow connected in a wider regional or even national level. According to Philippine criminal justice experts, all the Japanese groups are in some way or another connected to their counterparts in the Philippines or elsewhere in the world from where they import goods and persons. In major cities like Manila and Cebu, they station a branch or "representative office" at the same time.

The operation of the entertainment industry in Japan is said to be in the hands of the Japanese Yakuza. It appears to be highly organized (with rotation of women between cities and clubs). The Yakuza has been linked to excessive violence, drug and gun smuggling and appears to operate on a different scale than that seen in the Philippines. The fact that threats and violence perpetrated against the victims occurs almost exclusively in the destination country – not in the Philippines – points to a more acceptable use of violence among the Japanese organized crime groups than among the Filipinos operating in the Philippines.[20]

---

19 The Japanese criminal justice expert asserted that Japanese and Filipino crime networks frequently work together to traffic Filipino women, with the initiative being taken by Japanese groups.

20 A Japanese criminal justice expert had the following comment about the criminal networks operating in Japan:

> It is rare that a criminal organization has less than 5 members. There are small ones with around 10, and bigger ones. The organization of the "underground world" is not so visible, so it is hard to determine the exact number of members involved. Some members have

The criminal networks tend to move their recruits in groups. While only 9 (34 percent) of the 56 respondents from the Philippines and in Japan were moved individually, 37 (66 percent) were moved in groups. Of those interviewed in the Philippines, the majority traveled in groups of four to 10 persons (n=13) followed by groups of two to three persons (n=7). Four respondents going to Malaysia by boat claimed they were moved in groups of more than 20 persons. All of the victims interviewed, working in the entertainment sector in Malaysia, were also moved in groups ranging from eight to 15 persons.

Once in the destination country, respondents were sometimes rotated between clubs, cities or club owners/criminal groups. In Japan, 12 respondents were rotated between clubs within the same city, while nine women were rotated between different cities or towns. Five respondents reported being rotated between different criminal groups. In the Philippines victim survey, 12 women reported being rotated between different clubs, two reported being rotated between locations and one reported being rotated between criminal groups. No rotation occurred in the Malaysia study, which may be due to the fact that women were arrested and deported before they could be rotated. This appears to be a common practice in the sex industry but was not reported by those victims in the Philippines who worked in the domestic service sector.

Almost all women (27 of 29 respondents in the Philippines victim survey and 17 of 19 in the Japan study) reported that they were aware of other women who had been trafficked by the same group responsible for their own trafficking. The number of women ranges from a few to dozens. This points to either a large operation, or a stable one which has been in existence for an extended period of time.

In sum, this analysis highlights the role of highly organized criminal groups or those operating with (extensive) extended networks. Indications of this are that the criminal organizations were comprised of different ethnic groups, often moved victims in groups and under supervision or escort, had recruited numerous victims and were able to rotate women between clubs, cities or criminal groups. Based upon the number of persons with whom the victims came into contact during the various stages of the process, it appears that groups are small in size, but that these groups work together to help each other out. This hypothesis has been supported by the UNICRI data analyzing the smuggling of Filipinos into Italy.[21]

---

legitimate faces as corporate presidents, entertainment business owners or even politicians. Some others, who may own *pachinko* parlors for instance, are resident Koreans in Japan (*zainichi*). Unlike some decades ago, the loyalty and organizational discipline within such organizations have become loose. Some subordinates do not anymore obey their leader. While certain respect is still observed, one such discipline is not to harm ordinary citizens; the younger members may betray the boss (*oyabun*). (Cameron and Newman 2002)

21 The core of these two groups consisted of Filipino family members. There were, however, Slovenian and Pakistani smuggling groups involved in transporting the Filipinos from Hungary to Italy. Due to their involvement in smuggling other nationalities into Italy as well, this smuggling operation was quite international and sophisticated in terms of widespread contacts.

Connivance and Corruption

Since the majority of persons depart from the Philippines through international airports, the collusion of officials at points of departure could enhance opportunities for smuggling and trafficking. Heightened government control, on the other hand, could diminish opportunities. The role government officials play is therefore crucial in either facilitating or repressing smuggling and trafficking of persons. Respondents (n=48 from the Philippines victim and Japan survey) were asked if they came into contact with corrupt government officials during their departure from the Philippines and stay in the destination country. 30 (62.5 percent) reported having had contact with corrupt officials in the Philippines. As women reported contact with individuals from more than one agency, the number of government agencies identified as colluding or conspiring to smuggle and traffic (n=57) exceeds the number of victims who reported such activity (n=30). Numerous reports identified corrupt practices of Bureau of Immigration officials at Manila international airport (n=27) or airport personnel (n=3).

A number of points must be noted about these data. The interviews did not delve deeply into the specifics of these accusations. In many instances, particularly regarding the accusation of the Bureau of Immigration, women claimed that officers had "escorted" them through or had allowed them to pass control check points with fraudulent documentation. Of those women interviewed in the Philippines, many had left and returned to the country years earlier. The Bureau of Immigration has, over the years, taken numerous steps to thwart these practices. These include the removal of numbers from immigration counters, prohibiting the use of pagers, beepers or cellular phones and declaring restaurants near the airport known to be contact places for smugglers and traffickers "off limits" to immigration personnel.

The responses of the victims to claims of government collusion in the destination country are quite interesting. In the Japan study, three women claimed that the Japanese police notified the women of an impending raid so that those working without legal papers were not present.[22] The Malaysia report also identified police collusion/corruption at two levels:

> Senior officers in collusion with syndicates are provided with regular financial payments and free access to drinks as well as sexual services of women in the entertainment centers. Lower ranking personnel are not party to these arrangements and attempt to get their share through direct extortion of the women themselves through regular harassment with the threat of arrest and detention. (Wong and Saat, 2002)

The report cites three different incidents where women were told by club owners to provide sexual services to men identified as "police officers". In a fourth incident in

22 At the same time, the Japan study also reports police raids and the closure of clubs, not for trafficking or commercial sexual exploitation of women, but for employing illegal aliens. The women were often arrested, detained and then deported.

which a woman refused, a payment was made to the police by the club owner to have her released, after which she incurred a debt.

It is clear from the research that there are isolated cases of individual officers colluding with smugglers and traffickers. It is also clear from discussions with high-ranking officers from the Philippines Bureau of Immigration that the organization recognizes the problem and is currently taking steps to address it. Perhaps in the destination countries, the problem lies as much with the failure to recognize the situation and treat the women as trafficked victims, as it does with collusion with the traffickers.

Criminal Justice Responses

Respondents in the Philippines and Japan victim surveys were quite pessimistic about the monitoring of labor recruiters and travel agencies/immigration consultants. 25 (52 percent) of the 48 respondents in the sample found government regulation of labor recruiters to be non-existent while another 4 (29 percent) found the regulation insufficient. Eight respondents (17 percent) did not know and one thought the regulation was intensive. A similar pattern emerges with the victims' assessment of government regulation of travel agencies. 31 persons (65 percent) found regulation to be non-existent or insufficient while a large number, 16, did not know.

A special "illegal recruitment branch" within the Philippines Overseas Employment Agency (POEA), along with other enforcement agencies in the Philippines, investigates illegal recruitment. Statistics demonstrate that between 1997 and 2001, the POEA assisted and filed between 400 and 579 cases per year for preliminary investigation. While the number of cases has fluctuated, the number of victims involved in the cases has increased dramatically each year from 895 in 1997 to 1605 in 2001.[23] In short, while the number of cases remains relatively stable, the recruitment agencies have become increasingly successful in recruiting more victims. The number of surveillance missions carried out by POEA has also increased from 299 in 1998 to 544 in 2001. Disappointingly, however, the number of suspects arrested and persons convicted has declined. It appears that despite increased government awareness of and attention to the problem, criminals are becoming more successful at evading arrest and prosecution.

Victim Reporting Practices

Only seven persons (out of n=48) reported their victimization experiences to government authorities, and five of these women in Japan filed reports with the Philippines embassy. The remaining 41 persons (85 percent) gave multiple reasons for not reporting their experiences to government authorities: victims do not trust the authorities (n=18), the authorities will not or cannot help (n=13), the victim (n=7)

23 Statistics on cases filed for preliminary investigation. Information obtained directly from the POEA.

or victim's family (n=5) was threatened with violence, or the promise was made to smuggle the victim again (n=3). Other individual responses were given as well.[24] No victims in Japan reported their case to the Japanese authorities. Reasons for failure to report their experience include threats of violence from traffickers (n=5), lack of trust in the authorities (n=6) or the belief that the authorities cannot or will not help the victim (n=3), the promise to be smuggled again (n=2). The inability to speak Japanese was also cited by two women. A large number of those not reporting, feared contact with government officials due to their illegal status and the fear of deportation (n=6). If governments in destination countries are concerned about protecting victims of violence and exploitation and with prosecuting traffickers and exploiters, they must make it possible for victims to come forward without the fear of being arrested, detained and deported. A change in attitude and laws could greatly facilitate this.

What is clear from this study is that while victims may be hesitant to report to the embassy or authorities in the destination country, many victims do turn to NGOs for support, whether in the destination country or after having returned to the Philippines. It is critical, in terms of providing victims with necessary counseling, support and protection, that these services are available in both the destination country as well as in the Philippines for repatriated persons. If victims truly mistrust government agencies, it is essential that government agencies support and work closely with NGOs in terms of victim outreach.

Summary

This United Nations pilot project on trafficking in human beings in the Philippines, combining information from six studies, has identified certain trends in different phases of the process. One is the use of tampered and fraudulent documents. This indicates that there is a need for improved training of immigration officials, particularly at border crossings, and high-tech instruments to detect fraudulent and tampered documents at departure and entrance points, namely international airports. Eradication of corruption within police and immigration services is essential to tackling the problem of human trafficking. Second, it appears from the studies that relatives, friends and acquaintances facilitate contact with recruiters. Prevention projects designed for alerting persons to the dangers of illegal recruitment and illicit work abroad should therefore be directed at the families of these prospective migrants, as well as the population at risk. Awareness-raising campaigns pointing out the danger of illegal migration must reach the general population.

---

24 Another did not know where to ask for help while another victim had no more money (perhaps assuming that it would cost her money just to report to the authorities). Another simply discounted or ignored her experience and thought it was not necessary to report to the authorities. Another was simply relieved to be back in the Philippines. One was afraid of experiencing even more discrimination while one was bribed not to speak. One was ashamed and another was traumatized by her experience abroad.

Third, some form of organization or network appears to be behind the trafficking of Filipinos to various destination countries. While recruitment appears to occur on an almost informal basis, once the women reach the destination country their treatment changes and coercion, threats and violence, seldom experienced in the Philippines, becomes a prevalent practice. Human rights violations vary from long working hours and poor working conditions to physical violence and rape. Groups are comprised of different nationalities working together; Filipinos are often involved in recruiting, while nationalities from the destination countries are involved in the exploitation of victims. The groups, while small, appear to have more extensive networks and those involved in the sex industry rotate victims between clubs and cities.

Finally, a fourth dominant theme is that victims rarely turned to government agencies to report their victimization. Victims reported that government agencies were unsympathetic to their plight and that they often felt that the government would not or could not aid their situation. As long as victims fear arrest, deportation and harm from traffickers, it is almost impossible to gain their trust and cooperation in prosecuting traffickers. Their trust in NGOs is apparent, which calls for continued financial support of NGOs, and a closer working relationship between NGOs and government authorities, in both source and destination countries. This is particularly true when it comes to front-line police officers who must be able to refer victims to NGOs or shelters for services.

Recommendations

In March 2002, UNICRI, with the assistance of the Philippines National Police Commission and the United Nations Development Program organized a two-day expert meeting in Manila attended by the research teams, governmental and NGO delegates from the Philippines, Malaysia and Japan. Based upon the findings in this study and the expert meeting, the following recommendations are offered to counter trafficking in human beings and provide protection to its victims:

1. Adoption of or revision of legislation conforming to the definitions put forth in the UN Protocol to Prevent, Suppress and Punish Trafficking in Persons, especially Women and Children supplementing the United Nations Convention against Transnational Organized Crime, to go beyond the offense of sexual exploitation and include forced and indentured labor as well as the trade in organs.
2. The introduction of "sensitization programs" into training courses for immigration and law enforcement officials and prosecutors to sensitize them to the seriousness of trafficking offenses and the status of victims, and also help front-line officers to identify potential victims.
3. The appointment of government experts or focal points in various agencies to improve investigation of cases, protection of victims and prosecution of offenders; the organization of a governmental inter-agency or inter-ministerial

body comprising various ministries and perhaps representatives from NGOs and IGOs.

4. Continued government funding of and cooperation with NGOs; services should include improved legal as well as litigation services; psycho-social and welfare services and on-site protection.
5. Law enforcement agencies in destination countries should offer (telephonic) translation services to encourage victims to report cases of trafficking and exploitation; the government in these countries should fund such police translation services.
6. Government recognition and protection of trafficked victims; prohibiting the repatriation (deportation) of victims until their safety can be guaranteed.
7. Governments should examine the role that corruption and collusion plays in the trafficking and exploitation process and more closely monitor enforcement and immigration officials; improved technology at immigration check-points, in particular, international airports.
8. Governments should provide resources to develop or expand databases containing information on (but not be limited to) destination countries, cities and specific clubs, offenders, organized criminal groups and *modus operandi* with respect to the recruitment, trafficking and exploitation of migrant workers and trafficked victims; data should be made available on a need-be basis to other government agencies as well as agencies in other (source, transit and destination) countries.

Conclusion

Interpol calls trafficking in human beings "the fastest growing type of crime" in the world. According to the United Nations, it has boomed into a $7 billion global business (Sulavic 2003) and human trafficking is now the world's third largest business, victimizing hundreds of thousands of women and children each year" (Kassman 2003). According to the US Department of State, "at least 700,000 persons, especially women and children, are trafficked each year across international borders. Some observers estimate that the number may be significantly higher" (US Department of State, 2001 2002).

The situation in the Philippines is not unique. In countries all over the world, individuals in the sex industry and workers in other sectors are exploited and subjected to various forms of coercion and violence.[25] Most victims never come

25 Reports on trafficked victims in various areas of the world can be referenced or accessed from the websites of different organizations, among them, the International Labor Organization (ILO), United Nations International Childrens Educational Fund (UNICEF), International Organization for Migration (IOM), Office of the United Nations High Commission for Human Rights (OHCHR), Human Rights Watch and Organization for Security and Cooperation in Europe (OSCE). Various local, national and regional NGOs have also published extensively on the topic.

to the attention of government officials and social service providers. Those who do seek assistance are often in need of protection from traffickers, mental health care and legal assistance, financial and resettlement support (Tigno 2001). NGOs and governments in both source and destination countries must recognize the plight of and provide support to victims while investing resources in apprehending and punishing the offenders. It must be a concerted effort on the parts of victims, NGOs and government agencies working together at different levels extending across source, transit and destination countries.

The eradication of trafficking in persons requires measures to be implemented in less developed source countries so that individuals do not (need to) put themselves in high-risk situations to migrate at any cost. Governments and organizations must invest in education, job training and creation of work opportunities, while efforts must be made to address the root causes of trafficking, including poverty, inequality, discrimination and racism (Robinson 2000).

References

Aronowitz, A. A. (2001), "Smuggling and Trafficking in Human Beings: The Phenomenon, The Markets That Drive It and the Organizations That Promote It", *European Journal on Criminal Policy and Research*, 9(2): 163–95.

Aronowitz, A. A. (2002), "The United Nations Global Programme Against Trafficking in Human Beings: Research and Lessons Learned", *International Journal of Comparative and Applied Criminal Justice*, 26(2): 257–76.

Cameron, S. and E. Newman (2002), *Research on Trafficking Victims and Governmental Sources in Japan*, United Nations University (UNU), unpublished report submitted to the United Nations Interregional Crime and Justice Research Institute, Turin, Italy.

Kassman L. (2003), "UN: Human Trafficking Third Largest Criminal Business", *Voice of America News*, October 1, 2003, Stop-Traffic, October 5, 2003.

O'Briain, M. (2002), "The Contribution of the Protocol on Trafficking in Human Beings", paper presented at the symposium, "The United Nations Convention against Transnational Organized Crime: Requirements for its Effective Implementation", Turin, February 22–3.

Paredes-Maceda, C. (2000), "Prevention of Trafficking, Protection and Rehabilitation of Victims", Asia-Pacific Symposium on Trafficking in Persons, January 20.

Robinson, M. (2000), "Presentation by Mary Robinson, United Nations High Commissioner for Human Rights" (read by Justice PN Bhagwati) in *Asia-Pacific Symposium on Trafficking in Persons (proceedings)*, Ministry of Foreign Affairs, Japan, January 20, 2000.

Sulavic, C., (2003), "Facing Down Traffickers: Europe Takes on its Fastest-Growing Criminal Enterprise", *Newsweek International*, August 25–September 1, at http://www.msnbc.com/news/953515.asp, received by email from the Protection Project <Protection_Project@jhu.edu>, August 25, 2003.

Tigno, J. (2001). "A Survey on Trafficking and Smuggling in Human Beings from the Philippines and the Involvement of Organized Crime Groups; Examining Experiences and Perspective of Victims and Non-Governmental Organizations", ISDS, Institute for Strategic and Development Studies (Manila), unpublished report submitted to the United Nations Interregional Crime and Justice Research Institute, Turin, Italy.

United Nations Convention Against Transnational Crime, United Nations Protocol to Suppress and Punish Trafficking in Persons Especially Women and Children, supplementing the United Nations Convention Against Transnational Crime.

United Nations Office for Drug Control and Crime Prevention (UNODCCP) (1999), Global Program Against Trafficking in Human Beings, an outline for action.

United Nations Protocol against the Smuggling of Migrants by Land, Sea and Air, supplementing the United Nations Convention Against Transnational Crime.

US Department of State (2001), *Victims of Trafficking and Violence Protection Act of 2000; Trafficking in Persons Report*, at http://www.state.gov/documents/organization/4107.pdf.

US Department of State (2002), *Victims of Trafficking and Violence Protection Act of 2000; Trafficking in Persons Report*, at http://www.state.gov/documents/organization/10815.pdf.

Wong D. and G. Saat (2002), *Research on Trafficking Victims and Governmental Sources in Malaysia*, Institut Kajian Malaysia dan Antarabangsa (IKMAS), of the Universiti Kebangsaan Malaysia, unpublished report submitted to the United Nations Interregional Crime and Justice Research Institute, Turin, Italy.

Chapter 10

Transnational Organized Crime and Trafficking of Human Beings

Fusun Sokullu-Akinci
Istanbul University

Introduction

In every society there is a strong and persistent demand for illegal goods and services, such as illicit sex, drugs, arms trafficking and gambling. Such activities present an opportunity to make enormous profits because the cost of providing such goods and services is low and the price can be set high by those able and willing to violate the laws. This situation allows organized crime to flourish (Sykes 1978: 194).

Organized crime is both a criminological and a legal concept (Daragenlı 1998: 245). Defining organized crime is therefore a matter of some dispute among scholars and lawyers, especially when the subject is transnational organized crime. In many countries, there is no universally accepted definition of organized crime while other countries, such as the US and Russia, provide no legal definition of organized crime. Conversely, Turkey has a specific law on this matter. The law against organized crime enacted in 1999 (Act to Contend with Criminal Organizations with the Aim of Exploitation) in which the first article defines criminal organizations in detail and is fairly similar to the Italian Criminal Code, art. 416 bis. The definition is widely critized, however, by academics because of its wide scope and vagueness (İçel 2000: 9–10; Sözüer 2002: 68).

Distinguishing Characteristics of Organized Crime

Although there is not an internationally recognized definition of organized crime, there are a number of common characteristics (Sokullu-Akinci 2002: 13–15):[1]

1. organized crime is instrumental crime, the purpose of which is to make money;
2. participants are organized in more or less complex networks;

1 The Turkish Ministry of Interior lists distinguishing characteristics of the Turkish mafia, see Sokullu-Akinci (2002): 16–18.

3. most organized crime activities offer illegal goods and services. This does not mean, however that organized crime members have nothing to do with "traditional" crimes such as burglary or robbery;
4. one important characteristic of organized crime is its links to world governments and politics. Organized crime makes political corruption an integral part of its business. Indeed, political corruption is not merely a distinguishing feature of organized crime, but is critical to its survival;
5. another feature of organized crime is its generational persistence. The syndicates or families comprising organized crime, continue to operate despite the comings and goings of individual members. Although the death or retirement of persons in leadership positions may result in significant changes, organized crime does not disappear and individual organizations usually do not cease to exist. The persistence of organized crime despite the inevitable disappearance of its human participations could partially be explained by a final important feature of the phenomenon: sanctioned rules of conduct (sometimes called "the code").

The survival of any group or organization is problematic if the behavior of members is unpredictable or does not conform to the evaluations of other members of the group. Rules of conduct therefore establish conformity and predictability and sanctions for violations of the rules ensure that conformity and predictability persist over time.

Causes of Organized Crime

The general level of crime in a country is apparently associated with organized crime. High-crime countries are more likely than low-crime countries to have organized crime because organized crime and common crime are influenced by (many of) the same factors. Crime is related to urbanization, industrialization and social disorganization. These factors produce criminal opportunities and thus more crime. Organized crime is especially likely to occur in cities and countries with advanced levels of economic development (contrary to the history of the Mafia in rural Sicily). Economic development, industrialization, and urbanization both stimulate and facilitate demand for goods and services. (These include goods and services that provide no incentive for organized crime to supply.) When the opposite condition exists however, organized crime usually emerges to fulfill the unmet demand. This demand may be for drugs, firearms, sex workers, or a service such as protection or resolving disputes when there are no acceptable legal means available (Finckenauer and Voronin 2001: 3).

The nature of the criminal opportunities available in a particular place also influences the presence of organized crime. The extent to which particular criminal opportunities can be exploited by criminal organizations also helps explain the presence or absence of organized crime. While some crimes can be committed quite easily by criminals acting alone or in an unorganized crime manner, others cannot.

The latter is especially true of crimes committed across national borders. Certain geographical or infrastructure characteristics, such as the presence of seaports, international airports, strategic border location, rich natural resources, and so on, also provide unique criminal opportunities that can best be exploited by criminals who are organized. This is precisely Turkey's situation where her geography makes her vulnerable to organized crime, especially transnational organized crime. While Turkey's east and south-east are mountainous areas, the rest of Turkey is surrounded by seas which provide a perfect setting for transnational organized crime, especially for the trafficking of human beings.

More so than common crime, organized crime is fed by the presence of ethnic minorities who furnish a ready supply of both victims and offenders. Organized crime also thrives in environments characterized by a relatively high tolerance of deviance and a romanticization of the crime figures, especially when governments and law enforcement are weak or corrupt (the history of the Sicilian Mafia illustrates this feature). We are not suggesting that any of these factors cause organized crime but, rather, that they create a favorable climate for its growth. The fundamental causes of organized crime are actually quite simple, greed and demand. The greed for money and power on the part of some is often (although not always) met by the demand of others for goods and services that are illegal or unavailable (Finckenauer and Voronin 2001: 3, 4).

Strategies to Combat Organized Crime

Organized crime threatens human rights, the rule of law and the democratic system. The fight against organized crime, however, necessitates the use of different methods of prevention and investigation, which may violate the rules of fair trial (Özek 1998: 195–6). Organized crime should be combated on both the national and international (i.e., global cooperation against transnational organized crime) levels (Savona 1997: 224).

Combating Organized Crime on the National Level

Preventive Strategies

(1) Reducing the opportunities for criminal activities Both preventive methods and controlling methods should be used to combat organized crime. In general, it is better to prevent the comission of crime rather than respond to it after its commision because of its high cost to the tax payers. Different countries use different methods to reduce the opportunities for criminal activities. For example, some nations reduce the demand for illicit goods and services or legalize those goods and services that are monopolized by criminals (Savona 1997: 225). Prohibiting the sale of alcohol or cigarettes creates opportunities for organized crime (Barlow 1987: 298–9). For instance, when Turkey used to prohibit the sale of foreign cigarettes there was a widespread illegal trade especially of American cigarettes, which generated a large

profit for organized crime syndicates. The legalization of the importing of foreign cigarettes during the 1980s not only ended this illegal trade, but also created income for the government, through taxes.

Recent demand reduction policies in the area of drugs include education and treatment. For example, article 404/3 of the Turkish Penal Code allows drug users to choose between treatment or a prison sentence. Another proposed method for reducing the opportunity for criminal activities is legalization and liberalization of gambling, prostitution, pornography and drugs (Savona 1997: 225).

Traditional preventive measures against crime include strengthening morality and respect for the law. These concepts are essential for building a social and cultural consensus against organized crime. Maintaining high moral standards in political and administrative behavior through respect for law are the necessary first step for effective action against organized crime. A culture of legality and morality should therefore be cultivated with extreme care and transmitted to new generations. Crime, corruption and violence are interrelated expressions of opposition to these values. Since organized crime is the organized violation of these values, extreme attention must be paid to implementing policies that create incentives for morality (e.g., for those who are exposed to the risk of corruption). The criminal justice system must also protect against violence and the fear of violence (Savona 1997: 225–6).

Policies that improve education should also produce important results in the fight against organized crime. Policies that disseminate more information on, and create greater awareness of the cost of, organized crime to society will strengthen the social consensus against organized crime. The mass media plays an important role in this respect. The media must be aware of their important social function, which is not increasing their ratings with sensational and exaggerated news, but in creating and shaping public opinion. The right to information, freedom of artistic expression and commercial needs can and must be reconciled with civil and social responsibility (Savona 1997: 225–6).

(2) Reducing the vulnerability of the legitimate industries to the infiltration of organized crime groups (For detailed information see Albanese 1987: 103–14; Savona 1997: 226–8.) Organized crime cartels tend to infiltrate the legitimate economy for many different purposes: (1) to launder and invest the proceeds of crime in less risky activities; (2) to acquire respectability and social consensus for its members; (3) to control the territory where it operates to maximize economic and political advantages and minimize the risk of apprehension, arrest and conviction.

The activities of organized crime groups in the illegal markets and its infiltration in the legitimate business are not separate. Opportunistic criminal organizations operate where there is money to make quickly. Specialized organizations, such as those dealing with only drug trafficking want to invest the money produced by their criminal activities in legitimate businesses (money laundering). On the other hand, increasing the transparency of the legal economic system will reduce the ability of organized crime to infiltrate the legal economy. This could be achieved by licensing some key industrial activities (e.g., construction, banking and financial services).

A certain level of transparency is important since publicizing the names of the participants will help identify those who have criminal records.

Another possibility is to regulate of the transactions done by banks for anti-money laundering purposes. This should help identify money laundering operations and trace criminal organizations. Turkey has, for example, recently prohibited cash payments above a certain limit (about US$3,000). On the other hand, deregulation may be more beneficial to certain enterprises. In some instances regulation through licensing can produce inefficiency in the system. Construction industries are especially attractive to organized crime groups. These groups use violence and corruption to achieve monopolistic control of the bidding procedure of public contracts. Deregulation that increases the level of competition could be beneficial, because facilitating competition minimizes the risk of corruption due to competitive prices. Although it might appear as though this would cause more infiltration of organized crime groups, this is not the case since corruption requires monopolistic control for keeping prices high to pay the cost of corruption.

Crime Control Strategies

(1) Substantive legislation One effective way to combat organized crime is to amend and refine the criminal law in response to organized criminal activities. Many countries have approved statutes that (1) focus on the confiscation of crime proceeds. In Germany, "enlarged" confiscation is one example of a special sanction that was passed in response to organized crime (Erman 1999: 264). Germany also requires convicted organized crime offenders to pay expensive fines that are designed to incapacitate their future criminal activities (Erman 1999:272–4; Ünver 1998: 391–6); and (2) treat the commission of an organized crime as an an aggravating circumstance. The German statutes clearly distinguish participation/membership in an organized criminal entity from engagement in "ordinary" criminal activity. Other examples of special legislation include statutes passed in Germany (illicit narcotics trafficking, gang robbery, receiving stolen goods, trading illicit firearms, blackmail, management and procuring of prostitution, illicit gambling – for detailed information see Ünver 1998: 391–6); Italy (distribution of illegal drugs, kidnapping for profit, extortion, fraud, loansharking, counterfeiting of public money or securities); Jamaica (Dangerous Drugs Act, Offences Against the Persons Act, Forgery Act, Firearms Act, Corruption Prevention Act); Turkey (Organized Crime Act (1999), Prevention of Money Laundering Act (1966) are enacted. Trafficking of drugs, counterfeiting money, gang robbery, receiving of stolen goods, blackmail, etc. are already crimes in the Turkish Penal Code since 1926 (Tezcan 2000). There is also a special act for the illegal possession of firearms.

A more recent trend is the enactment of provisions that concern participation in an organized criminal association or conspiracy. This is the formation or combination of two or more persons, on a continuing basis for the purpose of committing an indefinite number of unlawful activities. Although such a provision existed in the Turkish Criminal Code (art. 313) for decades, it has only recently been applied much more frequently. In the US, the Racketeer Influenced and Corrupt Organizations (RICO) statute defines participation in the affairs of a criminal enterprise as a racketeering offense. Racketeering activity covers all serious criminal activity (federal or state) such as murder, robbery, drug dealing, fraud and other serious crimes listed in the statute. In the US there is also the Continuing Criminal Enterprise Statute (CCE) which covers persons who are engaged in large scale drug dealing. This statute applies to a person who commits at least three violations of the drug laws or is the manager or organizer of five or more persons (Savona 1997: 236). Finally, in addition to RICO and CCE, there are American statutes that prohibit criminal conspiracies in general and drug related conspiracies in particular.

It is also extremely important to prevent the "laundering" of illegal money since these proceeds can be used to undermine the whole economic system. The money generated from organized crime often circulates through the same channels as money concealed from taxation authorities. It is therefore important that banks record the identity of their clients and cooperate with the law enforcement agencies whenever suspicious deposits or transactions occur. Centralizing this information will make it easier for us to control the black market.

Many countries have approved money laundering statutes (in accordance with the Vienna Convention). Turkey has also passed a special statute called the Act on the Prevention of Laundering of Illegal Money in 1996. To combat money laundering effectively it is not sufficient to act only on the national level, there must also be an international enforcement mechanism. Such a global approach is required because the circulation of money and the current banking systems have no national limits and money is transferred from one part of the world to another with just a click of a button.

According to the Eighth United Nations Congress on the Prevention of Crime, corruption greatly facilitates the activities of organized criminal groups. All countries have domestic anti-corruption legislation. The Turkish Criminal Code contains a number of detailed provisions against bribery and corruption. The Turkish criminal code also contains provisions that prohibit civil servants from abusing their position of power or from performing acts contrary to his official duties.

Although corruption may have transnational dimensions, many countries not only do not punish businessmen who bribe foreign officials, but in some circumstances have legalized corruption practiced outside their national borders by financial and tax advantages. The OECD has proposed recommendations that concern international corruption and the harmonization of different countries' laws. Sanctions also play an important part in deterring organized crime. Traditional sanctions like incarceration and fines are not sufficient to deter organized criminality. Other sanctions such as limitations on the property, residence, or association may be more effective and the denial of license to public contractors with previous organized crime records should also decrease the risk of organized crime.

The Turkish Organized Crime Act contains provisions that call for prison sentences for those who establish and govern the organization and also for members of such an organization. All the properties used for the commission of the crime and also the proceedings of the crime are to be confiscated. The Act for the Prevention of Laundering of Black Money also contains provisions that call for the freezing all the rights and credits, confiscation of properties, legal instruments (negotiable securities), other valuables, and cancel the right of disposition.

In the US the RICO Statute, CCE Statute, anti-drug laws and a wide variety of other criminal statutes allow the confiscation of proceeds, and tools instrumental to organized crime.

(2) Procedural legislation There is a standard of evidence in criminal procedure, evidence must be collected within the boundaries of the law. Illegally obtained evidence will not be considered in the final verdict. Although these rules are designed to protect the defendant (accused), organized crime cases, because of their complexity, should be prosecuted and tried with different procedures. In these cases, methods that are different from ordinary procedural provisions should be used (e.g., electronic surveillance and undercover agents) (Sözüer 2002: 67–9). Such methods of preliminary investigation should, however, be constrained by strict observance of legal requirements and criminal procedural principles.

The Turkish constitution protects the right to privacy. Electronic surveillance is only allowed with judicial authorization in organized crime cases. In cases of exigent circumstances (where it appears that delay will cause injury), public prosecutors have the authority to use electronic surveillance so long as judicial confirmation is obtained within 24 hours. Otherwise, the electronic surveillance must be stopped (Dönmezer 2000: 550–4; Kazan 2000: 567–8). Germany and Italy have similar statutes, and in the United Kingdom electronic surveillance is admitted (under the Police and Criminal Evidence Act of 1984) if investigators obtain approval from the appropriate authorities before beginning the surveillance. In the US, electronic surveillance is considered an unconstitutional search, unless the authorities obtain an order, allowing surveillance, from a federal judge. Electronic surveillance conducted in an improper manner will also not be admitted as evidence (under the exclusionary rule). No judicial authorization is needed, however, for an undercover agent or consenting witness to voluntarily record a meeting with a subject under investigation (Savona 1997: 240–1).

Controlled delivery and the use of undercover agents are new powerful instruments successfully used against organized crime (see, for example, how provisions of Turkey's Act on Organized Crime enable the use of undercover agents (Dönmezer 2000: 555–7) and the method of controlled delivery).

Ensuring the protection of witnesses is also important for a successful campaign against organized crime. Although there are no specific provisions in Germany and United Kingdom, these countries rely upon other means to protect witnesses in their systems. Italy and the US do, however, have special provisions for this purpose. These provisions include, issuing documents for a new identity; providing temporary housing; providing an address for official notification and communication, and; assisting the witness in obtaining employment, etc. Organized crime offenders pose a major threat to witnesses. Unlike the witnesses of ordinary crimes, not only are the lives of these witnesses always in danger, but even their family members are in peril.

This is why such witnesses must have their identities kept secret (e.g., Turkey's Act on Organized Crime (art. 31) contains witness protection provisions).

Combating Organized Crime at the International Level

Transnational Organized Crime and Trafficking of Humans in General

Every year, millions of people, especially women and children become the victims of human trafficking. Although many think that these people willfully participate in such crimes, in reality they are usually unwilling victims of sexual, physical and economic harassment. Most of them have paid large sums of money to travel to a foreign country, where they hope to have a prosperous life. But they are instead either forced into prostitution or are forced to become organ donors. The global report of the UN on crime indicates that, 40 to 50 thousand women from Thailand are committing illegal prostitution in Japan. The same report states that the number of illegal prostitutes in the European Community is between 200,000 and 500,000. Two thirds of these are from the Eastern European countries and 33 percent of the rest are from Third World countries. Trafficking of women and children from middle and eastern Europe has also increased immensely in the last 10 years. The number has greatly increased after the opening of borders that followed the termination of the cold war.

Economic and sexual slavery is a profitable activity for transnational criminal organizations like the Yakuza and Mafia. These organizations make a yearly profit of 7 billion dollars. They use all means and technology and are therefore quite able to operate in Third World countries. Teenagers are attracted with untrue au pair advertisements and are forced into prostitution. Female victims are beaten, raped and sold to exploiters, who make them work 18 hours a day. They become the property of the persons who allegedly protect them since their passports were either confiscated by force or they never had one. They end up working like a slave for the person who purchased them.

In the US, the price of an Asian prostitute is around $20,000. In Belgium, human traffickers sell the women they bring from Africa for $8,000. In Germany, Russian prostitutes earn $7,500 monthly, $7,000 of which end up in the protector's pocket.[2] These women become physical and mental slaves and are unable to pay their debts to the protector. They are also unable to seek help from the local authorities due to their fear of extradition. Some Russian prostitutes in Turkey attempt to evade extradition by paying Turkish men to marry them.

In many countries, norms are insufficient for adequately combating the trafficking of human beings. International cooperation has also been difficult because of the inadequacy of the laws and instruments.

2 See www.Onuitalia.It/calendar,p.13(02.07.2003); www.unodc.org/adhoc/palermo/con vmain/html.

The UN Convention against Transnational Organized Crime and the Protocol to Prevent, Supress, and Punish Trafficking in Persons, Especially Women and Children
In 1998, during the seventh meeting of the UN on Prevention of Criminality and Criminal Justice, Argentina proposed a new convention for the trafficking of minors. The international community although recognizing the vulnerability of women and children, decided to enlarge the title to cover the trafficking of all individuals.[3] Member countries decided that the best way to cope with this problem was to add a protocol to the Convention Against Transnational Organized Crime. The UN General Assembly accepted the Protocol in November 2000 and according to article 38 of the Convention, it will enter into force on the 90th day after the date of deposit of the 40th instrument of ratification, acceptance, approval or accession. Since Armenia is the 40th country and 90 days have elapsed, the convention is now in force[4] and since Turkey has signed and ratified the Convention (according to the Turkish Constitution) it has also become a provision in her internal legislation.

(1) Aims of the Protocol The Protocol has three aims, to (i) prevent trafficking of human beings, particularly women and children; (ii) protect and aid the victims of such trafficking with a full respect to human rights; (iii) obtain cooperation between and among the signed states to achieve these goals.

(2) Approaches of the Protocol First, it defines the term "trafficking of persons" and outlines the instruments for having the laws respected and obeyed as well as maintaining effective control at the borders. The Protocol reinforces the judicial system and at the same time widens the protection and support to the victims and witnesses. It also establishes preventive policies.

Second, it enforces national and international measures against trafficking. The Protocol is applicable to everyone, especially women and children who are more vulnerable. To enforce these rules, trafficking must be made a crime in the strictest sense and the sanctions must be severe. Those who commit the act of trafficking must be subject to prosecution and conviction by a criminal court. Control at the borders is very important and can be achieved with the quality of travel documents. Instruments for the application of the laws and for effective control at the borders, exchange of information, prevention, investigation, victims' rights and human rights, cooperation with the civil society are also important.

Third, the protocol takes into account the victim's point of view. Presently, victims who collaborate with the judicial system are subject to secondary victimization (Sokullu-Akinci 199) (e.g., some are prosecuted for violating immigration laws). The main goal of the Protocol is to protect the victim and prosecute the traffickers. To enforce these laws it is necessary to obtain the cooperation of victims since they are the main source of evidence. In addition, assistance and protection of the victim includes respecting their privacy, keeping them informed about the procedure, aiding

---

3 See www.unodc.org/adhoc/palermo/convmain/html.

4 See htpp://www.unodc.org/unodc/en/crime_cicp_signatures_convention.html.

their physical and psychological rehabilitation, and providing special care for the victims and their babies. Providing for the security of the victims means avoiding their immediate expulsion and that safe repatriation must be provided for them.

(3) The situation in Turkey and the Turkish legislation Due to its location, Turkey has always been a country of emigration (İçduygu 2003: 12). While until 1979 most migrants were ethnic Turks from neighboring countries, during the last 25 years Turkey has faced a problem of illegal migration. Individuals who are unhappy with the political system of their country of origin use Turkey as a "passage to freedom" since it is uniquely situated in the middle of the Asia–Africa–Europe triangle. This situation begun in 1979 with the change of regime in Iran, and in 1988 a large wave of Kurdish refugees emigrated from Northern Iraq. Turkey opened its borders for obvious reasons. Subsequently, refugees from Asia, Africa, the Middle East and the Caucasus also used Turkey as a bridge to travel to Europe and other Western countries.

According to the statistics of the United Nations High Commissioner for Refugees, Turkey is a transit zone for asylum seekers from neighboring countries to Europe. In 1999, for example, 67,000 persons from Iran, Iraq and Afghanistan went to European countries as asylum seekers. This constitutes 15 percent of the total number of the asylum seekers. This number rose to 90,000 in 2000 and most of these people used Turkey as a passage way to Europe (İçduygu 2003: 18).

In the last five years the "final destination" countries have forced Turkey to become more concerned with this issue. The Western world has difficulty in understanding why so many people enter Turkey without being caught and are then apprehended either in western Turkish, Greek or Italian seas (for detailed information on sea routes and examples, see İçduygu 2003: 51–3). This occurs as a result of geography since eastern and southeastern Turkey and its borders are mountainous areas. Turkey is also surrounded by seas in the north, west and south. It is therefore difficult to control incoming and outgoing refugees.

The type of transportation used depends on the country of origin. For example, while 42.9 percent of the migrants from Afghanistan, 23.1 percent from Iraq and 15.4 percent from Iran come by foot, 50 percent of the Africans arrive by boat (İçduygu 2003: 35, table 9). Their reasons for choosing Turkey are mainly the ease of crossing the border from an adjacent country, low travel cost and onward migration (İçduygu 2003: 33 and 38).

The numbers of migrants are considerable. In 1995, the number of incoming and outgoing refugees was 11,362 it rose to 94,514 in 2001 and 92,364 in 2002. Obviously, the illegal numbers are much higher, perhaps two to three times as high. It is estimated that 600,000 to 700,000 illegal refugees reside in Turkey (İçduygu 2003: 18 and annex 1; 73–6). Thus, not surprisingly, something must be done and a radical change is indeed planned in the Turkish Criminal Code. Since new regulations were urgently needed to address trafficking of human beings, two new articles were added to the Criminal Code in 2002 (201/a and 201/b, following article 201, in the section on felonies against liberty. The heading of article 201 is "Felonies Violating to Engage in Business and Freedom of Labor").

The first paragraph of article 201/a defines the crime of illegal smuggling of persons. This prohibition includes illegal entrance, stay in and exit from the Turkish territories. The second paragraph punishes those who without being an accessory to the original crime defined in the first paragraph, aid these persons in the country, give them forged identity cards or passports or attempt to commit such acts. The punishments include imprisonment and heavy fines even if these acts constitute other punishable crimes (for example, if such a criminal will be punished for forgery too). If these acts threaten the victims' lives or physical integrity, or subject the victims to inhuman or degrading treatment, the punishments are increased (1/2) and if the victim dies the punishment is increased twice more. If these crimes are committed by an organization the punishments are also doubled.

Article 201/b punishes the acts of forced labor, organ donation under duress, kidnapping of persons, etc. (Koca 2003). If these acts are committed against minors, even if there is no duress, it is still punished with the same amount of prison sentence plus a fine. The punishments are also doubled if the crimes are committed by a criminal organization.

During the last seven years, the nationality of the apprehended refugees include 77,643 Iraqi; 19,409 Moldavian; 22,158 Afghani; 22,784 Iranian; 16,543 Pakistani; 12,651 Romanian; 11,006 Russian; 10,677 Ukranian; and 11,336 Bangladesh citizens (İçduygu 2003: 26). In terms of the profiles of the refugees, in 1996 they were mostly single males with little education that stayed for one year in Turkey before migrating to the West. Those who came during the last five years are generally married, educated and middle-aged and remain in Turkey between three to six months (İçduygu 2003: 31–3 and 40, table 4). On the other hand Turkey is not only used as a bridge to developed countries but it is also a paradise for overstayers. Many people enter Turkey legally as tourists, find work opportunities, and overstay illegally (e.g., without a visa or a working permit). These are estimated to be approximately one million (İçduygu 2003: 26). They work in many sectors, some young women as prostitutes, many Moldavian women work as house keepers for wealthy Turkish families and some Romanian and African men provide cheap labor in the construction sector (İçduygu 2003: 27–8).

Conclusion

Turkey has been the main road to freedom for many refugees because of its geography. However, Turkey is a responsible member of the international community and has made the necessary changes in its laws, signed and ratified the Convention and is trying to respond more effectively to these issues. Although Turkey's economy and unemployment rates are not an attractive place for refugees, its liberal political system make it an attractive transit point to more prosperous countries.

It is not possible to combat organized crime without international cooperation. The world is becoming smaller every day and as a result the activities of organized crime groups are increasingly committed across national borders. Countries must therefore cooperate in criminal justice matters, such as providing help in collecting evidence, arresting a fugitive, freezing and confiscating assets of criminal origin and extraditing criminals. Unfortunately, a few years ago Ukraine refused to extradite a member of Turkish Mafia, perhaps because the death sentence was still in practice in Turkey at that time. Now that Turkey has abolished the death penalty and also offers a guarantee of a fair and just trial, such extradition requests are more likely to be granted.

References

Barlow, Hugh (1987), *Introduction to Criminology*, 4th edn, Boston: Little, Brown.

Daragenlı, Vesile Sonay (1998), "Organize Suçluluk", in *Ceza Hukuku Günleri*, 70: 245.

Dönmezer, Sulhi (2000), "Çetelerle Mücadele Amacıyla 4422 sayılı Kanunla Kabul Edilen Koruma Tedbirleri", in *Yargı Reformu 2000 Sempozyumu*, Izmir.

Erman, Barış (1999), "Almanya ve Avusturya'da Organize Suçla Mücadele Kapsamında Kabul Edilen Malvarlığıyla İlgili Cezai Yaptırımlar", in *Prof. Dr. Sahir Erman'a Armağan*, Istanbul: Alpha: Basim, Yayim, Daðitim A:Þ.

Finckenauer, O James and Yuri A. Voronin (2001), *The Threat of Russian Organized Crime*, Washington DC: US Department of Justice.

İçduygu, Ahmet (2003), *Irregular Migration in Turkey*, Geneva: International Organization for Migration.

İçel, Kayıhan (2000), "Sunuş Konuşması", in *Avrupa Birliğine Uyum Süreci bağlamında Organize Suçlulukla Mücadele*, Istanbul: Beta Basim, Yayim, Daðitim A.Þ.

Kazan,Turgut (2000), "Organize Suçlarla Mücadelede Koruma Tedbirleri", in *Yargı Regormu 2000 Sempozyumu*, Izmir.

Koca, Mahmut (2003), "İnsan Yağması (Sömürüsü) Suçu, TCK. M. 201 b", *Ankara Üniversitesi Hukuk Fakültesi Dergisi*, 52(2): 142–71.

Ozek, Çetin (1998), "Organize Suç", in *Prof. Dr. Sahir Erman'a Armağan*, Istanbul: Beta Basim, Yayim, Daðitim A:Þ.

Savona, Ernesto U. (1997), "Assessment of the Various National and International Strategies Aimed at Combating Organized Crime", in Sieber, Von Ulrich, *Internationale Organisierte Kriminalitaet*, Cologne and Berlin: HRSG.

Sokullu-Akinci, Füsun (1999), *Viktimoloji*, Istanbul: Beta Basim, Yayim, Daðitim A:Þ.

Sokullu-Akinci, Füsun (2002), *Kriminoloji*, 3rd edn, Istanbul: Beta Basim, Yayim, Daðitim A:Þ.

Sokullu-Akinci, Füsun (2002), "Organize Suçların Kriminolojik Yapısı ve Türkiye'deki Boyutları", in *Avrupa Birliğine Uyum Süreci Bağlamında Organize Suçlulukla Mücadele*, Istanbul: Beta Basim, Yayim, Daðitim A.Þ.

Sözüer, Adem (2002), "Çıkar Amaçlı Suç Örgütü Kavramı ve Özel Yargılama Önlemlerinin Türkiye'deki Boyutları", in *Avrupa Birliğine Uyum Süreci Bağlamınnnda Organize Suçlulukla Mücadele*, Istanbul: Beta Basim, Yayim, Daðitim A.Þ.

Sykes, Gresham (1978), *Criminology*, New York: Harcourt, Brace, Jovanovich.

Tezcan, Durmuş (2000), "La Position de la Turquie au Regard de la Lutte Contre la Fraude et le Crime Organisé", paper delivered at the Seminar on Corpus Juris and Judicial Cooperation in the Field of Protection of Financial Interests of the European Union, Istanbul, October 12–13.

Ünver, Yener (1998), "Federal Almanya'da Terör ve Organize Suçluluk ile İlgili Düzenlemeler", in *Prof. Dr. Nurullah Kunter'e Armağan*, Istanbul: Beta Basim, Yayim, Daðitim A:Þ.

Chapter 11

Refugees and Human Rights: An International Law Perspective

Turgut Tarhanli

Istanbul Bilgi University Human Rights Law Research Center

Introduction

How a state treats the people entering its country who do so in an effort to save their lives is a very sensitive matter. The concepts, "security" and "human rights" are two different aspects of this case. These two different aspects denote, at the same time, the tension caused by the problems regarding refugees or asylum seekers.

Certainly, every state has the right to exercise authority concerning issues such as the entry, settlement or deportation of foreigners. This is an established rule of international law, however, it must be put into practice taking into consideration the provisions of the agreements that the state committed to undertake in international human rights law. There may be various compelling reasons for people to leave their country of nationality for another country. If the aim of entering another country is just to live or work in that country, then the legal status of that person can be defined as "immigrant".

A person, who is called refugee, legally bears the "foreigner" status. The reasons for calling a person a refugee or an asylum seeker are closely related with his/her legal ties with the state he/she is a citizen of. The duty of a state to protect its nationals is a natural function of this legal status. When a state cannot fulfill this function and when it acts contrary to this function the main reason for becoming a refugee arises. This may have of course many different reasons. Therefore, the definition of the term "refugee" is a crucial issue. According to the 1951 Convention relating to the Status of Refugees,[1] the term "refugee" shall apply to any person who is "... owing

1 1951 Convention Relating to the Legal Status of Refugees, (Law on the Approval of Accession, No. 359 - 29 August 1961), *Official Gazette*, 5 September 1961 – 10898 (hereinafter referred to as "1951 Convention"). Turkey acceded to the 1951 Convention with formulating a reservation in accordance with the Article 42 of the Convention: "No provision of this Convention shall be interpreted as the rights recognized to the refugees in Turkey are more than the ones recognized to the Turkish nationals" (see Law on the Approval of Accession, Article 2). In addition to this Convention, 1967 Protocol Relating to the Legal Status of Refugees (Decree of Approval, No. 6/10266 – 1 July 1968, *Official Gazette*, 5

to well-founded fear of being persecuted for reasons of race, religion, nationality, membership of a particular social group or political opinion, is outside the country of his nationality and is unable or, owing to such fear, is unwilling to return to it ..." (1951 Convention, article 1, paragraph (A) (2)).

With this definition, required and sufficient framework for the recognition of refugee status, the relevant person is determined. However, the answer of the question, "what is the fate of a person who is not granted refugee status yet, but who claims that he/she bears the required conditions to be a refugee" is another aspect of this issue. These people may have entered the country concerned through the border gates legally or by violating the law of the state concerning the entry of foreigners to its territory or they may be kept at the border gates or border zones of the state without getting permission of entry.

According to Turkish law[2] a person whose refugee status is not determined yet is called a "*sığınmacı*" (asylum seeker) and a person whose refugee status has been recognized is called a "*mülteci*" (refugee). Therefore, the difference between the terms *mülteci* and *sığınmacı* should be a legal one. On the other hand, in daily communication a difference of meaning may not arise between the two terms, because the term *mülteci*is a word used in Ottoman Turkish and the other term, *sığınmacı*, is a word of modern Turkish having the same meaning, but not in the legal sense. However, from the legal point of view, both terms refer to different legal statuses and shall be evaluated in the light of human rights law.

Another issue that should be considered in regards to Turkey is "geographical limitation". According to article 1, paragraph (B)(1) of the 1951 Convention, it shall be applied to people who had to leave their country due to the events occurring in any part of the world or in Europe. This provision of the Convention provides a right of choice to the signatories. Turkey has chosen the second choice and thus is not legally obliged to recognize "refugee" status to people coming to Turkey from countries other than Europe. The 1994 Regulation keeps this policy in its article 3, paragraph (II).

However, the geographical limitation is only related to the practice of legal obligations relating to the recognition of "refugee" status. In Turkish law, it is not possible to assert a geographical limitation clause in the case of recognition of the "asylum seeker" status (1994 Regulation, article 3, paragraph (III)). Because of this reason, though Turkey is not obliged to grant the "refugee" status to those entered to its country legally or illegally, it has to take into consideration the claims of people coming from non-European countries and seeking asylum.

August 1968 – 12968) was put into force as of July 31, 1968 (see *Official Gazette*, 14 October 1968 – 13026).

2 "The regulation on the procedures and the principles related to population movements and aliens arriving in Turkey either as individuals or in groups wishing to seek asylum either from Turkey or requesting residence permission in order to seek asylum from another country" which was approved by the Council of Ministers on September 14, 1994 by the decree No. 94/6169 and entered into force on November 30, 1994 (*Official Gazette*, 30 November 1994 – 22127 (hereinafter referred to as 1994 Regulation)).

Refugees and Human Rights

The main reason why the refugee law shall be evaluated within the context of human rights law is the "fear of persecution". Thus, to expel, return ("*refouler*") or refoul[3] a refugee in any manner whatsoever to the frontiers of territories where he/she fears of persecution is the violation of the 1951 Convention. Thus, the authorities of the contracting states have no such power to return (*refouler*) a person who is granted "refugee" status as mentioned above. An opposite decision given by a contracting state shall obviously be a violation of the 1951 Convention:

> No contracting State shall expel or return ("*refouler*") a refugee in any manner whatsoever to the frontiers of territories where his life or freedom would be threatened on account of his race, religion, nationality, membership of a particular social group or political opinion. (1951 Convention, article 33, paragraph (1))

This generally accepted rule of international law is known as "non-refoulement" or "prohibition of refoulement or expulsion". As a standard rule of international human rights law, this issue is also reiterated in the United Nations Convention on the Prevention of Torture, Other Cruel, Inhumane or Degrading Treatment and Punishment of 1984.

> 1. No State Party shall expel or return ("*refouler*") or extradite a person to another State where there are substantial grounds for believing that he would be in danger of being subjected to torture.
>
> 2. For the purpose of determining whether there are such grounds, the competent authorities shall take into account all relevant considerations including, where applicable, the existence in the State concerned of a consistent pattern of gross, flagrant or mass violations of human rights. (article 3)[4]

In accordance with the 1951 Convention, exception on the rule of prohibition of expulsion or refoulement can be made for reasons of "national security" and "public order":

---

3 In the official Turkish text of 1951 Convention the term "refoulement" is translated into Turkish by using the word "*iade*" (return).

4 The same legal obligation is among the basic rules of the international obligations law as well as refugee law. See 1957 European Convention on Extradition: "The same rule shall apply if the requested party has substantial grounds for believing that a request for extradition for an ordinary criminal offence has been made for the purpose of prosecuting or punishing a person on account of his race, religion, nationality or political opinion, or that person's position may be prejudiced for any of these reasons" (art. 3/2). Also see 1977 European Convention on the Suppression of Terrorism: "Nothing in this Convention shall be interpreted as imposing an obligation to extradite if the requested State has substantial grounds for believing that the request for extradition for an offence mentioned in Article 1 or 2 has been made for the purpose of prosecuting or punishing a person on account of his race, religion, nationality or political opinion, or that person's position may be prejudiced for any of these reasons" (art. 5).

> The Contracting States shall not expel a refugee lawfully in their territory save on grounds of national security or public order. (1951 Convention, article 32, paragraph (1))
>
> ... The benefit of the present provision may not, however; be claimed by a refugee whom there are reasonable grounds for regarding as a danger to the security of the country in which he is, or who, having been convicted by a final judgement of a particularly serious crime, constitutes a danger to the community of that country. (1951 Convention, article 33, paragraph (2))

This issue can be evaluated with a different approach. These cross-border population movements also take place not only with the aim of asylum but for reasons such as "economic migration", simply to earn money. The entries into economically developed countries or the so-called transit countries on the way to the developed countries are usually displayed as asylum. As a matter of fact, this problem is now a type of international organized crime.

Therefore, the major importance of this subject as regards to the protection of human rights becomes clear: if the related person is deported or returned at the border will there be a risk of persecution as it is claimed? This is a major question the answer of which is sought for by the refugee law and, of course, a lawful concern within the sphere of human rights law.

Giving credits to the legal practice established by the 1951 Convention, the 1994 Regulation foresees that individual aliens who either seek asylum from Turkey or request residence permission in order to seek asylum from another country shall be interviewed in accordance with the 1951 Convention and their statements taken (1994 Regulation, article 5, paragraph (B) and article 12, paragraph (II)). The main aim in carrying out these actions is of course to reveal the reasons forcing these people to come to Turkey. Because of this reason, the appropriateness of the evaluations made at this stage will be crucial in determining whether the administrative decisions regarding the deportation or refoulement of the asylum seekers to the countries of origin are legitimate or not.

The wording of the 1994 Regulation concerning the actions to be taken regarding the individuals or groups of aliens entering Turkey shall be interpreted as a guideline for the implementation of the rules foreseen by the 1951 Convention. For example, by the 1994 Regulation, attention was drawn to the fact that, for individual asylum, actions shall be taken according to the provisions of the 1951 Convention. However, no reference was made to the groups (see 1994 Regulation, article 12, paragraph (II)). This may be interpreted that Turkey limited the field of implementation of the 1951 Convention to only "individual" asylum. In fact, an interpretation of this kind has been a basis of discussion against the mass-influx phenomenon arising as a result of internal strifes or internal political turmoil, which became common in the 1990s, after the end of the cold war.

Even though defending this kind of interpretation seems legally possible, any evaluation should take the above-mentioned crucial question into consideration, whenever a state makes a decision on deporting or refouling the people who seek mass asylum or those who are waiting at the borders to take refuge from their country of nationality.

It is not easy to overcome this problem economically, politically and socially. Therefore, it is essential to cooperate with the international and national organizations, which have expertise and experience in these issues. These organizations can both be intergovernmental organizations and NGOs. But possibly a government should prepare beforehand a plan of action against this kind of humanitarian situation within the framework of the international agreement. The provisions of the 1994 Regulation regarding the individual and the groups of aliens who pass through the borders of Turkey shall be interpreted with the same concern in the cases of deportation or refoulement, providing an effective protection of the rights of those seeking refuge.

To prevent the possibility of violation the rights protected by the 1951 Convention, particularly the following provisions of the 1994 Regulation shall be implemented with utmost care:

1. "Individual aliens who entered Turkey legally or illegally shall make an application within ten days to the governorate where they entered the country or they leave within 10 days" (article 4).[5]

2. Regarding the conclusion to be reached by the Ministry of the Interior after the applications of individual aliens, "[t]hose aliens whose applications not accepted shall be deported by the governorate upon instructions decided by the Ministry of the Interior" (article 6, paragraph (IV)[6] and article 26, paragraph (II)).

3. "At the conclusion of a war, armed conflict or crisis the repatriation of refugees and those who seek asylum in groups shall be carried out by the Ministry of the Interior in coordination with the Turkish General Staff and the Ministry of Foreign Affairs" (article 26, paragraph (I)).

4. "Residence permission granted to individual aliens who seek residence permission in Turkey in order to seek asylum from another country may not be extended, if after having

5 Article 4 of the 1994 Regulation was amended by the government in 1999: "Individual aliens who are either seeking asylum from Turkey or requesting residence permission in order to seek asylum from a third country shall apply within five days to [any] local governorate if they entered the country legally; and if they entered illegally, shall apply within ten days to the governorate of the province where they entered the country. If it is necessary as regards national security Ministry of Interior shall shorten the time limit taking the views of the Ministry of Foreign Affairs" (*Official Gazette*, 13 January 1999–23582).

6 With the same amendment, a fourth paragraph was added to the article of the Regulation as: "Those aliens whose applications not accepted shall approach to the relevant governorate with a petition within 15 days. Statement and the information and documents supporting the statement of the alien who appealed to the decision shall be sent to the Ministry of Interior by the governorate. Appeal shall be investigated by a superior authority and the result shall be notified to the alien" (*Official Gazette*, 13 January 1999–23582).

been given reasonable time the aliens are still not able to go to a third country. Aliens in such situations shall be asked to leave the country" (article 28).

5. "A refugee or an asylum seeker who is residing in Turkey legally[7] can only be deported by the Ministry of Interior under the terms of the 1951 Convention or for reasons of national security and public order."

"An appeal against a deportation order may be made to the Ministry of the Interior within 15 days."

"The appeal shall be reviewed and ruled upon by an official one rank higher than the officer who previously made the deportation order, and this ruling shall be communicated to the person concerned by the competent governorate" (article 29).

The 10-day limit of application, which is regulated by article 4, can be easily surmounted by the aliens who cannot be expected to be aware of the Turkish law. The time limit foreseen in the original text of article 4 was five days and the new provision has extended to ten days in favor of the aliens, however, it is not easy to foresee an optimum period. It is essential to accept the applications, if the good will of the applicant is obvious in accordance with the obligations undertaken by Turkey, a State party to the 1951 Convention.

In all cases foreseen by the other articles of the 1994 Regulation, including the refusal of the application due to non-compliance with the time limit, the governmental body shall take an administrative action. Therefore, the alien concerned may file a case for annulment on charges of violation of his/her rights recognized by national and also international law. In accordance with the Constitution of 1982, "[r]ecourse to judicial review shall be available against all actions and acts of the administration" (article 125, paragraph (I)).

In general, when the aliens are going to be deported, a reasonable period of time shall be given, as it is a result of the execution of the above-mentioned article of the Constitution which requires giving the alien the opportunity to claim for his/her rights before the judiciary. Denial of such time would not only violate the rights of refugees and asylum seekers but it will also violate various rights and freedoms protected by the 1951 Convention defined as a "fear of persecution".

In accordance with the Constitution of 1982, as "the international agreements duly put into effect carry the force of law" (article 90, paragraph (V)), the alien may support his/her claim on the basis of relevant international agreements Turkey has ratified. In that case, "when the administrative action is clearly against law and it creates a loss which is hard to or impossible to redress" the provisions of international agreements to which Turkey is a party may be taken into consideration (Law on Administrative Trial Procedure, article 27, paragraph (2)) in the legal evaluation regarding whether a decision could be taken on the suspension of the execution or not.

7 What is meant by the term "reside legally" shall be understood as "lawfully" with reference to the relevant article (art. 32/1) of the 1951 Convention. See above, point 3.

However, the judicial verdicts given on the annulment cases against administrative actions may not be for the benefit of the alien who has chosen this way of claiming his/her rights. In other words, the judiciary may not annul the above-mentioned administrative actions. However, there are still some other ways in order to claim rights. The European Convention on Human Rights, with its judicial review mechanism provides an effective legal remedy.

The European Convention on Human Rights and Deportation or *Refoulement*

Turkey has been a party to the European Convention on Human Rights since 1954.[8] In 1987, Turkey recognized the competence of the European Commission of Human Rights to receive petitions according to the Convention. After that, in 1990, Turkey also recognized the jurisdiction of the European Court of Human Rights. According to the new text of the Convention as amended by Protocol 11, today, there is only one judicial body, the Court, under the review mechanism of the 1954 Convention.[9]

So, for the applications made to claim such rights in Turkey against that administrative action, it can be asserted that Turkey has violated its obligations arising from the 1954 Convention.[10] Thus, considering the admissibility criteria as regards the individual applications, in accordance with the procedural rules foreseen by the Convention, the Court may only deal with the matter, an individual application, after all domestic remedies have been exhausted, according to the generally recognized rules of international law, and within a period of six months from the date on which the final decision was taken[11] (1954 Convention, article 35).

Article 3 (Prohibition of Torture) of the 1954 Convention became a crucially important legal apparatus to protect the rights of refugees or asylum seekers in cases concerning expulsion or refoulement. The judicial practice before the European Court of Human Rights and its consistent approach to review with utmost care the possibilities of threats which a refugee or an asylum seeker faces, presents an effective remedy in terms of the refugee law.

The provision of article 3 is a short one and simply rules, "[n]obody shall be subjected to torture, inhumane or degrading punishment and treatment". This right, which is one of the generally accepted standards of international human rights law,

---

8 Convention on the Protection of Human Rights and Fundamental Freedoms, Published in the *Official Gazette* on 19 March 1954–8662. However, today Protocol 11 foresees a change in both the text and the control method related to the mechanism of the protection of human rights was put into effect (1 November 1998) this shall be implemented within the context of the new text.

9 See, article 19 of the 1954 Convention.

10 See below.

11 European Court of Human Rights (ECHR), which is now the sole control mechanism, has replaced the European Commission of Human Rights and European Court of Human Rights which were set up with the 1950 Convention with the entry of Protocol 11 into force (ECHR, Article 19).

is also recognized by the Constitution. In Turkey, article 17, paragraph (III) of the Constitution (Personal Inviolability, Material and Spiritual Entity of the Individual) has the similar provision: "No one shall be subjected to torture or ill-treatment; no one shall be subjected to penalties or treatment incompatible with human dignity".

At first sight, it may be difficult to find a correlation between the right of prohibition of torture and the refugee law. However, it is used as a legal basis by the European Court of Human Rights to prevent the expulsion or refoulement of the aliens in any manner to the frontiers of territories where his/her life or freedom would be threatened. For people who will be expelled, deported or returned what is important is not the ground for expulsion but the possible outcome of that decision. Therefore, applying article 3 in such a legal context becomes a preventive tool against possible unlawful executions.

In interpreting article 3, the special character of the Convention should not be overlooked. The "special character" of the Convention is related to its object and purpose, a human rights agreement focusing on the protection of individuals or groups of individuals. So, it is natural to implement article 3 within this context and for the same end.

On the other hand, including the implementation of it in the events of deportation and refoulement, the provision of "the prohibition of torture" which was foreseen with the article 3 of the Convention is one of the basic values of a democratic society.[12] And article 3 is one of those provisions of the Convention that shall be implemented absolutely.[13] There should be no exceptions in this implementation. Considering the absolute character of the provision of article 3 and in accordance with article 15, paragraph (2) of the Convention, no derogation from that article shall be made even in time of war or other public emergency.[14]

The European Court of Human Rights (ECHR) draws attention to a legal technical fact that the absolute character of article 3 is superior to exception clause of article 33, paragraph (2) of the 1951 Convention.[15] This kind of interpretation of the Court indicates, that giving a priority to the ground of security interest of the state concerned

---

12 ECHR, *Case of Ahmet v. Austria*, Judgement, December 1996: 11; ECHR, *Case of H.L.R. v. France*, Judgement, April 29, 1997: 13; ECHR, *Case of Soering v. the United Kingdom*, Judgement, July 7, 1989: 26.

13 ECHR, *Case of D. v. the United Kingdom*, Judgement, May 2, 1997: 14; ECHR, *Case of Ahmet v. Austria*, Judgement, December 17, 1996: 12.

14 In accordance with article 15/1 of the European Convention on Human Rights "in time of war or other public emergency threatening the life of the nation any High Contracting Party may take measures derogating from its obligations under this Convention to the extent strictly required by the exigencies of the situation, provided that such measures are not consistent with its other obligations under international law". However, these measures must not mean that the article 3 of the Convention shall be breached (European Convention on Human Rights, art. 15/2).

15 Article 33, paragraph (2) of the1951 Convention: "... the benefit of the present provision may not, however, be claimed by a refugee whom there are reasonable grounds for regarding as a danger to the security of the country in which he is, or who, having been

for expulsion or return (refoulement), can be legitimately overlooked when those acts evidently violate article 3 of the Convention, a provision of the Convention absolutely carried out by the parties, under the light of the Court's practice.[16]

Finally, it can be said that implementation of the provision of article 3 of the Convention with underlining its absolute character is, on the other hand, an application of the teleological or progressive method of treaty interpretation which can be efficiently used in human rights law.[17]

In Turkish administrative law, a governmental authority can take into consideration such method of interpretation, particularly in cases of expulsion or refoulement. And in the cases relating to the annulment of the administrative actions on the same issues, the Council of State (Supreme Administrative Tribunal) or the lower administrative courts, without any hesitation, can use the same method of interpretation. Applying the established principles of Turkish administrative law, such as principles of "public interest" or "requirements of the public service" (see Duran 1980: 10) in cases relating to expulsion or refoulement means, in fact, the due process of law. This may also be defined as the reasonable manner of the governmental authority.[18] So, even the Turkish administrative law provides various legal avenues in order to abstain from the violation of the peremptory norms of refugee law, in line with the human rights law.

In the context of the European Convention on Human Rights and regarding its article 3, a remedy of judicial review should be effective. So, through a judgment, the causes of complaints or the threat of violation of the rights and freedoms set forth in the Convention should be prevented. Expel or return a person to the frontier of a state where it is evident that there is a risk of torture and cruel, inhuman or degrading treatment or punishment, execution of the administrative actions on expulsion or return shall be against not only the refugee law but also the principle of due process of law. The primary function of the judicial body and effectiveness of its judgments impose such a legal approach.

But of course, the responsibility of the judicial body in evaluating that risk should be regarded within the framework of the claim of the applicant (or plaintiff) by making reference to the events and necessary information that may occur during expulsion or refoulement and submitted by the claimant through his/her case. In the European Convention system, the information that should be known by the contracting state should also be within the evaluation domain of the judicial authority.[19]

The asylum seekers who are not granted refugee status are more likely to face an implementation that will breach article 3 of the Convention. In that case, the asylum seekers who have entered the country unlawfully and apply for temporary residence

---

convicted by a final judgement of a particularly serious crime, constitutes a danger to the community of that country".

16 ECHR, *Case of Ahmet v. Austria*, Judgement, December 17, 1996: 11.

17 ECHR, *Case of Soering v. the United Kingdom*, Judgement, July 7, 1989: 31.

18 ECHR, *Case of D. v. the United Kingdom*, Judgement, May 2, 1997; p. 20.

19 ECHR, *Case of H.L.R. v. France*, Judgement, April 29, 1997: 13; ECHR, *Case of Cruz Varas and Others v. Sweden*, Judgement, March 20, 1991: 24.

permit in order to seek asylum from that country or to seek asylum from a third country, the governmental authority shall take action.

Due to the migration or security policy of governments, the asylum seekers are more likely to be excluded from the above-mentioned "legal protection" in comparison with refugees. In countries where recourse to judicial review is available against the actions and acts of the administration, there is no doubt that the legal understanding which is pursued for the refugees shall be valid for the asylum seekers as well.

There is another subject which gains importance and shall be taken into consideration for asylum seekers: the character of law in the country concerned and whether this is in harmony with the concept, the rule of law, which should be, in fact, the object and purpose of the European Convention on Human Rights. In this context, the law relating to the asylum seekers must be sufficiently accessible and precise[20] in order to avoid the risks that may arise due to arbitrariness. In other words, to prevent arbitrary intervention of the governmental authorities to the rights protected by the Convention, sufficient legal protection should exist in the domestic law of that country.[21]

According to the European Court of Human Rights, attention can be drawn to the review of the conditions that the asylum seekers will be subjected to and if necessary, to the limitation of the period in which the asylum seekers' applications are evaluated by the governmental authorities. The Court also draws attention to the fact that legal, humanitarian and social aid shall be provided for the asylum seekers and necessary procedures and time limits shall be determined by relevant regulations to facilitate the asylum seekers' initiatives about this matter.[22]

Conclusion

Regarding the refugee law, Turkey, similar to other countries, has undertaken some obligations of international law, in addition to its domestic legislation relating to refugee law. In this field, the provisions of the 1951 Convention and the 1967 Protocol are of prior importance. As it has been recognized by the Universal Declaration of Human Rights (1948) "[e]veryone has the right to seek and to enjoy in other countries asylum from persecution" (article 14, paragraph (1)). This means that refugee affairs are dealt with in light of the international human rights law, in a spirit of protecting human rights. For this reason, both the 1951 Convention and the 1967 Protocol should be implemented by bearing in mind that both of the instruments are international human rights agreements.

The significance of such an approach is underlined with the principle of *pacta sunt servanda*, a generally recognized principle of law and an established principle

20 ECHR, *Case of Amuur v. France*, Judgement, June 25, 1996: 27.

21 ECHR, *Malone v. the United Kingdom*, Judgement, August 2, 1984: 32; ECHR, *Case of Amuur v. France*, Judgement, June 25, 1996: 28.

22 ECHR, *Case of Amuur v. France*, Judgement, June 25, 1996: 28.

of the law of treaties. Article 26 of the Vienna Convention on the Law of Treaties[23] rules that "(e)very treaty in force is binding upon the parties to it and must be performed by them in good faith."

A separate legal assessment is required to determine how this principle will be implemented by all the countries, which have recognized it under their different culture of law. Considering this assessment, compliance with the provisions of a treaty ensures the carrying out of its object and purpose. In other words, the provisions of that treaty should be applied in the manner foreseen in that treaty and it should be furnished with legal effectiveness.

In this respect, the unique characteristic that needs to be emphasized in relation to the implementation of this principle in human rights treaties, can be nothing but the "protection of human beings" in the framework of that treaty. And this fact cannot be subject to the character of the provisions of these treaties (e.g. the 1951 Convention, in this context), whether they are self-executing (or having a legal character which can be directly applicable by the parties to them in the territories under their jurisdiction) or not. In both cases, the principle of *pacta sund servanda* should be regarded in due course.

In the first case, when the question is relating to a self-executing treaty and there is a request for the application of a provision of it or an allegation that it has not been implemented, such claim can be made by making direct reference to the relevant provision, because the wording of that provision has been made in such a way so as to grant a right directly to the related person or persons. The persons who prepared that treaty have drafted the text of the treaty in a style so as to reflect such a power. However, even when a treaty has such a characteristic, it is still possible to make some regulations by the competent national authorities in domestic law regarding that matter.

In the second case, when the question is relating to a non-self-executing treaty, the provision of that treaty does not have such a characteristic and for its implementation the state concerned has to make a national regulation, which is also called an act of transformation, in order to give effect to that treaty in the national legal order. So, a request for the application of a provision of such a treaty or an allegation about non-compliance to that provision can only have a legal effect after an act of transformation is duly put into effect in accordance with the national law.

Both in the first and second cases, we cannot ignore the unique characteristic of human rights treaties in the implementation and interpretation of domestic law regulations pertaining to that treaty. Article 31 of the 1994 Regulation states that the Regulation has been prepared in line with the provisions of the 1951 Convention and the 1967 Protocol. Even if such a phrase had not been put in the Regulation, the result would have been the same. But the fact that such a statement has been made is crucial for the above-mentioned legal implementation and interpretation style to be realized with utmost care for the implementation of this Regulation.

---

23 *United Nations Treaty Series*, 1155: 331, entered into force January 27, 1980.

An emphasis on "human rights" for both international treaties concerning refugees and the relevant domestic regulations would suggest that the object and purpose of these rules of law are to prevent people from being faced by a persecution or a fear of persecution. Therefore the necessary care should be implemented not to immediately return aliens who had to enter the country as asylum seekers or expel those who managed to enter the country unlawfully.

Unlike asylum seekers, the aliens who have the status of a refugee are the ones whose fear of persecution has been recognized by the competent authorities, national or international, such as UNHCR, pursuant to an investigation. Non-compliance to this legal decision would, inter alia, constitute a material breach of the 1951 Convention. All the aliens, be it refugees or asylum seekers, are entitled recourse to administrative and judicial remedies. Judicial review of the actions and acts of the governmental authorities is available. As stated in article 36 of the 1982 "freedom to claim rights" is a right everyone can exercise without discrimination between citizens and aliens.

Turkey has recognized the jurisdiction of the European Court of Human Rights. Hence, it is among Turkey's obligations not to prevent a person from exercising his/her right of "individual application" on charges of a violation of the European Convention on Human Rights due to an action which has been or will be carried out by the Turkish governmental authorities. An effective implementation of this right which is also valid for both asylum seekers and refugees could prevent any breach of that right which should be protected. In other words, it would suggest an approach whereby such persons should not be immediately expelled, deported or returned to countries from which they have escaped. This approach is considered to be a reflection of human rights law in the implementation of the rules of the existing law, national or international.

References

1948 Universal Declaration of Human Rights, *Official Gazette*, 27 March 1949 – 7217.

1951 Convention Relating to the Legal Status of Refugees, (Law on the Approval of Accession, No. 359–29 August 1961), *Official Gazette*, 5 September 1961 – 10898.

1954 Convention on the Protection of Human Rights and Fundamental Freedoms, *Official Gazette*, 19 March 1954 – 8662.

1957 European Convention on Extradition, *Official Gazette*, 26 October 1959 – 10365.

1977 European Convention on the Suppression of Terrorism, *Official Gazette*, 26 March 1981 – 17291.

1988 United Nations Convention on the Prevention of Torture Other Cruel, Inhumane or Degrading Treatment and Punishment, *Official Gazette,* 10 August 1988 – 19895.

Duran, L. (1980), "Yabancıların Türkiye'den Sınırdışı Edilmesi", *İnsan Hakları Yıllığı*, 2: 10.

PART IV
Responding to the Victimization of Migrants

Chapter 12

Preventing Migrant Deaths: A Possible Role for Situational Crime Prevention[1]

Rob T. Guerette
Florida International University

Introduction

In recent years, considerable attention has been given to incidents of migrants dying as they attempt to enter foreign countries illegally. These deaths have been recorded in Spain (Simons 2004) and Sicily (Bruni 2002) as migrants have attempted to enter from Africa. On the island of Lampedusa at the southern-most point of Italy, every summer brings the arrival of illegal migrants in decrepit boats, many of whom never survive the journey (Bruni 2003). Numbers of these migrants are reported to sink with their broken vessels, later to be found by fishermen when they drag the sea floor with their nets (Bruni 2003). In Turkey, the discovery of 19 frozen bodies of illegal migrants, of which nine were children, in the mountainous border with Iran provides similar evidence of the problem (BBC News 2002).

Just as in these countries, many illegal migrants have died trying to enter the United States. Most of these deaths have occurred along the border area between the US and Mexico.[2] In response to increased enforcement and fortification of the US and Mexico international boundary beginning in 1993, migrants have increasingly attempted to cross the border illegally through more dangerous routes, with a resulting increase in deaths (Cornelius 2001; Eschbach, Hagan and Rodriguez 1999, 2001; Reyes, Johnson and Swearingen, 2002).[3]

---

1 Throughout this chapter the term "illegal" migrant is used to describe those who immigrate into countries without official approval. It is used interchangeably and synonymously with other common terms used to describe this type of behavior such as "irregular", "unauthorized", "illicit", "illegitimate", and/or "criminal".

2 This is not to say that migrant deaths only occur in this geographic area. Migrant deaths are also repeatedly reported in the Caribbean as migrants attempt illegal entry into the US via south Florida (see Bracken 2004; Prengaman 2004).

3 The US Border Patrol launched a series of border enforcement campaigns under the idea of "prevention through deterrence". These campaigns include Operation Hold the Line, in El Paso, Texas, 1993; Operation Gatekeeper in San Diego and Operation Safeguard in Tucson, 1994; and Operation Rio Grande Valley in south Texas, August 1997. These operations

It is likely that any government forced to secure its borders will experience an increase in migrant fatalities and will find it necessary to reduce these deaths. This chapter discusses the reasons for this obligation and presents a case study of the United States' experience of dealing with death among those entering the country illegally. It describes the emergence of the problem in the US, the political environment in which it exists and the US government's efforts to deal with the problem. Finally, the chapter explores the scope for the use of Situational Crime Prevention (SCP) in reducing the scale of the problem.

The Obligation to Save Human Life

At first sight, it might seem paradoxical for a government to devote resources to saving the lives of those trying to enter the country illegally, but there are many reasons why governments might do this. First, the need to save lives of illegal migrants is required, or appears to be, under the human rights protocol accepted by the United Nations. This stipulates the right of all individuals to life, human dignity, personal liberty, freedom of movement, privacy and the right of self-determination, among others (United Nations 1948). Ignoring migrants whose lives are at risk could be interpreted as an infringement of their right to life, and more generally as denying their right to accessible medical care regardless of nationality or legal status (Cholewinski 2003).[4] It is true that the application of human rights mandates to willing participants in human smuggling is not as clear as its application to victims of human trafficking schemes whom are placed under servitude and transported against their will (Apap and Medved 2002). Even so, it is certain that saving human life – illegal migrant or not – is soundly embedded in the fundamental respect for humans intrinsic to democratic values.

Second, governments might accept the responsibility to save migrant lives in an effort to stem criticism by groups concerned with the welfare of illegal migrants.

---

included an increase in the number of agents patrolling directly on the border, erection of physical barricades or walls, and increased use of electronic surveillance equipment.

4 According to Cholewinski (2003:14 footnote 28) the following international provisions indicate the right to medical care for all:

> Article 12(1) of the ICESCR reads: "The States Parties to the present Covenant recognise the right of everyone to the enjoyment of the highest attainable standard of physical and mental health". In General Comment No. 14, the Committee on Economic, Social and Cultural Rights, responsible for monitoring the implementation of the Covenant, stated that "[i]n particular, States are under the obligation to *respect* the right to health by, *inter alia*, refraining from denying or limiting equal access for all persons, including prisoners or detainees, minorities, asylum seekers and illegal immigrants, to preventive, curative and palliative health services; abstaining from enforcing discriminatory practices as a State policy …". Original emphasis. See United Nations, Economic and Social Council, Committee on Economic, Social and Cultural Rights, 22nd Session, Geneva, 25 April – 12 May 2000, *The right to the highest attainable standard of health*, UN Doc. E/C.12/2000/4 (11 August 2000), para. 34.

Saving migrant lives could help to change perceptions of concerned citizens who view immigration enforcement measures as overly intrusive, abusive and unjust. In the US for example, some border watchers are very critical of what they see as the abrasive practices of the Border Patrol (LaFranchi 1996; MacLachlan and Mutch 1995; Nathan 1993).

Third, taking proactive preventive action to make border areas safer may reduce the financial burden of host countries forced to provide medical attention to those crossing the border illegally.[5] Several reports in the US and in England suggest that the expense involved in treating unauthorized migrants reaches into the millions (Hope 2003; Ibarra 2001; Janofsky 2003; Kelly 2004). In the European Union, efforts have been made to increase the level of health care provided to illegal migrants (Cholewinski 2003).

Fourth, adoption of a life saving program could serve to "shift the blame" from migrants to smugglers. The migrant then becomes viewed as the victim just as in human trafficking schemes. (There are cases where smugglers are already blamed for transporting their migrant clients in unsafe and hazardous conditions, IOM 2000.) Shifting of blame may also help minimize the role conflict of assigning life saving responsibilities to the same agencies responsible for enforcement. The strategy of shifting the blame is not new. For instance, the law enforcement response to the problem of prostitution was first to shift the blame to pimps, then to the clients. In a similar manner, in the field of drug abuse there was an attempt to shift the blame for drug use on to the dealers and away from the users. In each case, the conflict is between enforcing the law but at the same time ensuring that offenders do not suffer unduly – in the case of smuggled migrants that they do not die.

The United States Experience with Death among Illegal Migrants

To put migrant deaths in context it is necessary to give an account of recent trends in illegal migration and of the development of policies to control this migration.

The exact number of illegal aliens currently residing in the United States is unknown. Overall, estimates have generally indicated a large and increasing number of illegal immigrants in the US, with some figures ranging just over one million during the later part of the 1980s (Warren 2000; Woodrow and Passel 1990) and estimates of up to nine times that in 2001 (Bean, Van Hook and Woodrow-Lafield 2001; Reyes, Johnson and Swearingen 2002). The number of unauthorized immigrants entering the U.S. reached between 500,000 and 600,000 per year during the late 1990s, almost doubling from the first half of the decade (Bean, Van Hook and Woodrow-Lafield 2001; Passel and Fix 2001).

In efforts to control illegal immigration, the US Congress passed the 1986 Immigration Reform and Control Act (IRCA) which had three main provisions: (1) sanctions for employers who knowingly hired undocumented immigrants; (2)

---

5 Area hospitals bear the brunt of the expense but then commonly seek reimbursement by the national government (see Pear 2004).

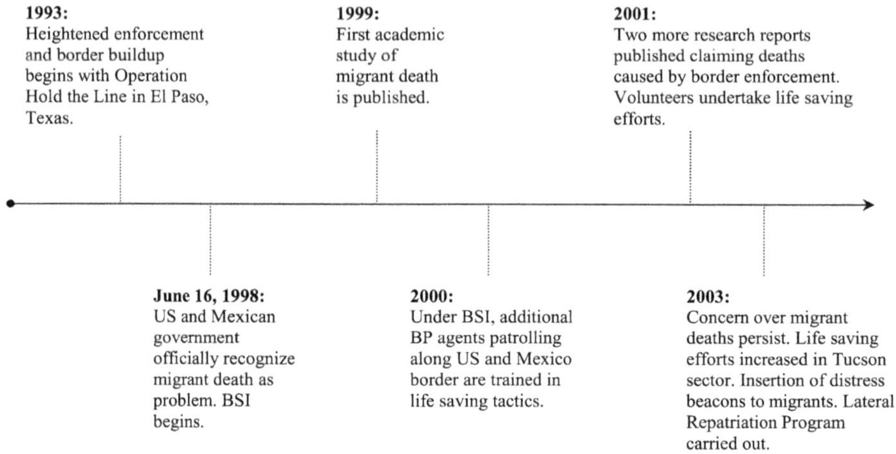

Figure 12.1 Selected developments of migrant death as a problem in the US

increased enforcement along the US borders; and(3) legalization of then current illegal aliens residing in the United States. The 1990 Immigration Reform Act imposed further restrictions on entry and in 1996 the Illegal Immigration Reform and Immigrant Responsibility Act and the Antiterrorism and Effective Death Penalty Act expanded the powers of the Immigration and Naturalization Service (INS) by allowing for the detention and deportation of any illegal and legal immigrant who has been charged with or convicted of a drug offense or who otherwise possesses a criminal record. Additionally, the 1996 Act established measures to control US borders and augmented enforcement of laws prohibiting businesses from employing illegal aliens.

The Recognition of Migrant Deaths

In fulfillment of US Congress directives to intensify enforcement of immigration policy, the US Border Patrol implemented several focused enforcement campaigns along the Mexico border beginning in the early 1990s. The first of these was Operation Hold the Line in El Paso, Texas in 1993, followed by Operation Gatekeeper in San Diego, California, and Operation Safeguard in Arizona, both in 1994, and Operation Rio Grande Valley in south Texas in 1997 (see Figure 12.1). It was anticipated that these enforcement campaigns would have two possible effects: (1) the deterrence of would-be migrants from attempting entry; or (2) the displacement of migratory routes to more remote areas where it was believed that Border Patrol would have the tactical advantage in detecting and apprehending illegal migrants.

In the aftermath of these enforcement campaigns, the numbers of recorded migrant deaths began to climb. Part of this increase might have been due to more deaths being discovered by the much larger number of agents patrolling the border but it was also due to the fact that migrants were using more treacherous desert and mountain routes to gain entry. In response to the growing numbers of deaths, the US government in collaboration with the Mexican government created the Border Safety Initiative (BSI) aimed at making the border safer.

Under BSI, the Border Patrol implemented a number of measures along the 2,013 miles of US–Mexico border which included (1) public message campaigns and signs warning about the dangers of remote terrain crossings; (2) search and rescue operations performed by Border Search, Trauma, and Rescue teams (BORSTAR); and (3) training of agents in life saving and rescue techniques. The Border Patrol has also implemented a data tracking system that records all rescues and deaths along the US side of the south-west border.[6]

At the same time, several non-governmental groups began splintered efforts to help migrants cross the border safely. They mounted volunteer search and rescue operations and placed water and food stations along known migration corridors (Flannery, Leonard, and Rozemberg 2001). By 1999, the academic community had also begun to take notice of the problem and began to study the increase in border deaths. Most of these researchers were seeking evidence that the rise in border deaths was the direct result of the heightened border enforcement (Cornelius 2001; Eschbach, Hagan and Rodriguez 1999, 2001).

Despite the various life saving efforts, recorded deaths continued to increase. In June of 2000, two years after the BSI began the then Department of Immigration and Naturalization service announced that Border Patrol agents in select locations would receive additional training in water-rescue programs because of continued drowning deaths (INS 2000).

In the summer of 2003, a well-publicized account of a group of migrants suffocating in a large truck in south Texas once again called national attention to migrant deaths. Partly in response to this event, the government augmented surveillance near Tucson, Arizona where substantial numbers of border deaths occur and began erecting light beacons for migrants to activate when in need of help (Thompson 2003). The Border Patrol also implemented a Lateral Repatriation Program (LRP) in September of 2003 which removed migrants from one of the most risky areas on the border and returned them to Mexico across an area of the border that was safer.

Trends of Migrant Fatality

It was not until 1999 that the US government began keeping figures of the number of migrant fatalities as part of the BSI Incident Tracking System. Prior to this, researchers such as Eschbach, Hagan and Rodriguez (1999) had traced the number of migrant fatalities by compiling counts of discovered bodies from Vital Registration Mortality files. Figure 12.2 presents two trend lines: one of likely migrant deaths reported by Eschbach, Hagan and Rodriguez (1999) from 1985 to 1998 and the second of migrant deaths recorded by the U.S. Border Patrol from 1998 to 2001. This

6 The south-west border region is divided into nine sectors that span the Mexico border through California, Arizona, New Mexico and Texas.

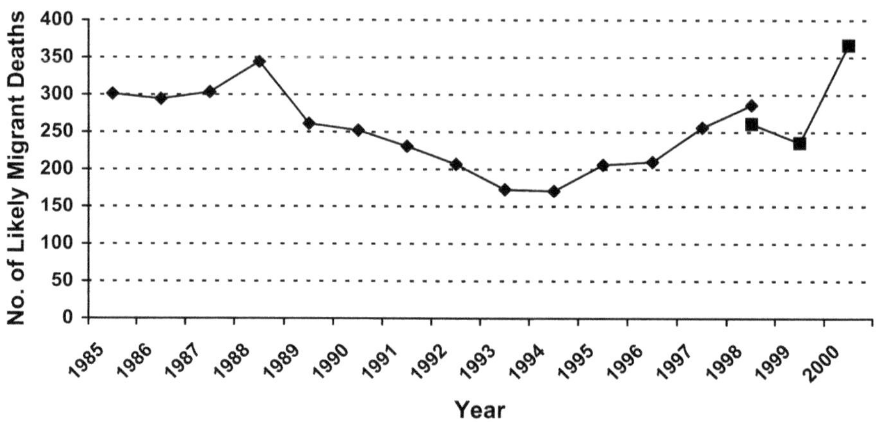

Figure 12.2 Likely migrant deaths along the US and Mexico border, 1985–2000

Source: *Figures for 1985 to 1998, Eschbach et al. (2001); 1998 to 2000, U.S. Border Patrol data.*

figure shows that deaths of migrants were declining prior to the border campaigns introduced in the early 1990s and then began to rise steadily throughout the later 1990s, with a peak in 2000.

Yet, simple numbers of migrant deaths carry little meaning without comparing them to the number of migrants crossing the border illegally. Though not a direct measure of all illegal crossings, yearly INS apprehension figures have been used to provide a basis for comparison (Reyes, Johnson and Swearingen 2002). Figure 12.3 provides the yearly rate of migrant deaths per 100,000 INS apprehensions of illegal migrants.[7]

The data presented in Figure 12.3 generally reflects the trend in Figure 12.2, but the increase throughout the later part of the 1990s is not as steep. The peak in the time series occurred in 1988 with a rate of 34 deaths per 100,000 apprehensions while the lowest rate of migrant fatality occurred in 1993 and 1996, each with a rate of 13 migrant deaths per 100,000 apprehensions. The cause of the increase in migrant deaths in the late 1980s has not been explained by research but it seems likely that it is the result of migrants learning that they could cross the border very easily near Tijuana and other border cities simply by running across with very little

7 Numbers of yearly INS apprehensions are total numbers throughout the United States and are not restricted to those occurring on the Mexico border. Divisions of apprehensions by border region do not become available until 1993. Clearly, comparison with only those apprehensions occurring on the Mexico border is most appropriate. However, to extend the time period of analysis to 1985, overall apprehension figures are used. South-west border apprehensions comprise the vast majority of all yearly apprehensions and differences in rates computed with southwest border apprehensions only from 1993 to 2000 were minor and are not reported.

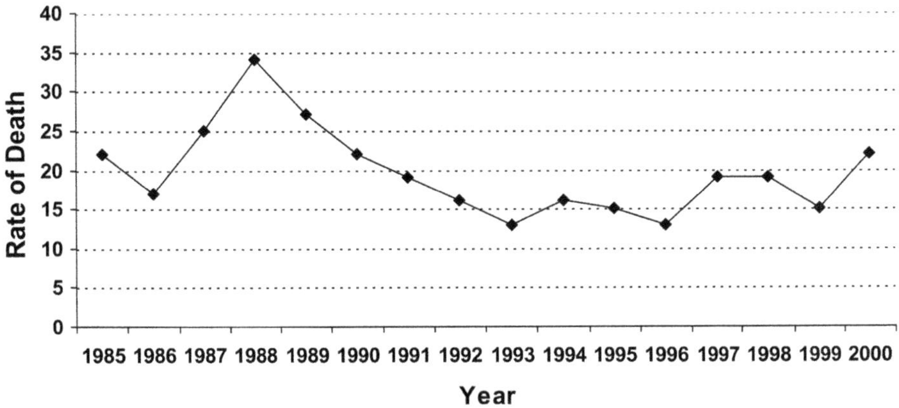

Figure 12.3 Migrant deaths per 100,000 INS apprehensions, 1985–2000
Source: Apprehension figures – INS; Death figures – 1985 to 1998, Eschbach, Hagan and Rodriguez (2001); 1998 to 2000, US Border Patrol data.

planning or preparation. Certainly there were many media reports documenting this phenomenon at the time. The IRCA act of 1996, which legalized the status of illegal migrants residing in the US, might have acted to lure migrants in hopes of gaining citizenship. Unfortunately, it was not uncommon for these migrants to be struck by cars as they crossed the busy highways in that area. Just after 1988, the rate of migrant death begins a steady decrease. While, again, this decrease has not been explained by research, it could well be the result of prevention measures taken by the Border Patrol and local police to prevent illegal migrants from crossing busy highways. What is clear is that auto–pedestrian fatalities, notably in San Diego, decreased at a particularly high rate. For example, in 1988 there were 36 such deaths; by 1995 these had dropped to 5 (Eschbach, Hagan and Rodriguez 2001). It was in this year that the Border Patrol erected a three-mile long barrier to prevent migrants from running across a highway near San Diego which had been the site of many deaths.

Two further important points emerge from the data in Figure 12.3. First, although the rate of migrant fatalities has continually increased in the aftermath of the border enforcement campaigns, the rate has not reached that observed in 1988. Second, the data also reveal the low probability of occurrence of migrant deaths, at least in relation to INS apprehensions of illegal migrants. Even at the highest rate in 1988, the occurrence of migrant fatality is less than 0.1 percent of all apprehensions for that year.

Reversing Immigration Policy to Reduce Migrant Deaths

Many argue that the only way to reduce migrant deaths is to relax immigration enforcement efforts (Nevins 2002) and increase opportunities for legitimate entry through issuing temporary work visas (Dinan 2003). However, this idea is directly contrary to the trend of US immigration policy since the early 1900s which has become increasingly restrictive and has called for evermore enforcement. At best, therefore, immigration policy could only change in the long term and it would likely be incremental. Such changes could only have a minor impact on migrant deaths. Second, the terrorist attacks that occurred on September 11 have made it even more unlikely that border enforcement measures will be relaxed. Finally, recent proposals to expand the temporary visa work program have never sought to increase the numbers granted by more than 115,000 per year (Jimenez 1998). As the INS routinely apprehends in excess of 1 million illegal migrants every year, the likely impact work visas would have in increasing the opportunity for legitimate entry is far offset by the demand.

The Possible Role for Situational Crime Prevention

Despite widespread efforts to save migrant lives by BSI and volunteer groups, the numbers (and even the rates) of migrant deaths have continued to increase. This does not necessarily imply that these life saving efforts have been a waste of time. Rather, it could be that migrants are increasingly exposing themselves to more hazardous conditions and that more of them are dying as a result. Whatever the case, it does suggest the need for a more coordinated, comprehensive approach to the problem. One framework for organizing such an effort is provided by situational crime prevention (SCP), a preventive approach that has proven widely successful in reducing many specific crime problems (Clarke 1997). The SCP model is based on an applied research methodology which serves as the template to define and understand the problem, formulate solutions, and evaluate the results. The application of a SCP approach to the problem of migrant death would include the following five stages:

1. the collection of data about the nature and dimensions of the problem of migrant death;
2. an analysis of the situational conditions that permit or facilitate the occurrence of migrant death;
3. a systematic study of possible means of blocking these situational conditions;
4. the implementation of the most promising, feasible and economic measures;
5. the monitoring of results and the further refinement of preventive efforts.

To assist stage three, SCP provides a classification of 25 situational techniques grouped within five categories that describe the intention or mechanism of the intervention (Cornish and Clarke 2004). These five categories are as follows:

- Increasing the effort: these techniques seek to increase the amount of effort needed to engage in the problem behavior. They include target hardening, controlling access to facilitators, screening exits, deflecting offenders, and controlling tools/weapons.

- Increasing the risks: these techniques seek to increase the risk of apprehension or likelihood of failure involved in the problem behavior. They include extending guardianship, assisting natural surveillance, reducing anonymity, utilizing place managers, and strengthening formal surveillance.
- Reducing the rewards: these techniques seek to eliminate the rewards from engaging in the problematic behavior. They involve concealing targets, removing targets, identifying property, disrupting markets, and denying benefits.
- Reducing provocations: these techniques seek to eliminate factors that provoke the commission of problem behaviors. They include reducing frustrations and stress, avoiding disputes, reducing emotional arousal, neutralizing peer pressure, and discouraging imitation.
- Removing excuses: these techniques seek to inform individuals of the consequences of their actions or otherwise remove excuses. They entail setting rules, posting instructions, alerting conscience, assisting compliance, and controlling drugs and alcohol.

An application of a SCP model to the problem of migrant death provides several benefits. First, SCP accepts the political and social environment by default, so that its implementation is not dependent upon broad social policy changes. This is particularly relevant for the problem of migrant deaths which calls for immediate response, within the current geopolitical environment. Second, SCP is compatible with policing operations. Though not informed by the SCP model, the Border Patrol has already begun using some situational tactics under BSI efforts. Examples of situational measures include the posting of warning signs for migrants identifying the dangers of crossing; the installation of barriers preventing migrants from crossing busy roadways where many had been killed by passing motorists; and the blockading of hazardous river crossings where drowning had occurred. There is some indication that the implementation of these measures has been effective. It is conceivable that many other promising situational measures could be identified through a systematic application of SCP.

Implications for Government

Adoption of a situational crime prevention approach in dealing with migrant fatalities would carry a number of implications for government, including the following:

1. Officially recognize the problem of migrant deaths. Governments need to acknowledge that the problem exists in order to initiate a formal prevention strategy. Many governments may be reluctant to do this when they are still struggling with managing and containing illegal immigration. In some ways, however, the operational tasks involved in reducing migrant deaths are one and the same as preventing illegal migration. For example, a reduction in

migrant deaths might be achieved through focusing immigration enforcement efforts at particular times and places. Thus, the implementation of a life saving campaign may be more about revising the shape of operational practice along borders zones rather than moving in a whole new direction.

2. Assign responsibility for reducing migrant deaths. The task of preventing migrant deaths must be unambiguously assigned to a specific government agency. For example, had the responsibility for saving migrant lives not been placed clearly on the Border Patrol it is unlikely they would have devoted so many resources to the BSI.
3. Create a multi-national collaboration to reduce loss of life. At the same time, it must be recognized that the illegal migration process and migrant death is a multi-national problem and dealing with it should be as well. Source and transit countries should be enlisted to help in the effort to reduce harm to illegal migrants.
4. Gain in-depth understanding of the migrant death problem. SCP is premised upon gaining an in-depth understanding of the problem to be addressed. This will require governments to invest much more heavily in research on migrant deaths. The BSI Incident Tracking system and the "IDENT" database are both steps in this direction. But much more research is needed including interviews with those knowledgeable about human smuggling and the circumstances of migrant deaths. This would include border officials who regularly encounter the problem (in both immigrated and emigrated countries), as well as apprehended smugglers and migrants. Analysis of intelligence reports of smuggling operations would also assist such understanding.
5. Assess the effectiveness of and refine implemented prevention tactics. SCP also requires the evaluation of any new tactics. This means that when a new intervention is formulated resources are set aside to evaluate the results. Otherwise there is no institutional capacity for building upon past efforts to reduce deaths.

Summary and Conclusion

This chapter examined the reasons why governments might undertake programs to reduce death among illegal migrants. Saving the lives of illegal migrants is consistent with international human rights protocols, may help to reduce criticisms of aggressive border security, and could reduce the financial burden of providing medical treatment to illegal migrants. The chapter also described recent United States experience of migrant deaths. It explored trends in illegal migration within the broader context of immigration policy, and traced the awareness of migrant deaths in the national conscience. It described the Border Safety Initiative, a program designed to safeguard lives of illegal migrants. It presented statistics of migrant deaths on the US side of the Mexican border which suggested that more might be done to save lives. Finally, it argued that situational crime prevention could provide a useful framework for coordinating a systematic approach for dealing with migrant deaths, and it spelled out some of the implications for government that would result from adopting this approach.

Media accounts reveal that migrant deaths routinely occur along the borders of many countries. As the process of globalization continues, migration – both legitimate and illegitimate – is likely to increase. In response, governments will be forced to devote more resources to managing their borders. One dimension of this border management is likely to involve making illegal migration less hazardous.

Acknowledgments

In writing this chapter I am grateful for input given by Ronald V. Clarke and Graeme Newman. I am also grateful to the US Border Patrol which commissioned me to undertake a study of migrant deaths along the US–Mexico border.

References

Apap, Joanna and Felicita Medved (2002), "Protection Schemes for Victims of Trafficking in Selected EU Member Countries, Candidate and Third Countries", International Organization for Migration, prepared for the Exchange of Information and Best Practices Regarding Protection Schemes for Victims of Trafficking in Selected EU Member Countries, Candidates and Third Countries, Madrid, December 19–20.

BBC News (2002), "Frozen Bodies Found in Turkey", *BBC News Online Network*, News Front Page, World, May 30.

Bean, Frank, Jennifer Van Hook and Karen Woodrow-Lafield (2001), *Estimates of Numbers of Unauthorized Migrants Residing in the United States: The Total, Mexican, and Non-Mexican Central American Unauthorized Populations in Mid-2001*, Washington DC: Pew Hispanic Center.

Bracken, Amy (2004), "18 Dominicans Missing at Sea Boat Capsizes; Survivor Found, 1 Body Recovered", *South Florida Sun-Sentinel*, Broward Metro Edition, National, July 14: 14A.

Bruni, Frank (2002), "Off Sicily, Tide of Bodies Roils the Debate Over Immigrants", *New York Times*, International, September 23: A1 and A10.

Bruni, Frank (2003), "Wave of Immigrants Breaks Against Italian Island's Shore", *New York Times*, International, July 11: A1 and A6.

Cholewinski, Ryszard (2003), "Ad Hoc Working Group on Irregular Migrants Report (MG-AD)", Strasbourg: Council of Europe, December 17–18.

Clarke, Ronald V. (1997) (ed.), *Situational Crime Prevention: Successful Case Studies*, 2nd edn, Guilderland: Harrow and Heston.

Clarke, Ronald V. (2002), "Protecting Immigrants from Victimization: The Scope for Situational Crime Prevention", in Freilich, Joshua D., Graeme Newman, S.

Giora Shoham and Moshe Addad (eds), *Migration, Culture Conflict and Crime*, Burlington: Ashgate.

Cornelius, Wayne (2001), "Death at the Border: Unintended Consequences of U.S. Immigration Control Policy", *Population and Development Review*, 27(4): 661–85.

Cornish, Derek B. and Ronald V. Clarke (2004), "Opportunities, Precipitators and Criminal Decisions: A Reply to Wortley's Critique of Situational Crime Prevention", in Smith, M. and D.B. Cornish (eds), *Theory for Situational Crime Prevention*, Crime Prevention Studies, vol. 16. Monsey: Criminal Justice Press.

Dinan, Stephan (2003), "Guest-Worker Proposals Face Big Hurdles", *Washington Times*, September 3.

Eschbach, Karl, Jaqueline Hagan and Nestor Rodriguez (1999), "Death at the Border", *International Migration Review*, 33(2): 430–54.

Eschbach, Karl, Jacqueline Hagan and Nestor Rodriguez (2001), "Causes and Trends in Migrant Deaths Along the U.S.-Mexico Border, 1985–1998", University of Houston, Center for Immigration Research, March.

Flannery, Pat, Christina Leonard and Hernán Rozmberg (2001), "Border Nightmare: U.S., Mexico Vow Justice in Fatal Desert Trek", *Arizona Republic*, May 25.

Goldstein, Herman (1979), "Improving Policing: A Problem Oriented Approach", *Crime and Delinquency*, 25: 236–58.

Goldstein, Herman (1990), *Problem-Oriented Policing*, New York: McGraw Hill.

Harrison, Paige and Allen Beck (2002), *Prisoners in 2001*, Washington, DC: US Department of Justice, Bureau of Justice Statistics.

Hope, Jenny (2003), "Hospitals Facing Cash Crisis from Bill for Illegal Migrants", *Daily Mail*, August 16.

Human Events Staff (1997), "Mexican Snipers Fire on U.S. Border Patrol: Shootings Underscore Mounting Violence on Southern Frontier", *Human Events*, June 13, 53(22): 5.

Ibarra, Ignacio (2001), "Migrants' Medical Costs Burden Providers", *Arizona Daily Star*, Tucson, April 17.

Immigration and Naturalization Service (INS) (2000), "INS Intensifies Life-Saving Measures Along the Southwest Border", INS announcement, June 26, Office of International Information Programs, US Department of State, at http://usinfo.state.gov.

Immigration and Naturalization Service (INS) (1998), "INS Launches Unprecedented Borderwide Public Safety Initiative: Comprehensive Effort Draws on Cooperation with Mexico", INS News Release, June 16, Office of Public Affairs, at www.immigration.gov.

International Organization for Migration (IOM) (2000), "Deaths in Trafficking/Smuggling", *Trafficking in Migrants: Quarterly Bulletin*, Trends, summer, 21.

Janofsky, Michael (2003), "Burden Grows for Southwest Hospitals", *New York Times*, dateline Phoenix, Arizona, April 11.

Jimenez, Andres (1998), "Guest-Worker Proposals Defeated in Congress This Time", *San Francisco Chronicle*, October 16: A1.

Kelly, David (2004), "A Hospital on Border Going Over the Edge", *Los Angeles Times*, dateline Bisbee, Arizona, June 20.

LaFranchi, Howard (1996), "Some American Border-Dwellers Say the US Patrol is the Real 'Invader'", *Christian Science Monitor*, February 20, 88(58): 10.

MacLachlan, Suzanne and David Mutch (1995), "Border Patrol Agents Routinely Abuse People", *Christian Science Monitor*, April 13, 87(96): 2.

Nathan, Debbie (1993), "A Death On the Border", *Christian Science Monitor*, March, 57(3): 15.

Nevins, Joseph (2002), "Time to End a Fatal Way of Life Along the U.S.-Mexico Boundary", *Common Dreams News Center*, June 18.

New York Times (2002), "Arizona: Criticism of Border Patrols", *New York Times*, national, December 20: A32.

Passel, Jeffrey and Michael Fix (2001), "U.S. Immigration at the Beginning of the 21st Century", testimony before the Subcommittee on Immigration and Claims Hearing on "The U.S. Population and Immigration", Washington DC: Committee on the Judiciary, U.S. House of Representatives, Urban Institute.

Pear, Robert (2004), "U.S. Is Linking Status of Aliens to Hospital Aid", *New York Times*, dateline Washington, August 10.

Pendleton, Scott (1995), "Rocks and Gunshots Fly at Texas Border Patrols", *Christian Science Monitor*, May 23, 87(124): 3.

Prengaman, Peter (2004), "Survivors Fought Desperation Some on Boat for Puerto Rico Demanded Breast Milk From Women", *South Florida Sun-Sentinel*, Broward Metro edition, foreign, August 12: 17A.

Reyes, Belinda, Hans Johnson and Richard Swearingen (2002). "Holding the Line? The Effect of the Recent Border Buildup on Unauthorized Immigration", San Francisco: Public Policy Institute of California, at www.ppic.org/publications/PPIC162/index.html.

Scalia, John and Litras, Marika (2002), *Immigration Offenders in the Federal Criminal Justice System, 2000*, Washington DC: US Department of Justice, Bureau of Justice Statistics.

Simons, Marlise (2004), "Under Pressure, Spain Tries to Close Open Door", *New York Times*, international, October 10: A10.

Thompson, Ginger (2003), "In Border Town, Migrant Crackdown Rankles", *New York Times*, international, June 5: A3.

United Nations (1948), *Universal Declaration of Human Rights*, adopted and proclaimed by General Assembly resolution 217 A (III) of December 10.

Warren, Robert (2000), *Annual Estimates of the Unauthorized Population Residing in the United States and Components of Changes: 1987 to 1997*, Washington DC: US Immigration and Naturalization Service.

Woodrow, Karen and Jeffrey Passel (1990), "Post-IRCA Undocumented Immigration to the United States: An Assessment Based on the June 1988 CPS", in Bean, Frank, Barry Edmonston and Jeffrey Passel (eds), *Undocumented Migration to the Unites States: IRCA and the Experience of the 1980s*, Washington, DC: Urban Institute Press.

Chapter 13

Providing a Helping Hand to Battered Immigrant Women: The Professionals' Perspectives[1]

Edna Erez
Kent State University

Linsey Britz
Victim Assistance Program, Akron, OH

Introduction

In recent decades migration has become a worldwide phenomenon. The rapid globalization of the world's economies and political environments will ensure that the number of migrants, at least half of whom are women (in some countries, women account for the overwhelming majority of migrants), will increase even further in the 21st century in all of the world's major geographical regions.

Migration exacerbates the gender-linked vulnerability of women. It makes them further dependent on and at times puts them at the mercy of their husbands or intimate partners, nuclear or extended families, sponsors or employers, and their own ethnic/racial communities (Erez 2001; Kelly 1999). Recent research in the US has confirmed that violence against women is one of the most common victimizations experienced by immigrants (Davis and Erez 1998). Research on the victimization of immigrants in general and women immigrants in particular has begun to be conducted (for reviews see Erez 2000; Menjivar and Salcido 2002; Raj and Silverman 2002).

Considering the high level of violence in women's lives for both immigrants and non-immigrants alike, battered immigrant women's appeals for help and the degree to which the social service and legal systems' responses address their particular needs deserve close attention. The complex context of immigration and related dilemmas and hurdles battered immigrant women face in deciding to seek help or invoke the justice system, present difficult problems for the allied professionals who

1 Data used in this study were collected in the course of research on "Violence Against Immigrant Women and Systemic Responses" supported by grant #98-WT-VX-0030 from the National Institute of Justice.

are called on to help them. This article attempts to fill this gap by examining the experiences of social service providers, legal advocates, and attorneys (e.g., family, and immigration lawyers) who attend to the needs of battered immigrant women. It presents the challenges and dilemmas these professionals encounter in the course of their work, and the manner in which they respond to the intricate problems of battered immigrants.

To understand the complex problems the professionals encounter in the course of addressing battered immigrant women, a review of the dynamics of the abuse immigrant women often experience, and the way it interacts with their immigration context and immigrant status is needed. This article thus first describes the social and legal context of the immigrant women's abuse, the coping methods they adopt, and their help-seeking behavior in addressing the abuse. It then presents the problems and dilemmas faced by the professionals who assist battered immigrant women or advocate on their behalf, and their mundane and more creative ways to respond to the intricate problems of their clients. The article concludes with policy recommendations about the response to battered immigrant women.

The Immigration Context of Domestic Violence

Economic, Cultural, Psychological and Practical Concerns

The immigration context of battered immigrant women presents unique problems vis-à-vis accessing social services or seeking help from the justice system. It involves a complex set of interacting cultural, legal, and practical concerns, making immigrant women remain in battering relationships, reluctant to report their abuse, hesitant to access services and fearful or unwilling to participate in justice proceedings (Erez 2000, 2002; Raj and Silverman 2002).

Battered immigrant women are often economically dependent and financially insecure. The husband is the breadwinner who typically conducts all communication with the outside world. Immigrant women frequently view their primary role as that of wives and mothers and they commonly lack linguistic and occupational skills for gainful employment.

Battered immigrant women are often highly isolated due to their immigration circumstances (e.g., Abraham 2000). Immigrant women often move to follow their husbands, leaving behind their own familial and social support systems (Erez and Hartley 2003). Further, immigrant women frequently live with or are close to their husbands' families due to cultural dictates and economic considerations (Abraham 2000; Raj and Silverman 2002). Proximity to the husband's family leads not only to increased support for the abuse, but also to increased likelihood of abuse by in-laws (Erez and Hartley 2003; Huisman 1996; Supriya 1996).

Despite severe, extended and lengthy abuse, battered immigrant women tend to remain in abusive relationships for a long time. There are social pressures on all women to remain in a marriage. In some cultures, however, divorce leaves such a stigma that a divorced woman may never be accepted by her cultural community or be unable to remarry (Erez 2000, 2002). Further, immigrants' memberships in religious institutions (such as churches, mosques, temples) provide women an amplified sense of community, much-needed continuity, and support. At the same time, cultural norms and religious prescriptions may not offer battered women the kind of support and encouragement they need to escape from violence in the home (Kelly 1999; Okin 1998).

If the woman leaves, she is usually held responsible for the break-up of the marriage even if she has been abused. Her family of origin oftentimes will not accept her back, because such an act brings shame and disgrace on the family name and mars the collective perception of the family's honor (Narayan 1995; Supriya 1996). In many cases, the women fear retaliation by their husbands' families (and sometimes their own families) if they return to their country of origin (Orloff 1995). Leaving an abuser to return to the home country also presents the women with tremendous difficulties in providing economic support for themselves and their children. In many countries, gender is a barrier to adequate employment (Orloff, Jang and Klein 1996).

Immigrant women themselves feel they must live up to their roles as wives and mothers, demanding the sacrifice of personal autonomy and freedom (Erez and Hartley 2003). As a woman is considered the pivotal point of the family, regardless of the physical or verbal abuse she may endure, her primary responsibilities are to care for and safeguard her family (Maglizza 1985) and steadfastly remain at her husband's side (Surpriya 1996). Proscription to reveal to outsiders any unbecoming or improper behavior of family members (whether their children or their husband) is also included within the cultural script for many immigrant women (Erez 2000).

For a battered immigrant woman, leaving her husband usually means relinquishing both financial resources (such as her home and personal effects) and vital practical services she needs to obtain work or maintain her job (Currie 1995). Immigrant women's social relationships are usually confined to those who share their language. Lack of linguistic skills thus contributes to the isolation of immigrant women, maintaining their dependence on the family, which in turn reinforces familial and cultural interpretations of assault (Erez 2000, 2002).

Immigration also affects immigrant communities' predilection to exposing abuse in their midst, for fear of attracting negative attention to their community. This tendency to hide and deny the abuse results in a weaker system of supports and aid for abused immigrant women, who in similar situations may have received assistance in their home country. Attempts to raise issues of violence against women in immigrant communities are often deflected by the community leadership as an imposition of irrelevant "Western" agendas, and the claim that "our tradition" or "our families" do not suffer from these problems that are endemic to "Western" marriages (Narayan 1995). Religious values and institutions often reinforce traditional responses to woman battering and act as disincentives to reveal the abuse or contact the justice system (Okin 1999).

Accessing Social Services and Reporting the Violence

Immigrant victims in general (Davis and Erez 1998), and battered immigrant women in particular (e.g., Das Gupta 2000; Erez and Hartley 2003), are reluctant to report crime and cooperate with authorities due to an intricate combination of cultural, social, and legal reasons. Immigrant battered women exhibit strong reluctance to reveal the abuse to social service agencies, religious leaders, or any outside family members as it will bring shame upon themselves, their husbands, and their children (Erez and Hartley 2003).

Women who violate social and gender norms may be disowned by their families and harassed by their communities. Although there are many positive and practical aspects of extended families, in circumstances of abuse its very self-sufficiency paradoxically works against the needs of battered women (Erez 2000). Appeals for help to outsiders (including police, social service or welfare agents) are therefore not perceived as an option for many battered immigrant women (e.g., Erez and Hartley 2003; Haile-Mariam and Smith 1999; Wachholz and Miedema 2000).

Immigrant women often do not know that battering is a criminal offense in their new country, nor are they aware of any social, legal, health, or other services available for women in their predicament. In addition to aversion from involving outsiders in private family affairs, prior negative experiences with the police and the justice system in their own countries often color battered women's willingness to call the police for help in their new country (Davis, Erez, and Avitabile 2001; Erez and Hartley 2003).

The overriding rationale for many immigrant women to stay in an abusive relationship and not report their battering is the prospect of losing their children (Erez 2000; Erez and Hartley 2003). Return to their own country often means never seeing their children again and loss of custody rights in favor of the father. Battered immigrant women sometimes believe, often because their abusers have told them so, that separation or divorce in the host country will also result in loss of custody and access to their children (Erez and Hartley 2003).[2] Immigrant women who have managed to overcome cultural incentives to remain silent are still wary of requesting help from law enforcement agencies (Erez 2000). They may have had negative experiences with authorities in their country of origin (Davis, Erez and Avitabile 2001) or fear unpleasant experiences with legal institutions in their new country (Erez and Hartley 2003; Pogrebin and Poole 1990). Language and communication barriers further add to their reluctance to contact the justice system (Davis and Erez 1998; Erez and Hartley 2003).

Some battered immigrant women are afraid that official action will lead to the deportation of their abusers, which they believe could mean loss of their own dependent immigrant status (Erez and Hartley 2003). Few women are aware of recent

---

2 In the US, the contrary is often the case, as the courts are likely to award custody to the non-abusive parent even when she does not have legal immigration status (American Bar Association 2000).

US laws that offer many abused immigrants an avenue to attain legal immigration status independent of their abusers through the Violence Against Women Act (VAWA) (1994, 2000). Deportation is an omnipresent weapon for abusers to threaten their immigrant partners, regardless of their partners' immigration status. Distrust of the government, ignorance of immigration law, and deception by abusers often combine to keep immigrant women in abusive relationships and prevent them from reporting the battering (Erez 2002; Erez and Hartley 2003; Orloff, Jang and Klein 1995).

More-informed abused immigrant women sometimes hesitate to call authorities because they are afraid that the batterer's likely arrest record resulting from reporting the abuse may hinder his attempts to gain lawful immigration status. Battered women who call the police often do not want to have the abusers arrested, as they are economically and/or emotionally dependent on them. Like most battered women, they merely want to stop the violence. Arrest of the batterer is an even less desirable outcome for immigrant battered women who believe that they are dependent on their abuser for their immigration status. The dual arrest practices that sometimes take place under mandatory/preferred arrest policies (i.e., police arresting both perpetrator and female victim rather than the primary aggressor, e.g., Miller 2001) may result in a criminal record for both parties, which in turn may adversely affect prospects for immigration status adjustment and related outcomes (Erez 2002).

Access to Information and Communication Problems

Access to information has always been a major factor impeding women's utilization of support services or appeals to justice. Typically, the husband is the primary conduit of information to the women in the household, often using his presumed knowledge of the system to maintain control and for exerting the domination characteristic of abusive relationships (Erez 2000). The control tactics abusers often use exploit and perpetuate immigrant women's vulnerabilities, including lack of information on services and remedies, which the women need to overcome in order to escape the abuse, and end their isolation and dependency on their abusers (Erez 2000; Erez and Hartley 2003).

For recently arrived immigrant women, the language barriers exacerbate their isolation (Abraham 2000). Frequently, immigrant women are pre-literate in their own language as well. An inability to read, combined with other language problems, reinforces barriers to accessing information and communicating effectively. For undocumented women, leaving is more difficult, because without immigration papers they cannot work legally and, in the US, may not be entitled to welfare assistance, including housing.

Not knowing the language of their new country, and lacking literacy skills in their own language, often means that battered immigrant women are not able to convey complaints about abuse to officials or service providers. These women must often rely on friends, neighbors, relatives or community members to translate their grievances in cases where the police are called (Erez and Hartley 2003). Family and community members may know about options to combat woman battering or may collude with the abuser to mislead the victim (Erez 2000). Children, who are often versed in the language of the new home country, are sometimes asked to translate (Erez and Hartley 2003). Such requests may endanger the children as the abuser may view them as colluding with their mother against him. The children may also not approve of their mother's resorting to official channels for assistance, and may be uncooperative in translating her wishes or communicating in her name (Erez 2002). Asking a child to translate for the mother may also impose difficult fissures of loyalty for the child, exacerbating his or her own adjustment to the new home country.

Reliance on official interpreter services may not be sufficient to counter communication problems with officials. Unless the officers called to the scene of abuse are versed in the immigrant woman's language or have interpreters employed by the police (neither of which are common occurrences), the officers are likely to gather necessary information from the husband or even the children (Erez and Hartley 2003; Wachholz and Miedema 2000). Further, the husband, with his greater proficiency in English, can sometimes dictate the sequence and nature of events to the officers and, hence, control the outcome of the incident.

With interpreters rarely available in crisis situations, police sometimes act on incomplete information, often mediated through scared or unsympathetic family members, or the husband himself (Erez 2002). Communication difficulties can undermine even the justice system's best efforts to assist battered women. Immigrant women in such situations are often susceptible to inappropriate or second-best legal remedies or solutions (Erez 2002; Erez and Hartley 2003).

Battered immigrant women either do not know about services for battered women or do not regard the justice system as an appropriate avenue for seeking assistance (Erez and Hartley 2003). For immigrant women who overcome these obstacles, existing crisis intervention services and legal options are often unable to meet their needs (Erez and Hartley 2003). As a result, immigrant women are even less willing to access or continue to utilize services, once accessed.

In the next sections, the experiences, dilemmas and challenges faced by the professionals who work with these clients, and the ways the professionals have responded to these challenges, as reported in their survey questionnaires, are presented and discussed.

The Current Study

Methodology

The data used to portray the range of problems and dilemmas faced by those who work with battered women and attend to their needs were derived from responses of professionals in various organizations or agencies that serve immigrants and battered women (social service providers, legal advocates, and attorneys who practiced family and immigration law) to a survey conducted during 2000–2001. Written questionnaires were distributed in-person or via email to potential respondents from social service and immigration-related agencies and attorneys listed in the National Network on Behalf of Battered Immigrant Women database. Professionals who attended various meetings and training sessions organized by the network during the years 2000 and 2001 also filled out the survey. The questionnaire included questions about the problems, barriers, resources, solutions and services for immigrant battered women, and enquired about the respondents' relationships with immigrant victims and their communities. It addressed their coordination efforts with other social service agencies, their contacts with the criminal justice system, success stories or cases in which they could not provide assistance. Throughout the survey instrument, respondents were asked to provide specific examples for each of the problems they encountered or issues they discussed.

The sample of respondents in this study consisted of 40 social service providers working in 12 states (Arkansas, California, Colorado, Florida, Hawaii, Illinois, Massachusetts, New Jersey, New Hampshire, New York, Washington, and Wisconsin), and 26 legal advocates, family and immigration law attorneys, working in either domestic violence help related agencies or immigrant organizations, or to attorneys working in private practice. The legal advocates or attorneys who responded came from 14 states (Florida, Arizona, Utah, Colorado, Virginia, California, New Jersey, Washington, Oregon, Washington DC, Texas, Georgia, New York and the Virgin Islands; for further details see Erez and Hartley 2003). These agencies serve a diverse range of abused women and children from countries around the world, both immigrant and non-immigrant women making up their clientele.

Results

Difficulties in Offering Services to Battered Immigrant Women

Resources and scope of expertise To serve an immigrant community, the professionals must have expertise in several areas of counseling and law. They also should possess knowledge of resources not necessarily required when dealing with non-immigrant populations. Some other expectations for those working in this area are knowledge of domestic violence and battered women's resources (i.e., counseling and shelters) and a basic understanding of various areas of the law (i.e., immigration law, family law and criminal law and the procedures within each).

Over half of the respondents stated that their activities and services exceed their mission statements. Some agencies have expanded their services to meet the specialized needs of battered immigrant women. To accomplish their mission, respondents explained, service providers must go beyond their organization's formal mandate to create new services, or increase existing ones, while continuing to operate under pre-existing fiduciary constraints.

Assistance such as bilingual advocacy, refugee settlement, language specific (e.g., Spanish)-based domestic violence intervention programs, and counseling services were developed by these agencies to respond to specific gaps in the social service infrastructure of their communities. To be able to offer such extended services, and to meet the many needs of their immigrant clients, the agencies have to work with other organizations and service providers.

Additional services are both short- and long-term shelter for women and their children, and counseling services for women, children, and families (individual, support groups, or both). Many agencies also provide 24-hour hotlines, crisis intervention services, transitional housing and housing placement, legal services (e.g. legal representation, advocacy, orders of protection, VAWA documentation, etc.), and appropriate information and referrals. For other agencies, their mission statements outlined a commitment towards a specific population or ethnic group, or providing specific services, such as the prosecution of criminals, law enforcement, or mental health services for victims of domestic violence.

Cultural, social and communal issues The professionals had to address various cultural differences and barriers related to differences between the US culture and the native culture the immigrants bring with them. These differences can interfere with services for immigrant women in several ways. As discussed above, cultural ideologies and familial pressures may prevent battered immigrant women from seeking help and blame the victim for leaving and disrupting the home and/or prosecuting the offender. These professionals therefore have to convince battered women that spousal abuse is unacceptable, never justified under any circumstances, not a "normal" part of marriage and is in fact a criminal offense that should be reported to the authorities. Professionals have to overcome the fear that battered immigrant women have in disclosing the abuse, reporting it and facing the consequences of disclosing it by their family and immigrant community.

The professionals also have to convince battered immigrant women that their immigration status would not be jeopardized if they reveal the abuse or leave their abuser. Abusers threaten to have the victim deported without her children thus creating a sense of powerlessness in the women regarding taking any action. As some respondents explained:

- The women experience marital rape, the batterer uses the women's immigration status as a control tool, the women fear losing custody or access to their children, the women lack knowledge regarding US laws and rights and fear doing anything that might get them deported.
- The women are terrified. Sometimes they prefer to capitulate and return to their husbands to get their INS (immigration) papers.

The professionals also attend to the problems of children of battered immigrant women, whose problems are similar to those of the adult mother, in terms of anxiety, fear of deportation and abduction by the abuser.

Legal restrictions, justice system-related constraints and recommendations to address them The legal issues and constraints concerning battered immigrant women can be overwhelming. Typical requests from clients were for information about, and assistance in obtaining legal services. Informing the victim of her legal rights and reducing the client's sense of isolation and confusion play dual roles in this process. Agencies act as translators between the immigrant victim and the immigration authorities and the judicial system. In so doing, requests for legal assistance by immigrant battered women are both numerous and diverse in nature. When battered immigrants use the legal system for help, their cultural community can overtly challenge them. This is due to the interplay of colliding cultures and perceptions that occur among the abuser, the abused, their ethnic community, and any outside intervention.

Bureaucratic obstacles related to advocating for clients with the INS pose further impediments for social service agencies. Several respondents commented upon the frustration and powerlessness caused by not being able to get in touch with an INS representative. Some respondents also reported keeping pace with labyrinthine regulations and guidelines pertaining to immigration law practice as a barrier.

Other legal services included functions such as providing advocacy for protection orders, help filing VAWA self-petitions,[3] writing support letters for immigration, and finding pro bono attorneys for divorce, custody, and child support issues. Agencies were often asked by clients to provide a sense of "judicial and institutional understanding" to what can be an intimidating, time-consuming, and labor-intensive process. The demand for legal advocacy bridges over to the need for housing and housing assistance. Both documented and undocumented women run into limitations when trying to get out of an abusive relationship seeking social assistance. A US government-sponsored initiative for funding victim services, for example, imposes rules that limit services for undocumented battered immigrants.

Another major obstacle that the agencies must confront is fear of the consequences in disclosing abuse. Both documented and undocumented women, due to fear of deportation by the INS, do not contact the justice system. Correspondingly, this fear and possible consequences such as losing one's children, being arrested and incarcerated, or the court's finding that the claims of abuse are unsubstantiated, minimal, or deserved, "can cause paralysis and lack of action to better their circumstances". Most saliently, the service providers stated that they had to deal with their clients' fear of official intervention that will result in deportation, particularly in light of the fact that many agencies are in contact with the police for various reasons.

Respondents also stated that they had to address and "justify" inappropriate comments or behavior by justice officials toward their immigrant clients. They repeatedly reported improper and overtly biased intervention from police officers, child protective services, and other criminal justice agents who were also unable to speak the language of the client.

3 These petitions were created by the Violence Against Women Act (1994) and its reauthorization VAWA 2000, to allow battered immigrant women to petition for immigration status adjustment on their own, if they can prove that they have been abused by the person who was supposed to petition for them as the head of the household or spouse.

Several service providers commented that justice system officials in their communities acted more like INS agents than law enforcement personnel. Respondents claimed that the police are often misinformed and try to screen females for their status. Their training therefore needs to be improved. The professionals offered advice and recommendations for the justice system agents, with whom they interacted on behalf of the battered immigrant women, advice that if followed would reduce the level of anxiety and fear experienced by their clients. They emphasized that prosecutors must learn more about the dynamics underlying immigrant women's reluctance to cooperate with the judicial process and to clarify to the victim this process. Prosecutors need to be cognizant of the many fears and tangible risks that may accompany criminal litigation: deportation, loss of children, potential ostracism from family and community, and recourses to few financial resources or supports if the wife leaves her abuser.[4]

The respondents also commented that prosecutors needed to review carefully any case of dual arrest and only proceed with the case against the primary aggressor. This favorable change would give victims a sense of fairness and equal opportunity for justice. Domestic violence training and education were viewed as mandatory steps towards initiating reform. Providers also recommended hiring prosecutors from more diverse backgrounds, having certified interpreters available in court, and encouraging prosecutors to become more involved in immigrant issues.

The service providers also listed ideas for improved processing of immigrant women cases through the judicial system. An overarching recommendation addressed enhancing court sensitivity to battered immigrant women's issues. As part of this heightened sensitivity, suggestions were to improve victims' access to and understanding of the judicial process.

Recommendations included providing orders of protection and no-contact orders in languages other than English having certified interpreters and victim/ legal advocates on hand for all proceedings and appropriating a safe space in the courthouse for female victims of crime. Other significant suggestions from agencies listed shortening case processing time and streamlining cases for quicker resolutions. Providers also expressed the need for mandatory yearly training and education classes for judges, clerks, and court officials about domestic violence and its repercussions on female immigrant populations.

Communication and translation issues The professionals repeatedly emphasized that communication and language skills are a common barrier to a successful outcome

---

4 The abuser's deportation may or may not have adverse effects on the victim, depending on her particular circumstances. VAWA 2000 removed much of the harm that his loss of status can have on the victim's immigration case, but many victims, advocates and prosecutors are not aware of these changes in the law. Fears about the effect of deportation of the abuser on the victim may be safety-planning issues. Some women's safety will be jeopardized by deportation; others' safety will be enhanced. Other deportation issues that may be of concern to some women, as mentioned in the previous chapter, relate to the abuser's role as a parent or the effect of his removal on the children.

in working with battered immigrant women. Accurately disseminating support and community resource information to any non-English speaking population is a problem; the cost involved in translating all the available information into other languages is often prohibitive. The other option is to have translators for multiple languages on staff or available on call at all times, though this option usually is cost prohibitive. Once a victim is lucky enough to be aware of the available resources and arrive at the hospital, counseling center, shelter, victim advocate's office or court, language is still a barrier.

Respondents from several agencies mentioned circumstances where communication and language issues involve the children of battered immigrant women, placing the children in a difficult situation, which adds to the hardships of the parents and their helpers. Immigrant children, who are usually more knowledgeable of the dominant language than their parents, are often used as translators between the mother and the outside world. A particular problem with this practice is that it puts the children in an awkward position and some may feel they are being forced to "pick sides", thus putting more responsibility on them than a child can handle.

The respondents noted that similar problems arise when family members or members of the immediate community are used as translators, or the community from which the client comes is a small one. The agency may hear a filtered or biased version of the victim's account or wishes. This issue becomes further aggrandized and detrimental to the victim during interactions with justice agents. Several agencies contextualized this issue as follows:

> Clients who speak no English—working with one in particular (Hispanic) and the abuser's aunt is constantly with her and insists on interpreting for her. I sometimes question if the client is getting all the information. Also the aunt-in-law may have ulterior motives – possibly including partnering with the abuser. Language is a huge barrier.

The respondents explained that miscommunication between parties and use of more than one language to interact invariably causes cultural misunderstandings and tendencies on the part of institutional actors (judges, police, service providers, etc.), particularly during police/victim interactions and in the courts. One respondent provided an account of the short and long-term problems caused by the lack of translators. It detailed a mutual arrest case[5] that had a negative effect on the immigrant woman's criminal record, which in the future could affect her INS eligibility status.

Guidelines and Good Practices Employed by the Professional

The professionals responding to the survey provided guidelines and suggestions about optimal methods of handling battered immigrant issues. They also expanded upon the protections and services they would recommend for battered immigrant women.

---

5 These are situations of domestic violence when both the abuser and the victim (who may have tried to protect herself, harming the abuser in the process) get arrested by the police called to the scene, rather than when only the primary aggressor gets arrested.

Service agencies must have a clear definition of success and formulate consistent goals. While several overall goals were frequently mentioned (for instance, to extend victims' support systems, empowering victims to make their own decisions, strive for a violence-free lifestyle, etc.), more concrete objectives that consider the context in which battered immigrant women are victimized and seek help are necessary for being successful in helping them.

Most respondents agreed that clients should receive information that is relevant to their situation and that gives them more than one option. It should be in a language (spoken or written) that they could understand, by somebody they can learn to trust and maintain contact with as necessary.

Some agencies recorded success as a quantifiable measure, such as a monthly number of contacts, number of approval notices from the INS, number of protection orders issued, etc. While most agencies realized the necessity of these measures for tracking clients, following their case progress or justification of funding, they also stated that what they do is beyond quantification or that type of measurement.

The respondents generally did not rank the justice system response to battered immigrant women as high. On a scale of 1 (poor) to 7 (excellent), the average score was 3.3. Only one-quarter of the ranking agencies felt the criminal justice system was helpful to their clients. They found police, prosecutors and judges often not responsive to the needs or problems of their clients and made several recommendations to increase the justice system's helpfulness for them. One suggestion was to put together a resource manual for police officers to carry in the patrol car, which would list names or resources to call for culturally appropriate victim advocates. Domestic violence units could coordinate training with other law enforcement and criminal justice agents, including prosecutors and public defenders, to increase understanding of the special needs of their clients and the future ramifications a criminal charge against immigrant batterers and victims could have on immigration status. They suggested that more police officers and police chiefs should be proactive and invest time and energy in dialogue with immigrant communities, getting to know the members (male and female) of the community one-on-one. Another suggestion was to remind police officers that since they are not INS or border patrol agents they should not be concerned with an immigrant victim's legal status. Rather they should protect and serve community members regardless of such status.

Additional recommendations focused on areas of continued or renewed training and education of those involved in the criminal justice system including judges, agents and attorneys. Also mentioned were increased uses of interpreters at all levels of interaction; case monitoring by advocates; and the utilization of victim-advocates to accompany police to domestic violence incidents. A frequent recommendation the responding professionals made was the hiring of more professionals within the criminal justice system to address domestic violence and the creation of innovative approaches to address the plight of battered immigrant women. They emphasized the need for a more fluid exchange of resources between law enforcement, prosecutors, public defenders, legal services lawyers and immigrant rights groups, as well as increased collaboration to facilitate consideration of a victim's immigrant status on a case-by-case basis and work toward finding alternative solutions such as:

- having personnel on hand for problems that are unique to immigrant women and understanding the additional weapon of control the abuser has when the woman is undocumented;
- working with immigration specialists to create options and alternative resolutions that mitigate the immigration consequences in appropriate cases. Deciding issues on a case-by-case basis, taking into consideration what the woman wants and not reporting "willy-nilly" to INS;
- confidentiality and immunity from immigration problems as a result of using the criminal justice system. Sensitivity training. Better availability of bi-lingual outreach brochures and resource referrals. Women officers.

Recommendations made by both social service providers and some attorneys was for legal services corporations (LSC) to waive their immigration status requirements for eligibility so that LSC-funded programs would be free to represent all battered immigrants regardless of their status.

A question about any special activities or procedures relating to working with battered immigrant women triggered responses that illustrate the precariousness of servicing this group. Typical responses included:

- Be sure to verify immigration status before giving advice, clarify that we are not connected with the government, emphasize confidentiality, give clear advice about encounters with Border Patrol and concerning leaving the US (don't), give careful advice about consequences of divorce, getting orders of protection and child custody and family law, always give sensitive info in a client's native language. Address immigration questions first so women feel comfortable seeking services. Then address safety issues once women know they can seek help without being deported … Understand that various legal issues are interrelated.
- Pair them with a volunteer to be special mentor. Assess immigration rights, possible eligibility to enhance safety. Tell them about VAWA, stress confidentiality. Always include it as part of community education, but advise further in one-on-one … explain confidentiality, options, law, regulations, enquire regarding manner of future communication …
- Children – custody issues, etc. Physical safety, being followed, abuser finding out that women went to an attorney, finding business card from the center, gathering evidence safely so that abuser doesn't find out.
- Safety planning, advising on safety of documents, keeping journals, gathering evidence, when men call the office, being careful what info we give out, we just recently got a P.O. Box.

The delicate situation of battered immigrant women requires that work with them be compartmentalized. Confidentiality and related safety issues are vital, lawyers dealing with battered immigrant women are always on guard with who they contact, what is said, how information is acquired and kept. The method of communication they maintain with their clients is documented, so they can note if there is a breach of an agreed-upon method, which may be an alert as to her safety. A phone call to or from a contact might endanger her with her spouse or abuser.

The professionals interviewed attributed their ability to help battered immigrant women to the new legislation on the topic. They mostly credited the ability to help battered immigrants to the Violence Against Women Act of 1994. They considered the Act as instrumental in raising awareness of violence against women, facilitating abused immigrant women to self-petition and adjust their immigration status independent of their abusers.

These professionals considered the recent legal developments as the beginning of an era that would provide immigrant women further means of liberating themselves from their abusers.

Conclusion

Battered immigrant women face tremendous barriers to accessing social services and using the US criminal justice system to respond to the violence in their lives. In dealing with requests for help, the professionals quickly learn to understand the multiple and varied constraints by which the women live, and the ways the professionals must adapt their responses to accommodate immigrant women's special needs and requests for assistance. These complex and multiple problems often result in the professionals having to settle for partial solutions, provide restricted scope of service or simply turn clients away, as they do not have legal backing or sufficient resources to help. The professionals also must find creative ways to address the real or perceived constraints experienced by their immigrant clients, and to offer assistance that goes beyond the call of duty or the mission statement of their agency.

This study suggests that effective advocacy and intervention for battered women should include developing collaborative working relationships among the various professions involved in addressing battered immigrants' plight. A coordinated approach endorsed by all parties involved may enhance battered immigrant women's willingness to access the justice system, minimize the system's adverse effects, and maximize its benefits for them. Since battered immigrant women are a highly vulnerable population, adopting response strategies that consider their multiple vulnerabilities, cultural and social constraints, and legal restrictions are necessary in helping them to extricate themselves from the violence.

The professionals also need to be sensitive to the consequences and ramifications of the various options, remedies, or actions available for abused immigrant women and the women's perceptions regarding their options. The professionals' experiences, as reported in this study, demonstrate the creative as well as more mundane solutions they find for battered immigrant women's intricate problems. The multiple obstacles faced by the professionals' clients in their attempt to escape violence, and the professionals' own frustration when unable to help the immigrant women because their hands are tied or because they lack the resources to do so, provides a glimpse into the challenges they face.

With the unprecedented increase in the US immigrant population in recent decades, attention to the plight of immigrant women is necessary at all levels of government in all states of the US. Although the events of 9/11 have resulted in restricted immigration to the US, the large number of immigrants that arrive to the US and make it their home is high and is likely to increase in the next decades. This trend compels us to pay close attention to the reports of the professionals who work with battered immigrant women.

References

Abraham, M. (2000), "Isolation as a Form of Marital Violence: The South Asian Immigrant Experience", *Journal of Social Distress and the Homeless*, 9(3): 221–36.

American Bar Association (2000), *Domestic Violence and Immigration: Applying the Immigration Provisions of the Violence Against Women Act Training Manual*, Chicago: American Bar Association.

Anderson, M.J. (1993), "A License to Abuse: The Impact of Conditional Status on Female Immigrants", *Yale Law Journal*, 102(6): 1401–30 and 1420–1.

Ciurak, I. (1985), "Problems Facing Migrant Women in Domestic Violence", in Hatty, Suzanne E. (ed.), *Domestic Violence, Proceedings of a National Conference. Australian Institute of Criminology, Canberra*, 1: 37–40.

Currie, J. (1995), "Ethno Cultural Minority Women, Spousal Assault and Barriers to Accessing and Problems in Using the Justice System", a technical report by the Research and Statistics Section and the Law Reform Fund, Department of Justice, Canada: 1–57.

Das Gupta, S. (2000), "Charting the Course: An Overview of Domestic Violence in the South Asian Community in the United States", *Journal of Social Distress and the Homeless*, 9(3): 173–85.

Davis, R.C. and E. Erez (1998), "Immigrant Population as Victims: Toward a Multicultural Criminal Justice System", in *Research in Brief*, Washington DC: National Institute of Justice.

Davis, R.C., E. Erez and N. Avitabile (2001), "Access to Justice for Immigrants Victimized by Crime: The Perspectives of Police and Prosecutors", *Criminal Justice Policy Review*, 12(3): 183–96.

Erez, E. (2000), "Immigration, Culture Conflict and Domestic Violence/Woman Battering", *Crime Prevention and Community Safety: An International Journal*, 2: 27–36.

Erez, E. (2001), "The Victimization of Women in the Context of Transnational Crime", in Ollus, Natalia and Sami Nevalas (eds), *Women in the Criminal Justice System: International Examples and National Responses*, Helsinki: European Institute for Crime Prevention and Control, Affiliated with the United Nations (NEUNI).

Erez, E. (2002), "Migration/Immigration, Domestic Violence and the Justice System", *International Journal of Comparative and Applied Criminal Justice*, 26(2): 277–99.

Erez, E. and C. Copps Hartley (2003), "Battered Immigrant Women and the Legal System: A Therapeutic Jurisprudence Perspective", *Western Criminology Review*, 4(2): 65–79.

Haile-Mariam, T. and J. Smith (1999), "Domestic Violence Against Women in the International Community", *Emergency Medicine Clinics of North America*, 17(3): 617–45.

Huisman, K.A. (1996), "Wife Battering in Asian American Communities: Identifying the Service Needs of an Overlooked Segment of the U.S. Population", *Violence Against Women*, 2: 260–83.

Kelly, L. (1999), *Violence Against Women*, London: British Research Council.

Maglizza, E. (1985), "Migrant Women and Domestic Violence: The Dilemma of Whether to Stay or Leave", in Hatty, Suzanne E. (ed.), *Domestic Violence. Proceedings of a National Conference, Australian Institute of Criminology, Canberra*, 1: 35–6.

Menjiver, C. and O. Salcido (2002), "Immigrant Women and Domestic Violence: Common Experiences in Different Countries", *Gender & Society*, 16(6): 898–920.

Miller, S. (1999), *Gender and Community Policing: Walking the Talk*, Boston: Northeastern University Press.

Miller, S. (2001), "Gender and Policing", in Renzetti, Claire and Lynne Goodstein (eds), *Women, Crime, and Criminal Justice: Original Feminist Readings*, Los Angeles: Roxbury Publishing: 255–63.

Narayan, U. (1995), "'Male Order' Brides: Immigrant Women Domestic Violence and Immigration Law", *Hypatia*, 10(1): 104–19.

Okin, S.M. (1998), "Feminism and Multiculturalism: Some Tensions", *Ethics*, 108(4): 661–84.

Okin, S.M. (1999), "Is Multiculturalism Bad for Women?", with respondents in Cohen, Joshua, Matthew Howard and Martha Nessbaum (eds), *Is Multiculturalism Bad for Women?*, Princeton: Princeton University Press.

Orloff, L. (1995), "Addressing the Needs of Battered Immigrant Women", *Network News*, 20(2): 3–4.

Orloff, L.E., D. Jang and C. Klein (1995), "With No Place to Turn – Improving Legal Advocacy for Battered Immigrant Women", *Family Law Quarterly*, 29(2): 313–29.

Pogrebin, M.A. and E.B. Poole (1990), "Culture Conflict and Crime in the Korean American Community", *Criminal Justice Policy Review,* 4(1): 69–78.

Raj, A. and J. Silverman (2002), "Violence Against Immigrant Women: The Roles of Culture, Context, and Legal Immigrant Status on Intimate Partner Violence", *Violence Against Women*, 8: 367–98.

Stanko, E.A. (1995), "Policing Domestic Violence: Paradoxes and Dilemmas", *Australian and New Zealand Journal of Criminology* (special addendum).

Supriya, K.E. (1996), "Confessionals, Testimonials: Women's Speech in/and Contexts of Violence", *Hypatia*, 11(4): 92–106.

Wachholz, S. and B. Miedema (2000), "Risk, Fear, Harm: Immigrant Women's Perceptions of the 'Policing' Solution to Women Abuse", *Crime, Law and Social Change*, 34(3): 301–17.

Chapter 14

Dealing with Domestic Violence in India: A Problem-Solving Model for Police

Mangai Natarajan
John Jay College of Criminal Justice
City University of New York

Introduction

Until recently domestic violence was largely a private matter, but it has now begun to attract considerable public attention in many Western countries due to the improved social position of women, an increased awareness of women's rights, campaigning by feminist groups, and research documentation of the widespread and serious nature of the problem (Jasinski and Williams 1998; Steinman 1991; Straus and Gelles 1990). In America, all 50 states have now passed civil and/or criminal statutes to protect battered women (Buzawa and Buzawa 2002; Roberts and Kurst-Swanger 2002).

In traditional societies, however, domestic violence is still considered a "family matter" and not the business of the criminal justice system. Many victims of domestic violence cannot seek help from the authorities. They are also unable to break free of an abusive relationship and cannot leave their homes for the following reasons:

- the majority of families are still extended and they will lose their support network, which is part and parcel of many women's lives;
- the legal system in these societies does not generally recognize any entitlement of the wife to a share of the household goods and income. If she leaves her husband she cannot therefore claim her share and live independently;
- many women are uneducated, lack employment skills and cannot support themselves and the children;
- if they are living alone, they become vulnerable to sexual exploitation;
- many women subscribe to the traditional value system and are not prepared to live independently, unlike women in many modern societies;
- divorce is still considered shameful and something to be avoided at all costs.

Even in Western societies, most women victims of domestic violence will only report their abuse to the police after repeated episodes (Hoyle and Sanders 2000; Kelly 1999; Klinger 1995). This is all the more so in traditional cultures where women believe that reporting their problems to the police will do little good and harm their marital status. Specifically:

- they are hesitant to talk to a male police officer about their private problems;
- they believe that male officers will not be sympathetic because there is a general tendency for men to support one another; male officers are also more likely to believe the man's story;
- they believe male officers do not understand women's psychology and the suffering resulting of domestic violence;
- they fear that the male police officers might take sexual advantage of them;
- they fear police intervention would make the partner more violent;
- they fear that if they report their husbands the police will arrest their husband and they will be left on their own.

Though many individual and family factors help explain domestic violence, culture plays a major role in explaining why domestic violence occurs and why women stay in an abusive relationship and cannot take the necessary action to safeguard themselves and their children. The problems are exemplified by the violence often resulting from the dowry system in India, a customary practice of giving gifts by the bride's family to that of the groom during and after marriage. This has been in existence from time immemorial in the Hindu culture. When not satisfied with the dowry, the bridegroom and his parents may humiliate, harass and physically abuse the bride. Many instances of torture have been reported, as well as murders of young brides. While these dowry murders are committed in a variety of ways, they are generally known as "bride burning". Violence associated with the dowry has been recognized as a serious problem nationwide and many state governments have developed programs to deal with it that are tailored to the local culture.

This chapter describes the initiatives undertaken by the government of Tamil Nadu (a southern Indian state) to reduce domestic violence and the ways in which police now handle domestic violence cases. It also proposes a problem-solving method as a way to organize multiple approaches in *identifying*, *analyzing*, and *solving* the domestic violence problem (the IAS model). This model might be of more general application not only in India, but also elsewhere in the world where traditional cultures prevail.

Police Response to Domestic Violence in Tamil Nadu

In an attempt to deal more adequately with crimes against women, particularly violence related to problems over dowries, the Tamil Nadu government decided to experiment with all-women police stations, the first of which was opened in Central Madras in 1992. It was thought that abused women might be more likely to seek police help if they could be certain of dealing with female officers. The station was quickly judged a success and more stations were opened throughout the state. Most women police officers were placed in these stations, of which there are now 148. A typical station has an inspector, a subinspector and 15 constables and head constables.

These stations have clearly met an important need. For example, 10,508 cases were reported in three years (1999–2001) in three stations in the capital city of Tamil Nadu. Of these 2,075 (20 percent) were dowry related. Others include general family disputes, marital problems, false promises of marriage, sexual assaults or rape, kidnapping, and other cases involving women. Essentially, the all-women units deal with Indian Penal Code and Indian Criminal Procedural Code cases involving crimes against women.

In-depth interviews with 60 women victims of dowry violence in their homes (whose petitions had already been cleared by the police) were undertaken to examine how well women police handled the complaints (Natarajan 2003a). These interviews revealed that 18 of the 30 women who were physically abused reported that they were still living with their husbands. The husbands had now stopped hurting them because the wives would report them to the police if they did. The rest of the women had left their husbands to seek separation or divorce. Though this is a small sample, it provides some evidence that intervention by women police reduced repeat victimization and had a deterrent effect on the perpetrators.

Training in Dispute Resolution and in Record Keeping

Though it was clear that the all-women stations were providing a valuable service, systematic observation of the work of these stations (Natarajan 1996, 2002, 2003a) revealed that women officers were essentially performing a dispute resolution function, but without sufficient training to be fully effective in handling domestic disputes. Even though women officers might be sympathetic to women petitioners, they still generally approached the case in the way they had been trained, which required them to use an authoritarian approach. This is believed to be the best way of extracting the truth from petitioners, counter-petitioners and criminals, but it is unsuitable for dealing with family disputes and family violence. It intimidates many women complainants, who, as a result, often hide their personal feelings and opinions from women police, which makes it difficult to help them. On the other hand, employing simple dispute resolution methods, like negotiation and mediation, can put the disputants at ease and more able to talk openly to a third party. This can help couples to deal with conflicts successfully, as they reach the solution themselves. This not only strengthens the relationship, but also teaches the couple how to deal with difficult issues at later stages in their lives. In this way, both repeat victimization and dependency on the police can be avoided. Successful use of dispute resolution by the police, who are the gatekeepers of the criminal justice system, would also help reduce overcrowding in the family court system.

Not only did the women police lack the necessary basic training in dispute resolution, but in most stations only limited support was available to them from social workers or psychologists. This meant that women officers often found it difficult to decide about the best way to proceed. In addition, they were being called upon to perform a wider range of duties than before, which meant that they frequently could not give the necessary attention to women petitioning for help with their problems. Further, some of the women police imposed their own cultural values on the victims with the result that they might remain in the abusive relationship and be subjected to repeated victimization. To provide more appropriate solutions to solving family disputes, women police need to avoid unnecessary criticism and to be cautious in their professional dealings with petitioners of domestic disputes and violence.

An additional, but separate problem was that many of the officers lacked basic training in note taking and record keeping. These skills are important in dealing with cases that often require protracted discussions with disputants over several sessions. The women officers complained that they could not remember all the details about the petitions. Nor did they record the information they obtained about the case in preliminary interviews with the petitioner and the accused when they returned from other duties. When they resolved a case, they did enter certain items of information by hand in large ledgers. These items included case number, name and address and a brief statement about outcome under one of three categories: case withdrawn, agreed to settle at family court, and file FIR, which is equivalent to a charge sheet. However, no other information was recorded about the case such as the age of the petitioner, educational level, nature of the quarrels, seriousness of the violence, etc. In addition, as the records are manually maintained, it is difficult to access them to produce baseline statistical data (e.g., age of petitioners, kind of abuse, occupations, etc.).

To deal with these problems, the Tamil Nadu Police applied successfully in 2002 for a UK Queen's Award[1] to develop training in record keeping and dispute resolution for women police. Because of increased workloads and shortage of staff, women police could not be released to attend regular college courses in these subjects. The training was therefore designed to be web based so that women police officers could access the reading materials from their own premises and at their own pace and time. The police created a web site (www.twp.net) for this purpose. Because of the experimental nature of the project and the expense involved in purchasing computers, the training was limited to 30 officers[2] in three all-women police stations.

The syllabus in dispute resolution included negotiation, mediation/arbitration, and counseling. A Western model of dispute resolution was used as the basis, but the six course modules (listed below) had to be tailored to the needs of the local culture in relation to the nature of disputes in the Indian culture.

---

1 This is a competitive grant given by UK Home Office to commonwealth nations for providing innovative training for police.

2 Of the 30 women, 50 percent had a Masters degree, 20 percent Bachelors degree and 30 percent held a high-school diploma. 20 percent of the officers were inspectors or subinspectors and the remainder were police head constables and constables. Their age range was from 25 to 48 years (mean 37.9 years) and their experience in the police force ranges from 4 to 26 years (mean 17 years).

- Module 1: Introduction to domestic/family violence;
- Module 2: Introduction to dispute resolution techniques;
- Module 3: Basics of negotiation;
- Module 4: Basics of mediation;
- Module 5: Basics of arbitration;
- Module 6: Counseling approach to interviewing.

Training in data management and data entry skills was organized around a database created solely for the purpose of dealing with domestic violence and domestic disputes. A "contact sheet" was developed to assist collection of information for the database. This included fields for the background of the petitioner, the nature and duration of disputes/violence, the place and parties involved in violence was developed. This is a much more detailed record than ones previously being used by the women police stations. If a case involves any form of physical/sexual violence, the officer in charge is required to make a risk assessment and direct the petitioner for proper care. A danger score sheet, which helps to calculate the risk of injury or death, was included for this purpose. This involves 15 questions involving the risk associated with the victim and her children. The risk factor is divided into three categories: low, moderate and high risk. When a case is diagnosed as high risk the system flashes a signal for immediate action.

While the training was geared to providing needed skills, the officers were encouraged to see themselves preparing to become professional mediators, not simply agents of law enforcement. This requires a radical change in their perceptions and attitudes as well as their personal and professional ideologies. These changes would assist them in:

- understanding how important it is for female officers to be involved in resolving domestic and family disputes;
- confirming their role as gatekeepers in the context of the criminal justice system;
- fulfilling their policing role in dealing with domestic disputes and domestic violence issues;
- detecting, intervening and preventing domestic violence at an early stage;
- building community–police relations;
- clarifying their own role conflicts in dealing with family disputes;
- strengthening their own skills for a better performance.

The project team consisted of the project director (the senior police official who won the award), the project supervisor (a senior woman officer based at police headquarters), a project consultant (the present author) and the staff of Crime Prevention and Victim Care (PCVC), a non-profit organization. PCVC was awarded the contract in August 2001 to write the course modules (under the guidance of the consultant) and manage the e-training program.

To deal with various concerns, including the trainees' discomfort about undertaking counseling in the course of their regular work, the e-training was supplemented with a one-week class held at police headquarters for the 30 trainees. The consultant provided an overview lecture covering women police around the world, their law enforcement functions and their roles in handling domestic disputes and domestic violence cases. Other lectures covered the importance of networking with NGOs, physicians, religious institutions, psychiatrists and psychologists to provide the best service possible to women victims of violence. One outcome of these discussions was the production of a condensed guide (see below) on using dispute resolution techniques with domestic violence and dispute cases.

To assess the impact of the training, before-and-after assessments were made of the 30 women's working knowledge of dispute resolution techniques, data entry and data management (Natarajan 2003b). Significant gains in knowledge were found in these areas. It was also found that, while the women officers were extremely enthusiastic and open to learning, they struggled with some major impediments: their hectic work schedule within the department, a general lack of understanding among senior officers about the time taken to handle the cases and the nature of disputes and a pervasive feeling that the work of the all-women stations was undervalued.

Solving these problems was beyond the remit of the present project, but in order to reinforce the lessons learned and assist the trainees in handling future cases, a stepwise problem-solving guide was developed by the consultant to the project (i.e., the present author). Its overall purpose was to assist early detection, appropriate immediate attention, and prevention of repeated domestic violence. This is reproduced below.

A Problem-Solving Model for Family Disputes

When a petitioner arrives at the station, women police should use a *counseling* approach to interview the petitioners rather than a traditional authoritative approach. Women who approach the stations are emotionally distressed and they need to be *comforted* on their first appearance at the station. Most often they want the women police to intervene and warn their husbands, so that their husbands will stop harassing them. They want an authority figure to intervene and advise the man to behave properly. Also, most families in India are afraid of going to courts and taking their problem to the police rather than to court would seem a better way. Further, many victims believe that warnings by the police have a deterrent effect on the husband and his family.

To ensure the well-being of petitioners, women police need to address a petition systematically and handle it professionally. The following model should help them to do this. First, women police need to orient themselves appropriately in handling such matters. In all-women police units, officers are often pressured with other policing assignments on a given day and often become impatient and irritable. If they are under pressure it is hard to focus properly on abused women. Hence, they need to prepare themselves to handle effectively such delicate and important family matters. There are three stages involved in taking care of these cases:

1. planning/preparation;
2. processing;
3. persuasion/following-up.

Stage 1: Planning

The planning stage requires women police to improve their own self-esteem and self-image. In a sense, women police are intermediaries creating harmony in the lives of men and women. This requires women police (who are generally very sympathetic to women's problems) to dedicate their time and energy to developing creative, culturally sensitive solutions to suit the needs of each case. Women police need to put their personal opinions on one side and learn to see the facts, to recognize the intensity of the harm inflicted on the woman petitioner and prepare to act as a neutral party.

Stage 2: Processing and the IAS Model

Figure 14.1 depicts the IAS model that women police should follow in processing a petition of family dispute or violence. The problem analysis involves three phases:

1. identifying the problem;
2. analyzing the problem;
3. solving the problem.

Phase 1: Identifying the Problem

At this stage women police must gather the information needed for investigating a petition that arrives at the station. They should adopt a counseling approach, intended to help the petitioner make an autonomous decision that solves his/her problems. This is a relationship-building process, whereby the women petitioners come to trust the women police and disclose information so that women police can make appropriate enquiries and suggest alternative solutions. The objective of a counseling approach is to make the petitioner who may be confused, afraid, anxious, depressed, insecure and helpless, into a confident, peaceful, happy, safe, empowered, free and calm person. The following are the sequential stages of the process:

Petition intake This is the first contact between the woman petitioner and the police. Being polite and offering a seat to the petitioner will help her to feel at ease and therefore more likely to open up to the police. Under a formal counseling approach, this would be called the "relating stage".

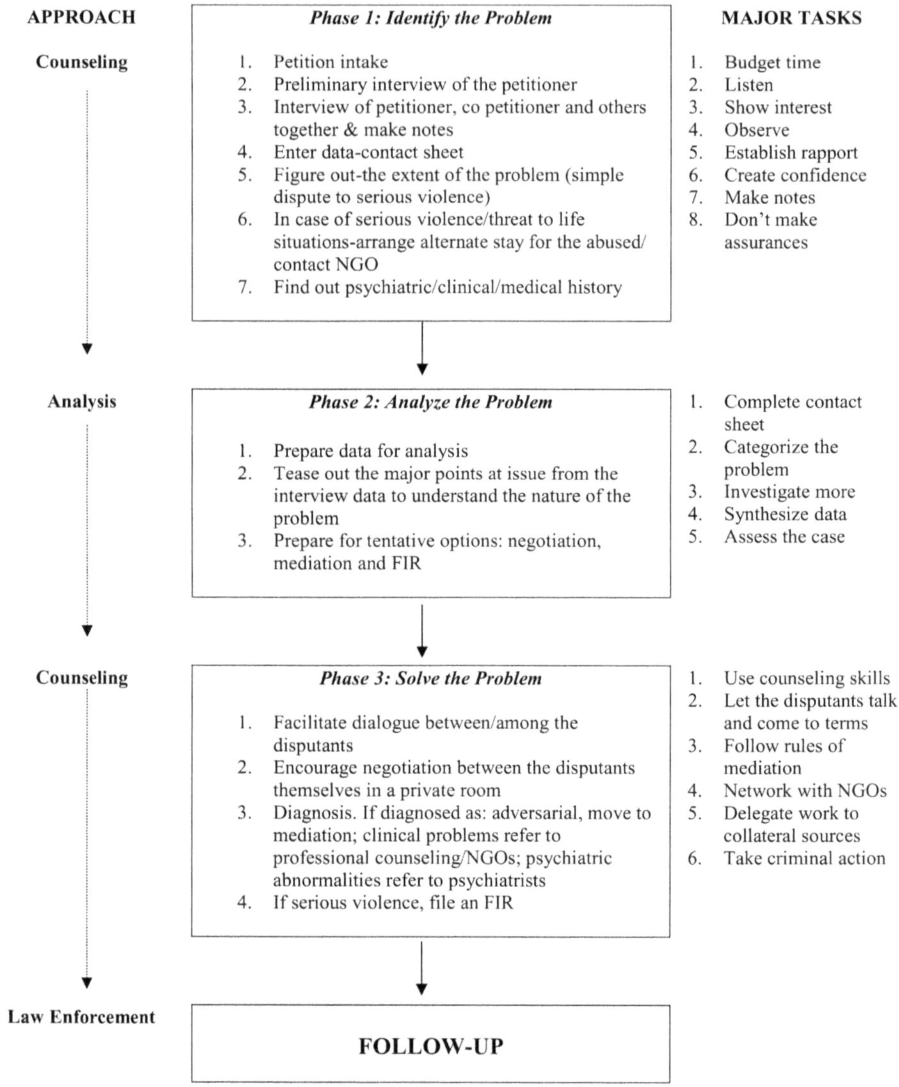

Figure 14.1 Processing of domestic dispute and domestic violence cases at all-women police stations in Tamil Nadu, India (The IAS model)

Preliminary interview of the petitioner At this "understanding stage", the petitioner describes the problem and seeks the help of the police. Women police need to listen to the facts carefully and to show empathy, but they should not give an undertaking that they will solve the problem in the petitioner's favor. To keep the proceedings businesslike, they might say to the petitioner that she has approximately 20 minutes to tell her story. This will allow the petitioner to bring out the salient points to the women police, which will allow them to manage their time in performing their duties. At the same time, women police need to listen carefully and use body language to show they are doing this. Women police should be sure to:

- give full attention to the petitioner (i.e., not taking phone calls or talking to others in the station);
- adopt a relaxed and open attitude;
- lean slightly forward;
- use appropriate gaze and eye contact;
- convey appropriate facial expressions;
- use good gestures; to pat/touch sparingly;
- be sensitive to personal space.

Women police need to understand the position of the woman from her internal frame of mind. They need to question the petitioner quietly to bring out all the salient points of the problem. This helps the police to discover whether the dispute centers on a single factor or multiple factors. It is important to remember that women victims of violence come to police only after exhausting other avenues. Probing the woman petitioner in a quiet and firm way will help her play her part in addressing the problem effectively. This is called the “changing stage” under the counseling approach.

1. Interview of counter petitioner and others, such as in-laws and the petitioner’s parents: After the preliminary one-on-one interview with the woman petitioner, women police can interview the counter petitioner and others and enter data in the computerized database (i.e., the “contact sheet”).
2. Use of the contact sheet to establish the extent of the problem: The contact sheet assists women police to understand the extent of the problem and develop an action plan. For example, if the contact sheet records a danger score of less than 3, women police can fix the dates for a second and third meeting with the petitioner if necessary. This will establish a clear time-line in the petitioner’s mind.
3. If the contact sheet reports a danger score of 3 and above, the women police must take *immediate action* in arranging alternate lodging for the abused woman by contacting appropriate NGOs. This will provide temporary relief and safety for the woman and permit police to take further action against the perpetrator/abuser.
4. Women police should also inquire whether the woman petitioner has any psychiatric/clinical and medical history that may be contributing to her problems. Knowing this will help in finding solutions.

Phase 2: Analyzing the Problem
By this stage women police should have enough data to analyze the problem. Analysis involves the following stages:

1. Prepare data for analysis: women police need to check whether the contact sheet is filled properly. After this, they need to take a printout of the petition and begin analysis.
2. Tease out the major points or issues: from the interview data, women police should be able to understand the magnitude and the nature of the problem and arrive at a danger score for the seriousness of the problem.
3. Preparation for tentative options (negotiation, mediation and FIR): if the petition involves less/medium violence, women police need to prepare themselves for negotiation and mediation to resolve the disputes of the parties petitioned. They should arrange a date for the petitioner and counter petitioners and others to visit the station. Each station should develop a registry of station meeting dates that is similar to procedures of assigning court dates.
4. If there is sign of extensive violence, women police should prepare themselves for criminal action against the abuser.

Phase 3: Solving the problem

With the analysis complete, women police should be able to find ways to resolve the petition at hand. The skills they need are listed below:

1. Simple counseling skills: if diagnosed as petty quarrels between the husband and wife, simple counseling would help.
2. Negotiation techniques: if the dispute focuses on one issue, women police may want to use negotiation techniques to help the disputants discuss the matter between themselves – on the station premises. For example, the husband and wife might blame each other, but they might also admit their own faults during the interview. In many instances, this communication muddle is the result of not talking to one other before. In such domestic disputes, the parties may love each other, but need someone else to help them solve their problems. This is why negotiation techniques are appropriate. They will not only help to solve the immediate dispute, but they will help the couples get to know each other and make them understand their own shortcomings. This will help them resolve their own problems in the future without seeking assistance from police.
3. Mediation skills: if the dispute involves many issues and one party is blaming the other without taking any personal responsibility, women police need to take the role of mediator in resolving the dispute. At this stage, women police need to follow the rules of mediation (which have been learned earlier)
4. Networking skills: if the women police suspect any clinical/psychiatric and serious sex-related marital problems, which are not within their scope to deal with, they should enlist the help of professional counseling centers, psychiatrists or medical specialists. In many cases women police should be able to diagnose the problem, which can then be referred to other appropriate institutions for action. Also, women police can sometimes refer the case to the family court for legal action to resolve the dispute.

5. Law enforcement skills: if serious violence is involved, women police should take criminal action against the counter petitioner(s). In many instances, the women petitioners do not want criminal action to be taken by the police, but only want them to warn the abusing party (usually the husband). Research has found that women police intervention can reduce physical violence at home. The abusers know that their wives have support from the police and are aware of the consequences of criminal action. Whatever the case, if there is a threat to the petitioner's life, the women police must file an FIR and take criminal action. If the abused woman wishes to withdraw her petition against her husband, the police can do nothing at that point. They can only give her advice and ask her to take precautions against violence.

Stage 3: Follow-up

Once the police resolve the petition, they should conduct a follow-up of the case. Though it is their job to reopen a case that is closed, with the best interests of the petitioners in mind, women police can do the following:

1. ask the petitioner and the counter petitioner to report to the station every month;
2. ask the petitioner to seek help if there is any ill treatment after the intervention;
3. delegate follow-up to local NGOs.

Summary and Conclusion

The Tamil Nadu government established 148 all-women police stations during the 1990s to deal with crimes against women and with domestic disputes. These stations have filled an important need, especially for poorer women who would be unlikely to seek professional marriage counseling, even if they were aware of such services. While the stations have helped many women, observation of their work found their efficiency was limited by the insufficient training of the women police in dispute resolution and record keeping.

To improve these skills, the Tamil Nadu police secured a competitive grant from the UK Home Office in 2002 to run an experimental web-based training in dispute resolution, interviewing and record keeping for 30 officers in three all-women police units. Six modules containing study materials on dispute resolution and counseling, and a user guide for women police, was posted on the website created for the project. A database was developed for processing cases and data management and data entry skills were taught at the officers' own premises by the project's training team. A before-and-after evaluation found marked improvements in the women's skills and a problem-solving model was developed to reinforce the learning that had occurred and to assist the women officers in their future handling of cases. In sum, the Tamil

Nadu experience shows that a dispute resolution model can be very useful for police in responding to domestic violence in a traditional society and that this training can be effectively delivered through web-based training. However, the training must be carefully tailored to issues of culture.

More generally, this experimental training project might serve as a working model for police in other developing countries to develop new ways of dealing with domestic violence and disputes. According to a study by Grace (1995), training may be the main way to change the police's attitudes and responses to domestic violence. In addition, it is also affords a way to transfer accurate information about civil remedies and other options available to the victim (how to refer victims to support agencies, and which support agencies do what) as laid out in the recent model developed by the International Association of Chiefs of Police for dealing with domestic violence. This consists of a comprehensive, proactive approach with an emphasis on victim safety and on developing ongoing partnerships with local victim advocacy organizations.

Finally, it is worth considering the implications of the Tamil Nadu experience for dealing with immigrant victims of domestic violence in developed countries. Voluntary women's organizations can play a valuable role in helping these women, but they are no substitute for legal protection and there is an urgent need for law enforcement agencies to reach out to these immigrant women. The most useful interventions that could be undertaken at the present time would be for the police to find ways of encouraging abused women in these communities to seek their protection. Many women want to stay in their marriages and want a simple intervention by police. Training in the dispute resolution techniques discussed above would certainly be of great help to the police officers in identifying the high-risk cases of violence as well as in preventing future violence at home. At the very least, when dealing with complaints from immigrant women, police departments can be sensitive to the need for these complaints to be allocated to female officers – preferably ones sensitive to the cultural backgrounds of the complainants.

Acknowledgments

Extended discussions with the 30 women police officers who were part of the Queens Award project helped in designing the guidelines for dealing with domestic violence disputes. The author is indebted to these officers: Anandajothi, S.; Arokiakumari, A.; Brindha, S.R.; Geetharamani, T.; Glory, J.; Indiragandhi S.; Jayadevi, K.; Kalaiselvi, M.; Maheswari, B.; Mallika, M.; Marudambal, S.; Padmavathy; Pandiammal, R.; Pushpa, D.; Rajakumari, V.; Rajalakshmi, J.; Inspector Rangathal; Rani, G.K.; Renuga Devi, D.; Santha; Santhi; Inspector Saraswathy, S.; Subashini, N.; Sumathi, C.; Usha, S.; Ushakumari, U.; Vanaja, M.; Inspector Vasantha, V.; Vijayalakshmi, G.

References

Buzawa, E. and C. Buzawa (2002), *Domestic Violence: The Criminal Justice Response*, Thousand Oaks: Sage.

Grace, S. (1995), *Policing Domestic Violence in the 1990s*, *Home Office Research Study 139*, London: Home Office Research and Planning Unit.

Hoyle, C. (1998), *Negotiating Domestic Violence: Police, Criminal Justice and Victims*, Oxford: Clarendon Press.

Hoyle, C. and A. Sanders (2000), "Police Response to Domestic Violence: From Victim Choice to Victim Empowerment?", *British Journal of Criminology*, 46(1): 14–36.

International Association of Chiefs of Police (2001), "Family Violence Summit Recommendations", at www.theiacp.org.

Jasinski, L.J. and Linda Williams (1998) (eds), *Partner Violence: A Comprehensive Review of 20 Years of Research*, Thousand Oaks: Sage.

Kelly, L. (1999), *Domestic Violence Matters: An Evaluation of a Development Project, Home Office Research Study 193*, London: Home Office Research and Planning Unit.

Klinger, D.A. (1995), "Policing Spousal Assault", *Journal of Research in Crime and Delinquency*, 32: 308–24.

Natarajan, M. (1996), "Women Police Units in India: A New Direction", *Police Studies*, 19(2): 63–76.

Natarajan, M. (2002). "Women Police in India: A Tale of Two Cohorts", *International Journal of Comparative Criminology*, 2(2): 201–24.

Natarajan, M. (2003a), "Dispute Resolution by Women Police in Tamil Nadu, India in Dealing with Dowry-Related Domestic Violence Cases", report for CUNY DRC, New York.

Natarajan, M. (2003b), "Web-Based E-Training Programs in Dispute Resolution, Interviewing and Record Keeping for Officers in All-Women Police Units in Tamil Nadu: A Pilot Project", report submitted to Home Office London.

Roberts, A. and Kurst-Swanger, K. (2002), "Police Response to Battered Women: Past, Present and Future", in Roberts, A. (ed.), *Handbook of Domestic Violence Intervention Strategies*, New York: Oxford University Press.

Steinman, M. (1991) (ed.), *Woman Battering: Policy Responses*, Cincinnati: Anderson Press.

Straus, M., and R. Gelles (1990), *Physical Violence in American Families: Risk Factors and Adaptations to Violence in 8,145 Families*, New Brunswick: Transaction Press.

Index

For Product Safety Concerns and Information please contact our EU representative GPSR@taylorandfrancis.com
Taylor & Francis Verlag GmbH, Kaufingerstraße 24, 80331 München, Germany

www.ingramcontent.com/pod-product-compliance
Ingram Content Group UK Ltd.
Pitfield, Milton Keynes, MK11 3LW, UK
UKHW022132190926
475702UK00013B/1768
* 9 7 8 1 1 3 8 2 7 7 8 8 5 *